FRANKLIN PARK PUBLIC LIBRARY
FRANKLIN PARK, ILL.

Each borrower is held responsible for all library
material drawn on his card and for fines accruing on
the same. No material will be issued until such fine
has been paid.

All injuries to library material beyond reasonable
wear and all losses shall be made good to the
satisfaction of the   Replacement costs will be
billed after 42 days overdue.

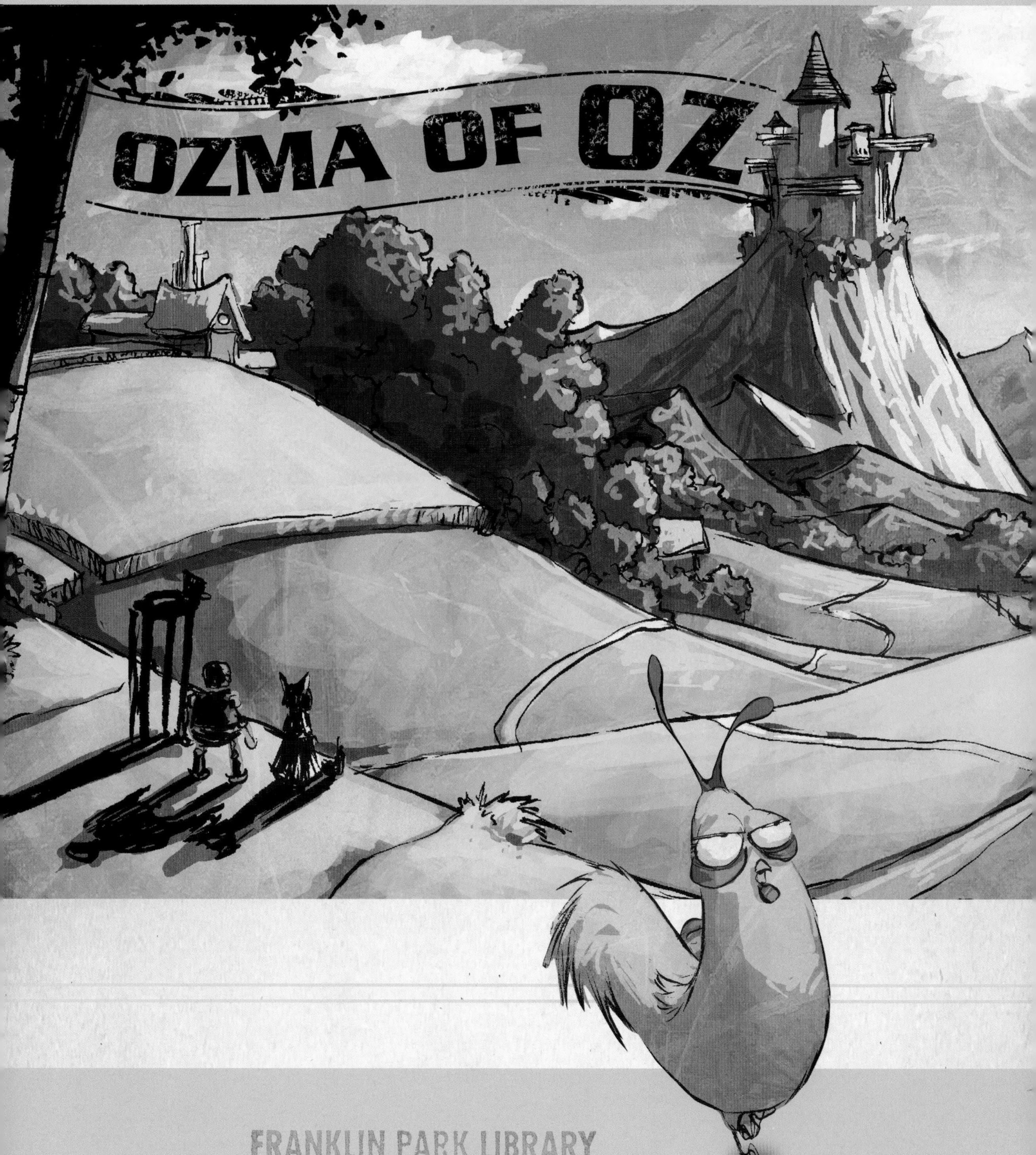

OZMA OF OZ

OZ: OZMA OF OZ. Contains material originally published in magazine form as OZMA OF OZ #1-8. First printing 2011. ISBN# 978-0-7851-4247-8. Published by MARVEL WORLDWIDE, INC., a subsidiary of MARVEL ENTERTAINMENT, LLC. OFFICE OF PUBLICATION: 135 West 50th Street, New York, NY 10020. Copyright © 2011 Marvel Characters, Inc. All rights reserved. $29.99 per copy in the U.S. and $32.99 in Canada (GST #R127032852); Canadian Agreement #40668537. All characters featured in this issue and the distinctive names and likenesses thereof, and all related indicia are trademarks of Marvel Characters, Inc. No similarity between any of the names, characters, persons, and/or institutions in this magazine with those of any living or dead person or institution is intended, and any such similarity which may exist is purely coincidental. **Printed in the U.S.A.** ALAN FINE, EVP - Office of the President, Marvel Worldwide, Inc. and EVP & CMO Marvel Characters B.V.; DAN BUCKLEY, Publisher & President - Print, Animation & Digital Divisions; JOE QUESADA, Chief Creative Officer; JIM SOKOLOWSKI, Chief Operating Officer; DAVID BOGART, SVP of Business Affairs & Talent Management; TOM BREVOORT, SVP of Publishing; C.B. CEBULSKI, SVP of Creator & Content Development; DAVID GABRIEL, SVP of Publishing Sales & Circulation; MICHAEL PASCIULLO, SVP of Brand Planning & Communications; JIM O'KEEFE, VP of Operations & Logistics; DAN CARR, Executive Director of Publishing Technology; SUSAN CRESPI, Editorial Operations Manager; ALEX MORALES, Publishing Operations Manager; STAN LEE, Chairman Emeritus. For information regarding advertising in Marvel Comics or on Marvel.com, please contact John Dokes, SVP Integrated Sales and Marketing, at jdokes@marvel.com. For Marvel subscription inquiries, please call 800-217-9158. **Manufactured between 7/25/2011 and 8/22/2011 by R.R. DONNELLEY, INC., SALEM, VA, USA.**

10 9 8 7 6 5 4 3 2 1

OZMA OF OZ

ADAPTED FROM THE NOVEL BY L. FRANK BAUM

Writer: **ERIC SHANOWER**
Artist: **SKOTTIE YOUNG**
Colorist: **JEAN-FRANCOIS BEAULIEU**
Letterer: **JEFF ECKLEBERRY**

Production: **DAMIEN LUCCHESE, TAYLOR ESPOSITO, MAYA GUTIERREZ & MANNY MEDEROS**
Assistant Editor: **MICHAEL HORWITZ**
Editors: **SANA AMANAT & NATE COSBY**

Collection Editor: **MARK D. BEAZLEY**
Editorial Assistants: **JAMES EMMETT & JOE HOCHSTEIN**
Assistant Editors: **NELSON RIBEIRO & ALEX STARBUCK**
Editor, Special Projects: **JENNIFER GRÜNWALD**
Senior Editor, Special Projects: **JEFF YOUNGQUIST**
Senior Vice President of Sales: **DAVID GABRIEL**
SVP of Brand Planning & Communications: **MICHAEL PASCIULLO**
Book Design: **ARLENE SO**

Editor in Chief: **AXEL ALONSO**
Chief Creative Officer: **JOE QUESADA**
Publisher: **DAN BUCKLEY**
Executive Producer: **ALAN FINE**

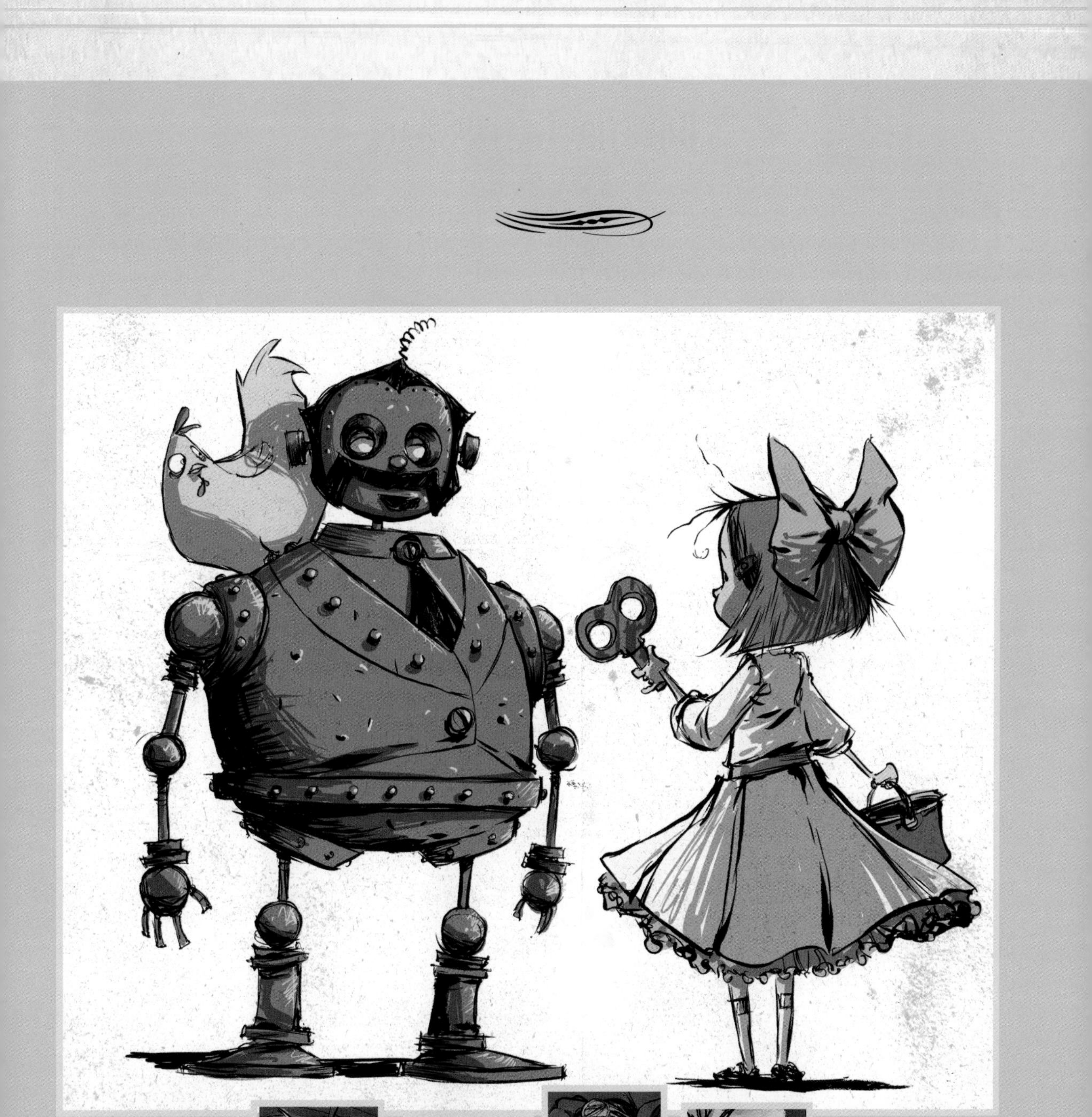

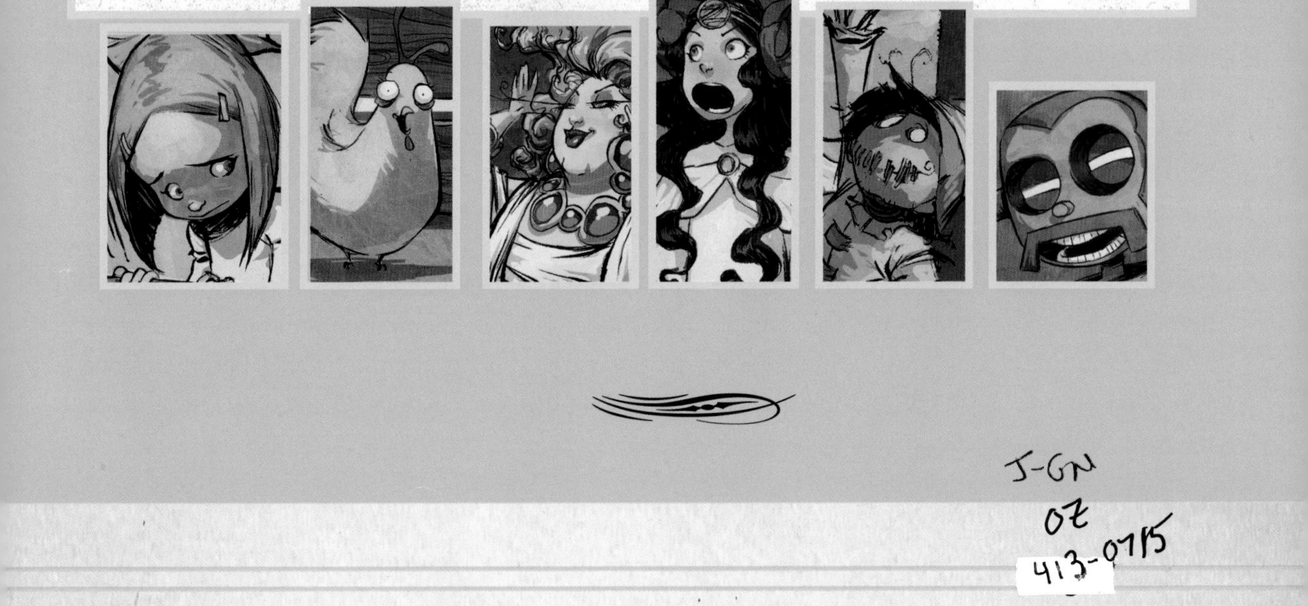

DOROTHY GALE IS BACK

The main character of author L. Frank Baum's best-selling 1900 children's book, *The Wonderful Wizard of Oz*, was a Kansas farm girl named Dorothy who found herself in the strange and magical Land of Oz. Her goal was to return home. Baum's 1904 sequel, *The Marvelous Land of Oz*, barely mentioned Dorothy. Instead, the returning characters from the first book were Dorothy's Oz friends, the Scarecrow and the Tin Woodman. But readers demanded "more about Dorothy."

So in the third Oz book, *Ozma of Oz*, published in 1907, Dorothy Gale returned to Oz, and the Oz books officially became a series.

In *Ozma of Oz* L. Frank Baum could have mimicked the plot of *The Wonderful Wizard of Oz* by again giving his young heroine the goal of returning home. But Baum consciously tried to make each of his Oz stories unique. *Ozma of Oz* is tightly plotted and introduces many new characters destined to become mainstays of the Oz cast. When I read it first as a child, it immediately became my favorite Oz book. I know that I'm not alone in that experience.

Dorothy's main role in the story is as an ally to her new friend, Ozma, ruler of Oz. Ozma's goal is to free a group of slaves from another country by leading her army against the ruler of a third country. Much criticism has been leveled over the years at Ozma's foreign policy, which tends to be well intentioned but naïve. What her critics seem to forget is that Ozma is new to ruling a country. Her upbringing as a witch's servant was no fit preparation for dealing with affairs of state. She's a kid suddenly saddled with adult responsibility, still feeling her way as a monarch after her surprise discovery at the end of the previous Oz book. Some of her advisors have experience as rulers—the Tin Woodman, Glinda, the Scarecrow, and the Cowardly Lion. But youthful, inexperienced Ozma must largely rely on her own judgment. Yet even in the face of danger and her own mistakes Ozma never falters, as you'll see.

Ozma of Oz also features the return of the Cowardly Lion. Near the end of *The Wonderful Wizard of Oz* the Lion became King of Beasts. But from now on, he evidently takes up permanent residence in the Emerald City. He mentions his forest kingdom once in this story, but after that we never hear about it again.

The Scarecrow, the Tin Woodman, and the Sawhorse are back, too. Lots of other Oz characters from the first two books make appearances: Jack Pumpkinhead, the Woggle-bug, Jinjur, Jellia Jamb, even Boq the Munchkin—see if you can spot him.

But it wouldn't be an Oz book without plenty of new characters. Viewers of the 1985 Disney motion picture *Return to Oz* will recognize several of them in cartoonist Skottie Young's captivating new designs. Foremost are Billina the Yellow Hen, who doesn't stand for any nonsense, and Tik-tok, the copper Clockwork Man, who can do anything but actually live. The vain and self-absorbed Princess Langwidere with her cabinet of detachable heads also appeared in the movie *Return to Oz*—though there she was called Mombi, possibly because the play on words "languid air" was too obscure.

And here's the first appearance of the Nome King, the arch villain of the Oz books. Initially the Nome King doesn't seem like such a bad guy. Outwardly he's reasonable, even jolly. But like any good literary villain, the Nome King has deeper layers. And some of them are anything but reasonable. Many of the Nome King's justifications for his actions are as valid as any politician's, before or since. If you'd like an exercise in critical thinking, pay attention to the Nome King's debate with Dorothy about the King of Ev's long life.

Ozma of Oz has been adapted many times—to motion pictures, to the stage, to animation, to picture books, to comics art. I'd like to mention two instances.

First, L. Frank Baum, as he'd done with his previous Oz books, adapted *Ozma of Oz* into a stage musical. After several incarnations, the production finally reached the stage in 1913 as *The Tik-tok Man of Oz*, with music by Louis F. Gottschalk. The show played successfully in California and toured the Midwest, but never reached Broadway. Baum recycled much of the show's plot and many of its characters into his Oz book for 1914, *Tik-tok of Oz*.

Second, there was a previous Marvel Comics adaptation of *Ozma of Oz*. In 1975 Marvel Comics and DC Comics teamed up for the first time to publish *MGM's Marvelous Wizard of Oz*. It was an oversized comic book—in the format called a Treasury Edition—adapting the 1939 MGM movie adaptation of Baum's first Oz book. The art was penciled by John Buscema, who captured a close retelling of the movie, despite having seen it only once decades before. The script was by Roy Thomas, who also wrote the script for the follow-up, *The Marvelous Land of Oz* Treasury Edition, issued the next year by Marvel Comics alone. Its lush artwork by Alfredo Alcala was based on John R. Neill's original illustrations for the book, except in the depictions of the Scarecrow and the Tin Woodman, who resembled their MGM movie versions.

An advertisement in the *Marvelous Land* Treasury Edition announced *The Marvelous Ozma of Oz*, coming later in 1976, again with art by Alcala and script by Thomas. The completed project was a faithful adaptation of Baum's book, sprinkled with a handful of characters based on their MGM movie counterparts. This adherence to the MGM movie necessitated the Hungry Tiger walking on his hind legs to match the Cowardly Lion. As scripter Roy Thomas has noted elsewhere, the result was a bit odd-looking when the two characters pulled Ozma's chariot.

Back then, as I understand it, Marvel's legal department had determined that three Oz titles were in the public domain. The first two were *The Wonderful Wizard of Oz* and *The Marvelous Land of Oz*. But the third title wasn't Baum's third Oz book, *Ozma of Oz*, as had been assumed. It was actually *The New Wizard of Oz*, merely a retitling of *The Wonderful Wizard of Oz*. When Marvel realized that *Ozma of Oz* was still under copyright, rather than secure publication rights from Baum's heirs, they simply cancelled publication.

Today there's little chance of the first Marvel Comics adaptation of *Ozma of Oz* being published. While L. Frank Baum's *Ozma of Oz* has since entered public domain, the rights to the likenesses of the MGM movie characters would need to be secured again. An even greater hurdle to publication is the state of the artwork, assuming the art could be located. Photocopies of the art show that many word balloons—originally pasted onto Alcala's artwork—have fallen off. Restoration would be a major undertaking.

One fragment of the project, however, saw print. The front cover by John Romita—with coloring by yours truly—appeared on the back cover of a 1987 issue of *The Baum Bugle*, the journal of the International Wizard of Oz Club (whose web address is www.ozclub.org for those interested).

But now Marvel Comics presents a new comics version of *Ozma of Oz* for the enjoyment of all. So what are you waiting for? Turn the page and start enjoying Dorothy Gale's return.

Eric Shanower
July 2011

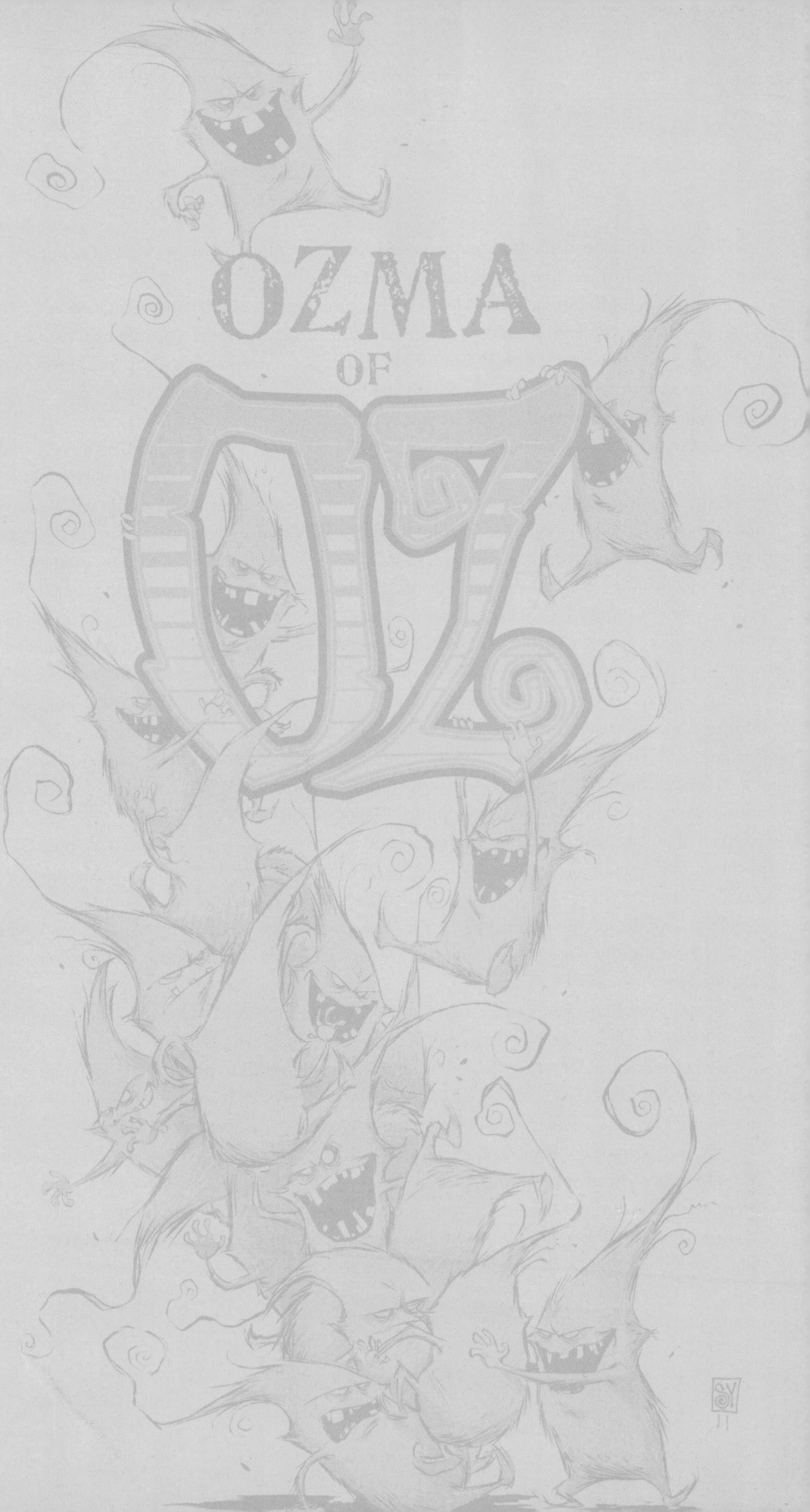
OZMA
OF
OZ

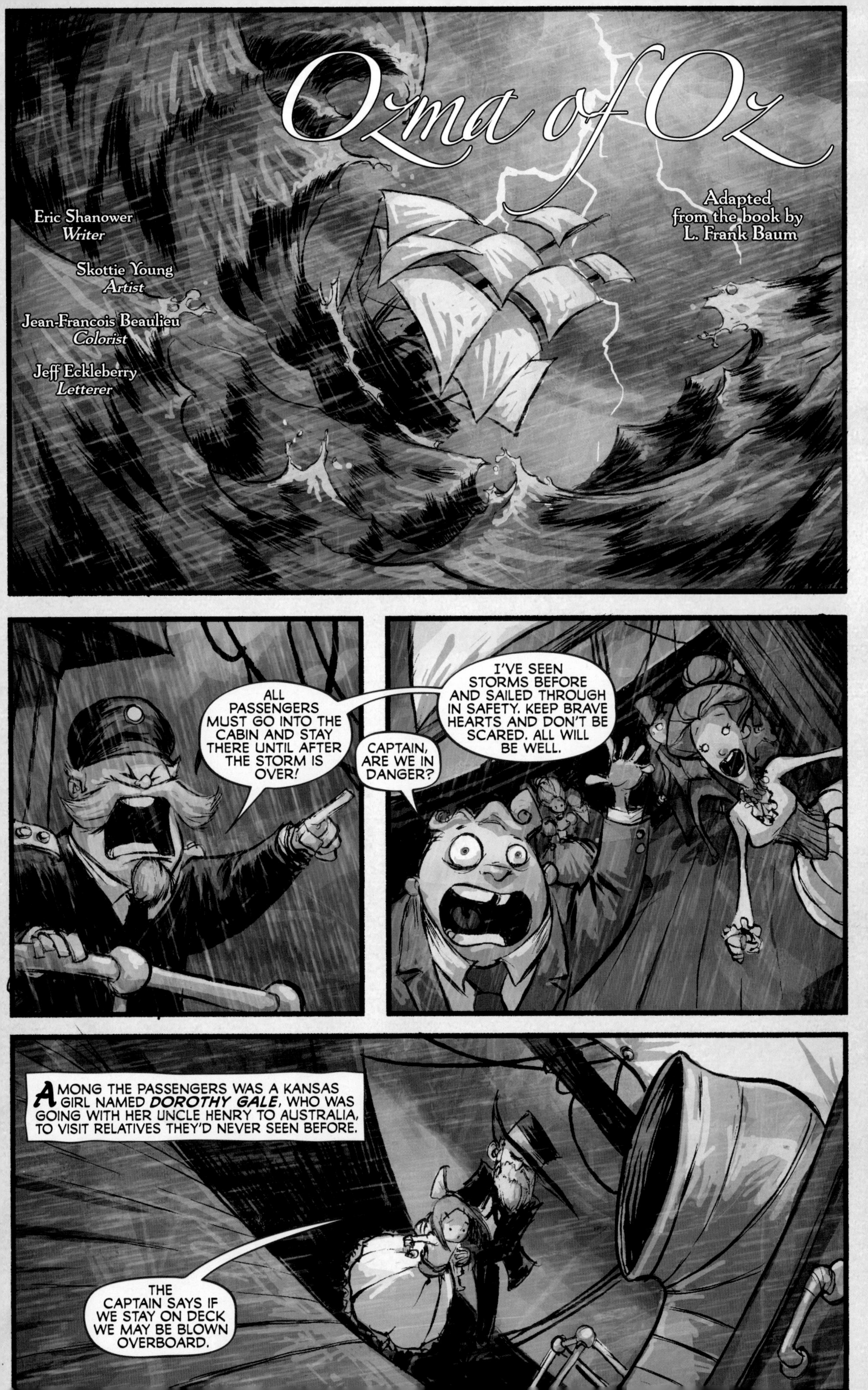
Ozma of Oz
Eric Shanower Writer
Skottie Young Artist
Jean-Francois Beaulieu Colorist
Jeff Eckleberry Letterer
Adapted from the book by L. Frank Baum
ALL PASSENGERS MUST GO INTO THE CABIN AND STAY THERE UNTIL AFTER THE STORM IS OVER!
CAPTAIN, ARE WE IN DANGER?
I'VE SEEN STORMS BEFORE AND SAILED THROUGH IN SAFETY. KEEP BRAVE HEARTS AND DON'T BE SCARED. ALL WILL BE WELL.
AMONG THE PASSENGERS WAS A KANSAS GIRL NAMED DOROTHY GALE, WHO WAS GOING WITH HER UNCLE HENRY TO AUSTRALIA, TO VISIT RELATIVES THEY'D NEVER SEEN BEFORE.
THE CAPTAIN SAYS IF WE STAY ON DECK WE MAY BE BLOWN OVERBOARD.

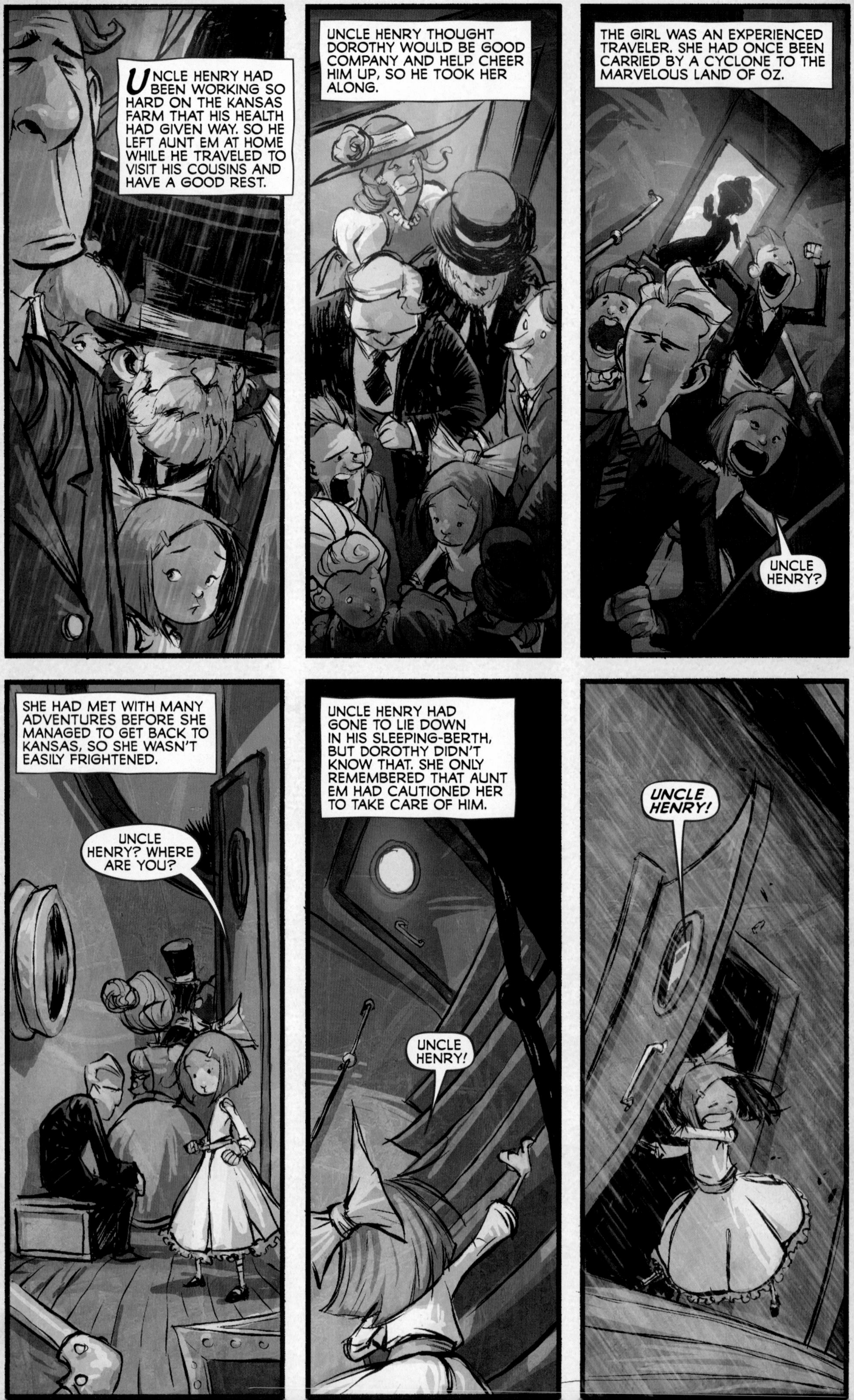
UNCLE HENRY HAD BEEN WORKING SO HARD ON THE KANSAS FARM THAT HIS HEALTH HAD GIVEN WAY. SO HE LEFT AUNT EM AT HOME WHILE HE TRAVELED TO VISIT HIS COUSINS AND HAVE A GOOD REST.
UNCLE HENRY THOUGHT DOROTHY WOULD BE GOOD COMPANY AND HELP CHEER HIM UP, SO HE TOOK HER ALONG.
THE GIRL WAS AN EXPERIENCED TRAVELER. SHE HAD ONCE BEEN CARRIED BY A CYCLONE TO THE MARVELOUS LAND OF OZ.
UNCLE HENRY?
SHE HAD MET WITH MANY ADVENTURES BEFORE SHE MANAGED TO GET BACK TO KANSAS, SO SHE WASN'T EASILY FRIGHTENED.
UNCLE HENRY? WHERE ARE YOU?
UNCLE HENRY HAD GONE TO LIE DOWN IN HIS SLEEPING-BERTH, BUT DOROTHY DIDN'T KNOW THAT. SHE ONLY REMEMBERED THAT AUNT EM HAD CAUTIONED HER TO TAKE CARE OF HIM.
UNCLE HENRY!
UNCLE HENRY!

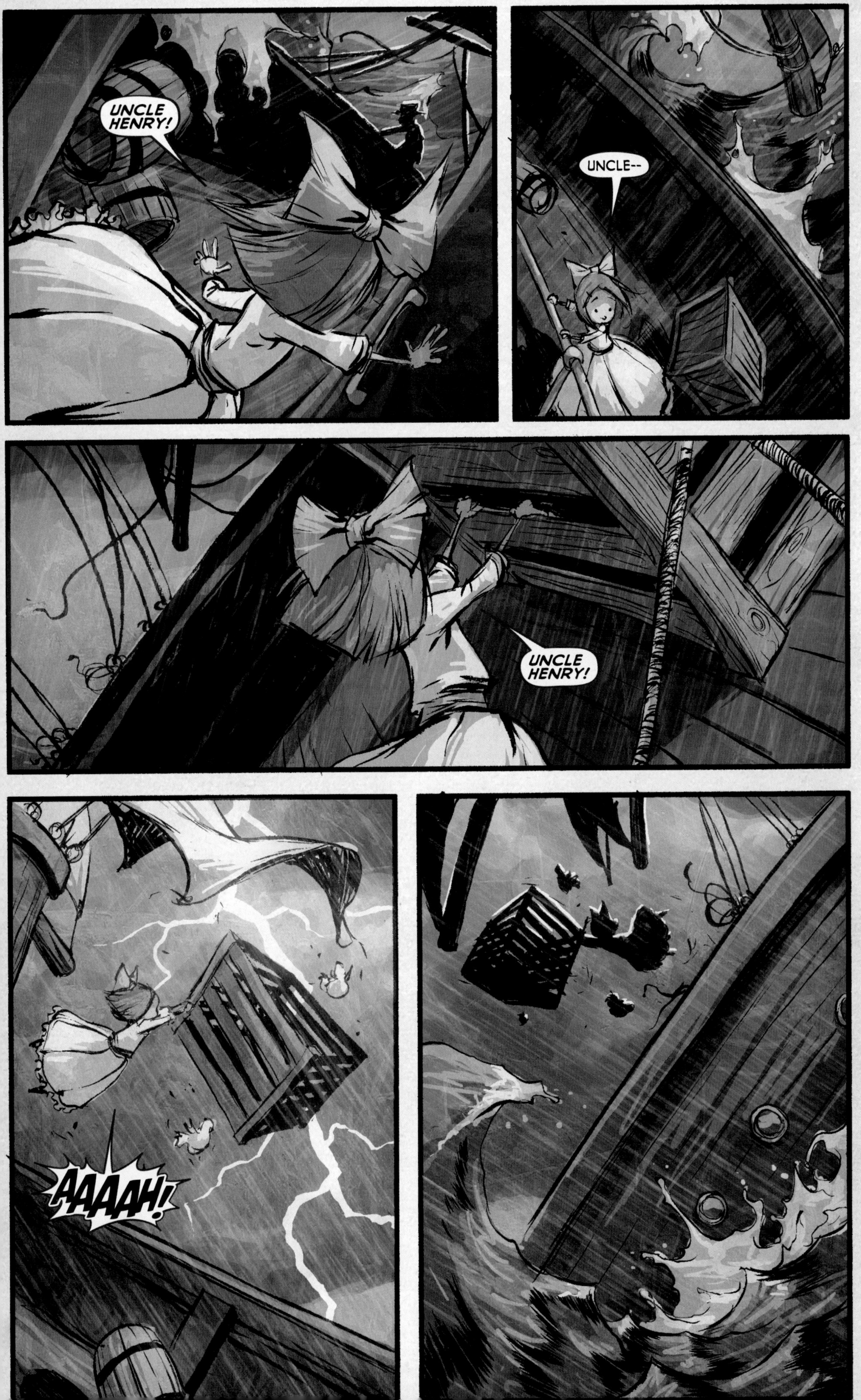
UNCLE HENRY!
UNCLE--
UNCLE HENRY!
AAAAH!

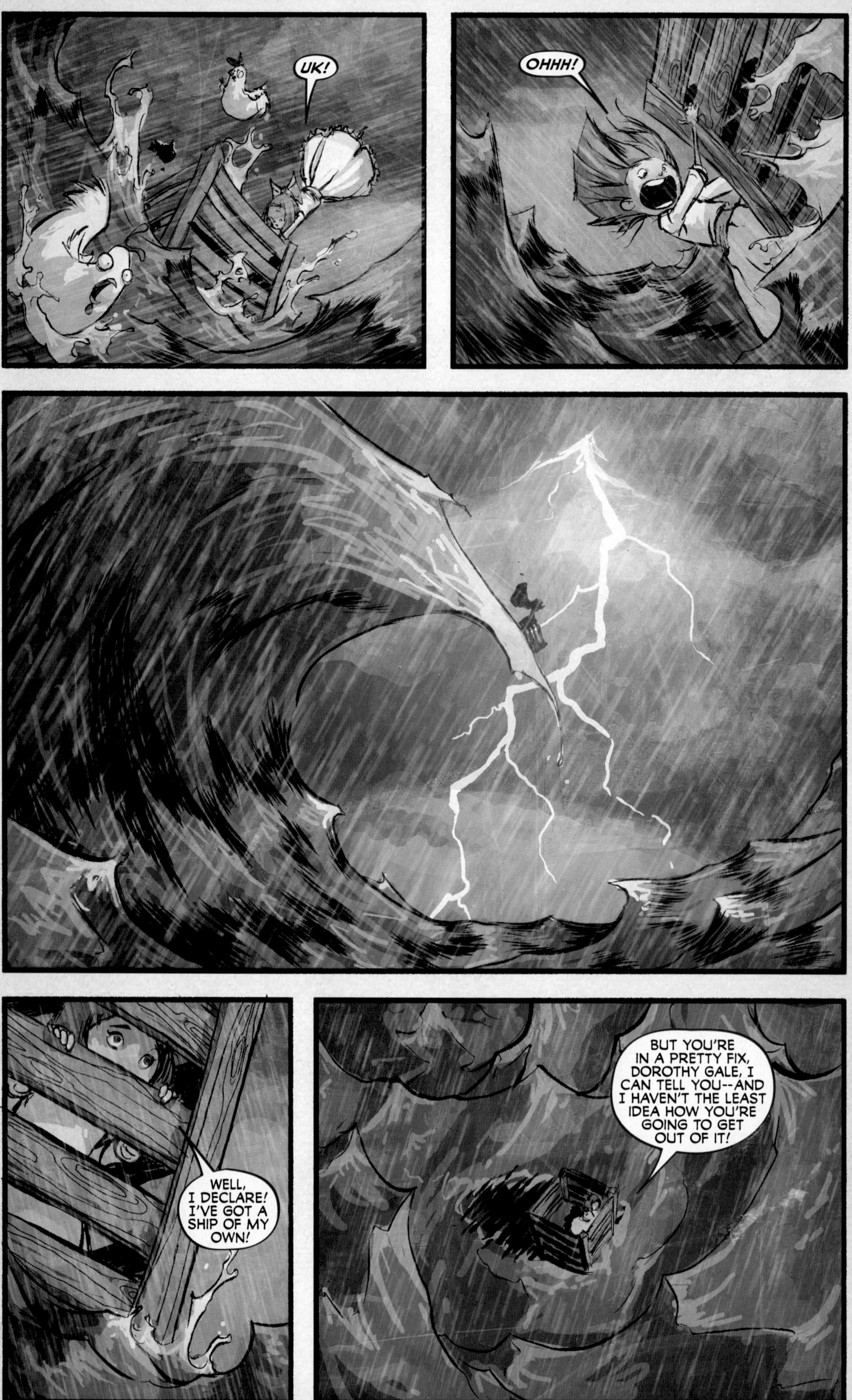
UK!
OHHH!
WELL, I DECLARE! I'VE GOT A SHIP OF MY OWN!
BUT YOU'RE IN A PRETTY FIX, DOROTHY GALE, I CAN TELL YOU--AND I HAVEN'T THE LEAST IDEA HOW YOU'RE GOING TO GET OUT OF IT!

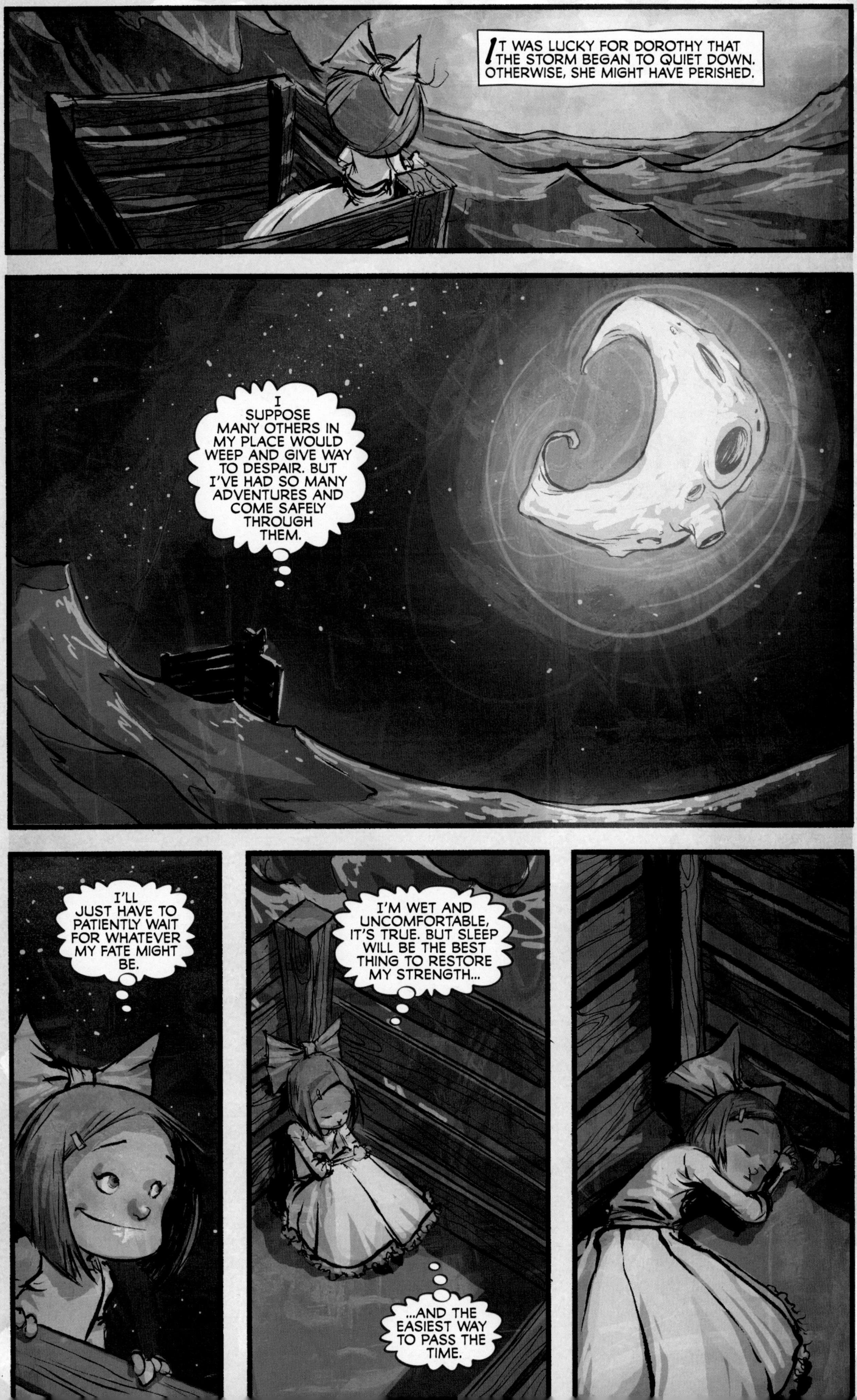
IT WAS LUCKY FOR DOROTHY THAT THE STORM BEGAN TO QUIET DOWN. OTHERWISE, SHE MIGHT HAVE PERISHED.
I SUPPOSE MANY OTHERS IN MY PLACE WOULD WEEP AND GIVE WAY TO DESPAIR. BUT I'VE HAD SO MANY ADVENTURES AND COME SAFELY THROUGH THEM.
I'LL JUST HAVE TO PATIENTLY WAIT FOR WHATEVER MY FATE MIGHT BE.
I'M WET AND UNCOMFORTABLE, IT'S TRUE. BUT SLEEP WILL BE THE BEST THING TO RESTORE MY STRENGTH...
...AND THE EASIEST WAY TO PASS THE TIME.

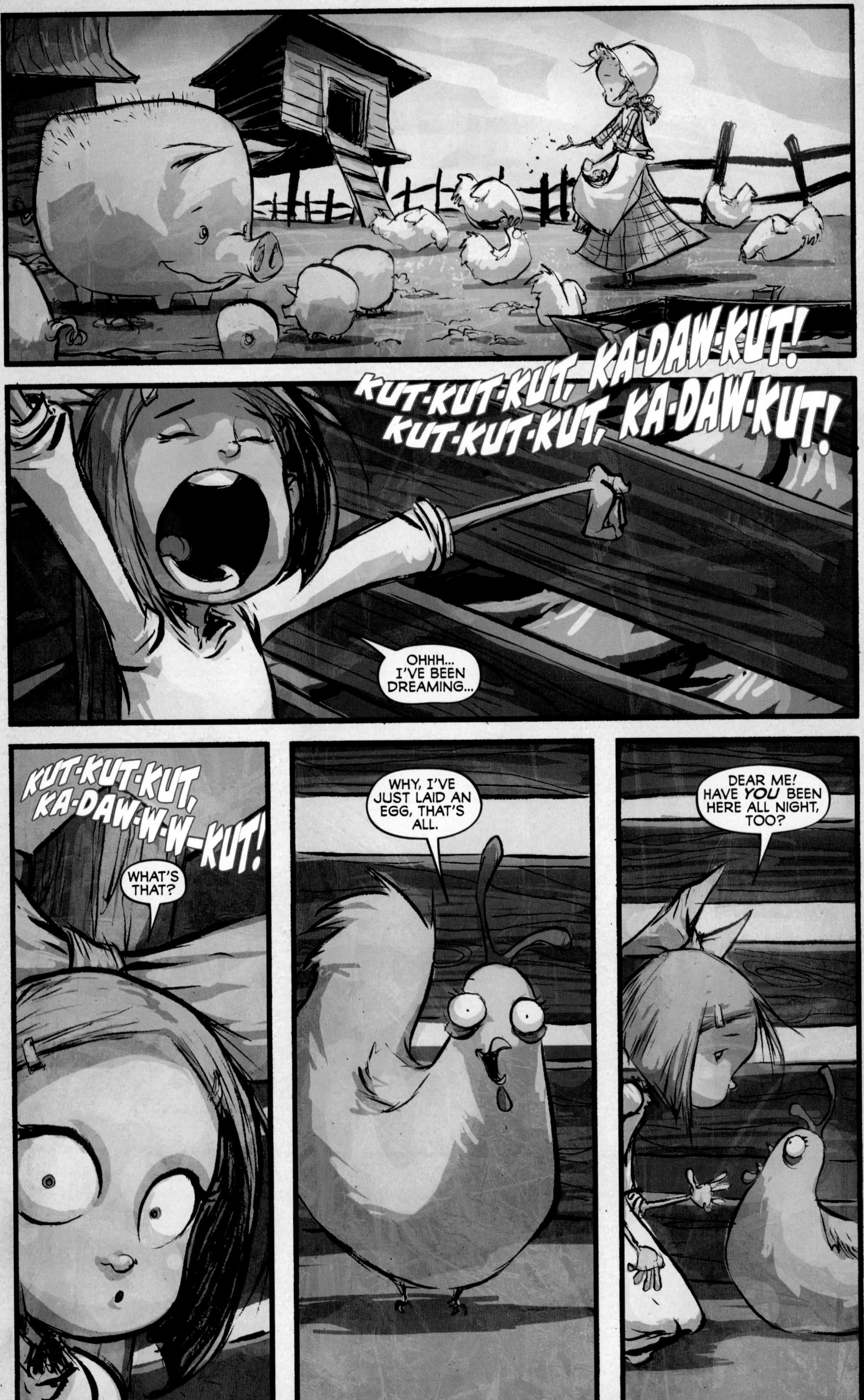
KUT-KUT-KUT, KA-DAW-KUT!
KUT-KUT-KUT, KA-DAW-KUT!
OHHH... I'VE BEEN DREAMING...
KUT-KUT-KUT, KA-DAW-W-W-KUT!
WHAT'S THAT?
WHY, I'VE JUST LAID AN EGG, THAT'S ALL.
DEAR ME! HAVE *YOU* BEEN HERE ALL NIGHT, TOO?

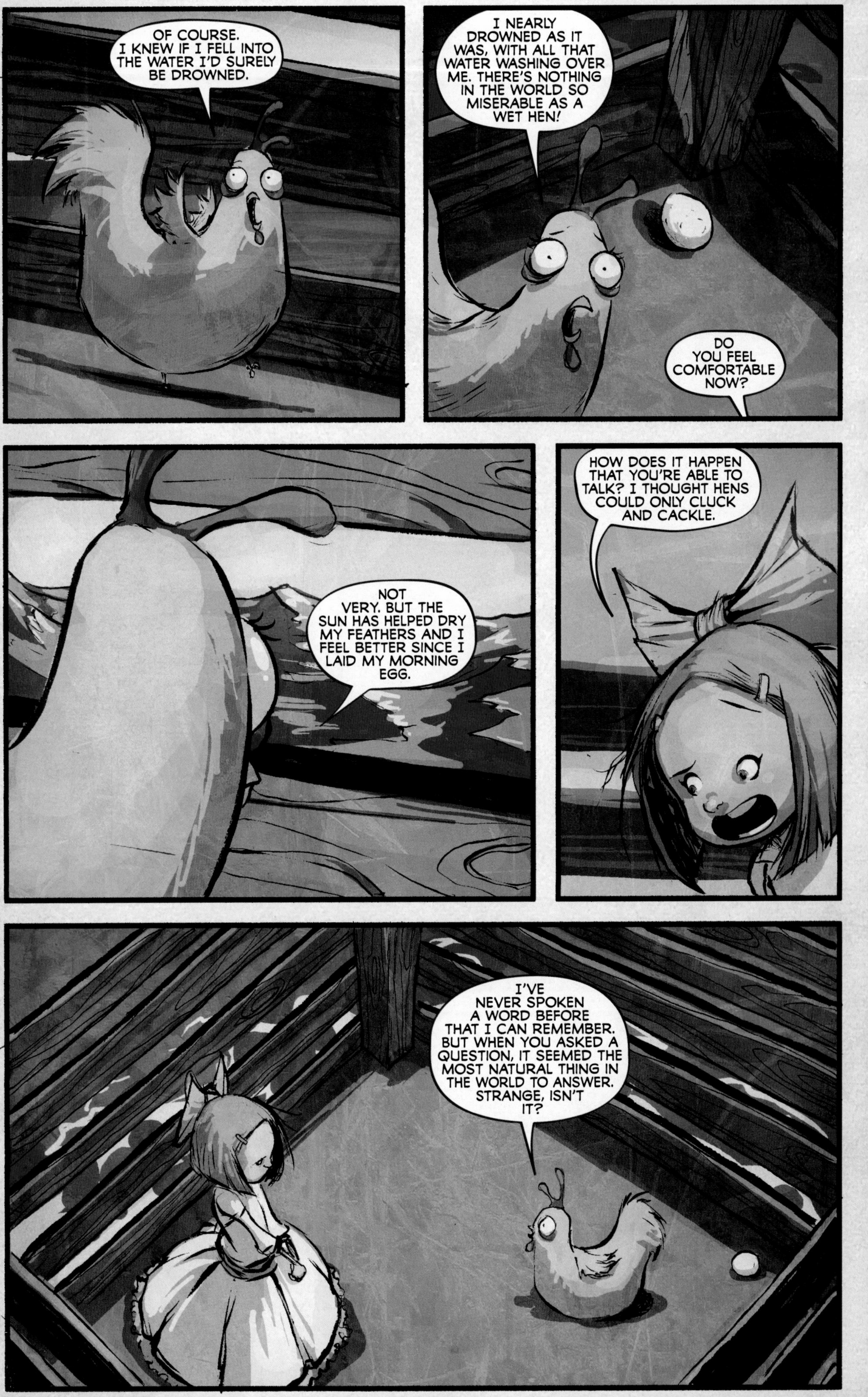
OF COURSE. I KNEW IF I FELL INTO THE WATER I'D SURELY BE DROWNED.
I NEARLY DROWNED AS IT WAS, WITH ALL THAT WATER WASHING OVER ME. THERE'S NOTHING IN THE WORLD SO MISERABLE AS A WET HEN!
DO YOU FEEL COMFORTABLE NOW?
NOT VERY. BUT THE SUN HAS HELPED DRY MY FEATHERS AND I FEEL BETTER SINCE I LAID MY MORNING EGG.
HOW DOES IT HAPPEN THAT YOU'RE ABLE TO TALK? I THOUGHT HENS COULD ONLY CLUCK AND CACKLE.
I'VE NEVER SPOKEN A WORD BEFORE THAT I CAN REMEMBER. BUT WHEN YOU ASKED A QUESTION, IT SEEMED THE MOST NATURAL THING IN THE WORLD TO ANSWER. STRANGE, ISN'T IT?

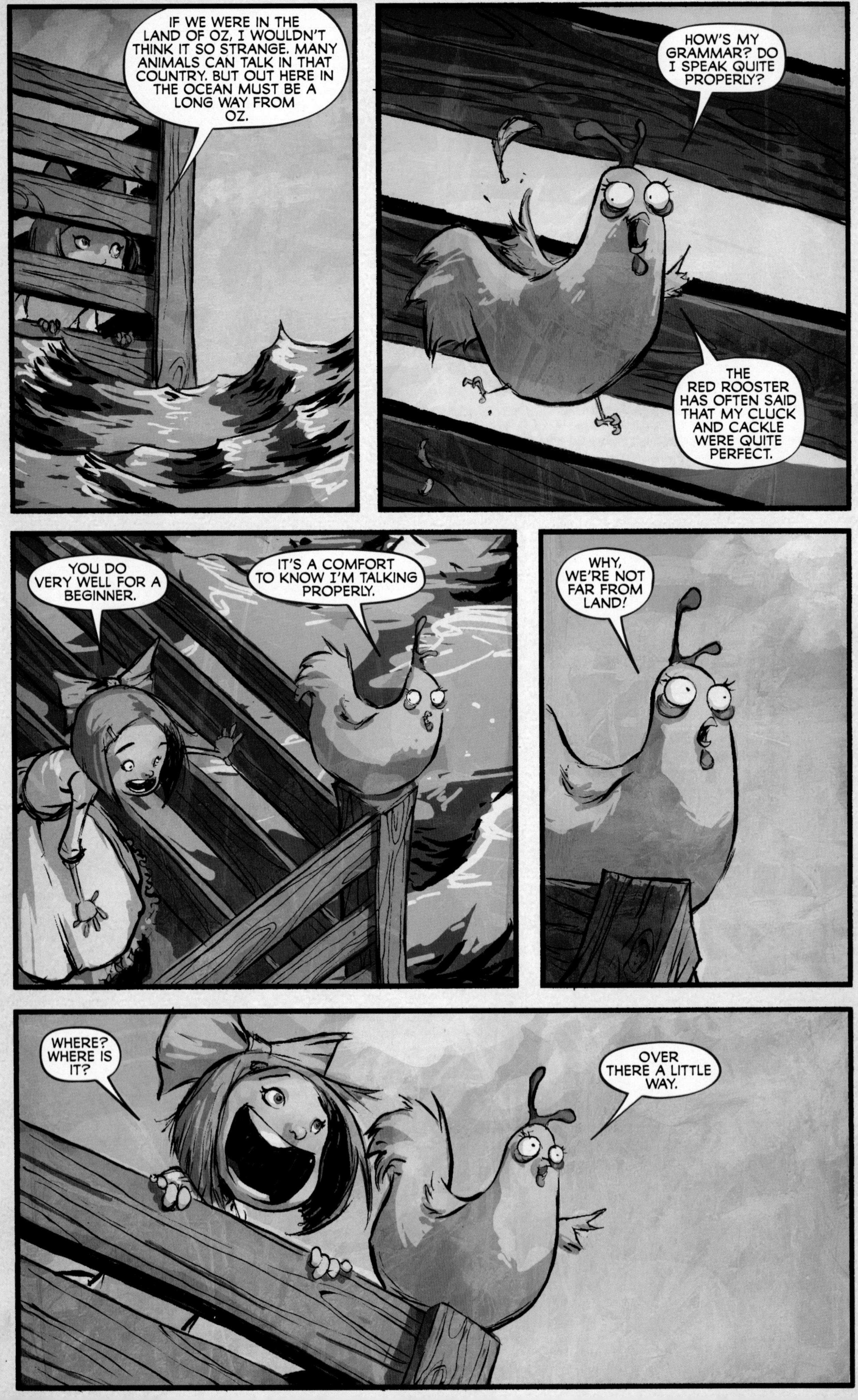
IF WE WERE IN THE LAND OF OZ, I WOULDN'T THINK IT SO STRANGE. MANY ANIMALS CAN TALK IN THAT COUNTRY. BUT OUT HERE IN THE OCEAN MUST BE A LONG WAY FROM OZ.
HOW'S MY GRAMMAR? DO I SPEAK QUITE PROPERLY?
THE RED ROOSTER HAS OFTEN SAID THAT MY CLUCK AND CACKLE WERE QUITE PERFECT.
YOU DO VERY WELL FOR A BEGINNER.
IT'S A COMFORT TO KNOW I'M TALKING PROPERLY.
WHY, WE'RE NOT FAR FROM LAND!
WHERE? WHERE IS IT?
OVER THERE A LITTLE WAY.

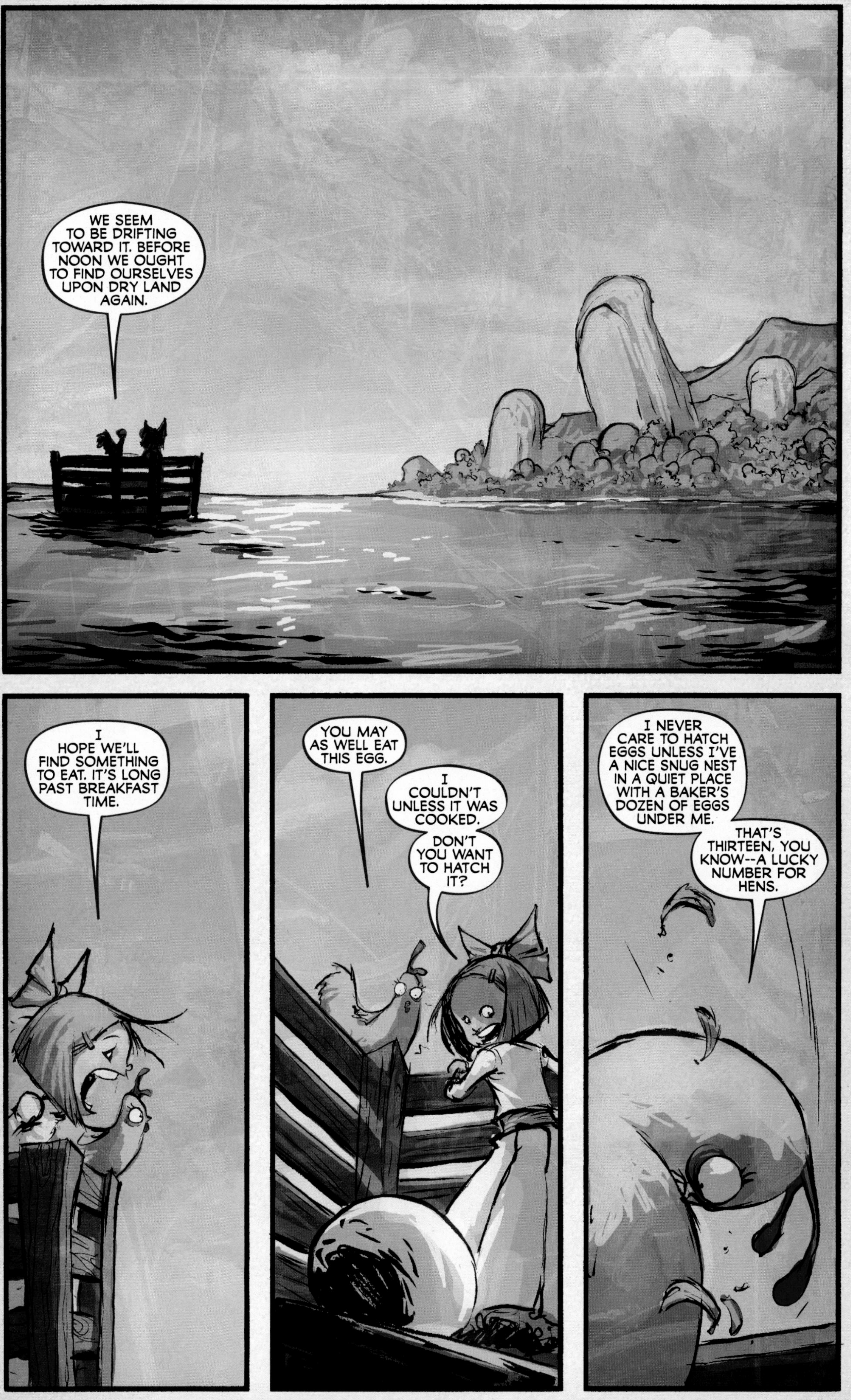
WE SEEM TO BE DRIFTING TOWARD IT. BEFORE NOON WE OUGHT TO FIND OURSELVES UPON DRY LAND AGAIN.
I HOPE WE'LL FIND SOMETHING TO EAT. IT'S LONG PAST BREAKFAST TIME.
YOU MAY AS WELL EAT THIS EGG.
I COULDN'T UNLESS IT WAS COOKED.
DON'T YOU WANT TO HATCH IT?
I NEVER CARE TO HATCH EGGS UNLESS I'VE A NICE SNUG NEST IN A QUIET PLACE WITH A BAKER'S DOZEN OF EGGS UNDER ME.
THAT'S THIRTEEN, YOU KNOW--A LUCKY NUMBER FOR HENS.

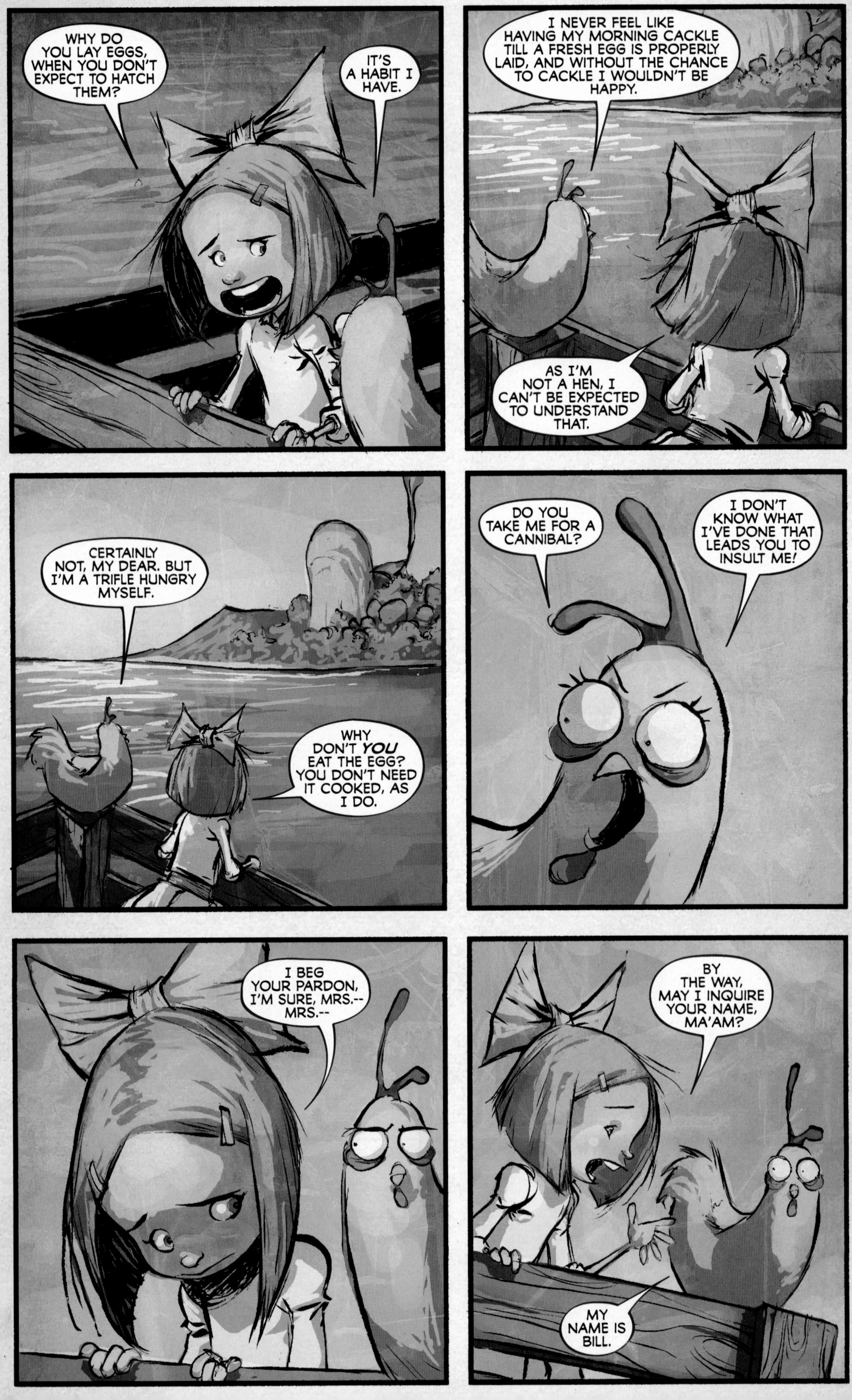

WHY DO YOU LAY EGGS, WHEN YOU DON'T EXPECT TO HATCH THEM?
IT'S A HABIT I HAVE.
I NEVER FEEL LIKE HAVING MY MORNING CACKLE TILL A FRESH EGG IS PROPERLY LAID, AND WITHOUT THE CHANCE TO CACKLE I WOULDN'T BE HAPPY.
AS I'M NOT A HEN, I CAN'T BE EXPECTED TO UNDERSTAND THAT.
CERTAINLY NOT, MY DEAR. BUT I'M A TRIFLE HUNGRY MYSELF.
WHY DON'T *YOU* EAT THE EGG? YOU DON'T NEED IT COOKED, AS I DO.
DO YOU TAKE ME FOR A CANNIBAL?
I DON'T KNOW WHAT I'VE DONE THAT LEADS YOU TO INSULT ME!
I BEG YOUR PARDON, I'M SURE, MRS.-- MRS.--
BY THE WAY, MAY I INQUIRE YOUR NAME, MA'AM?
MY NAME IS BILL.

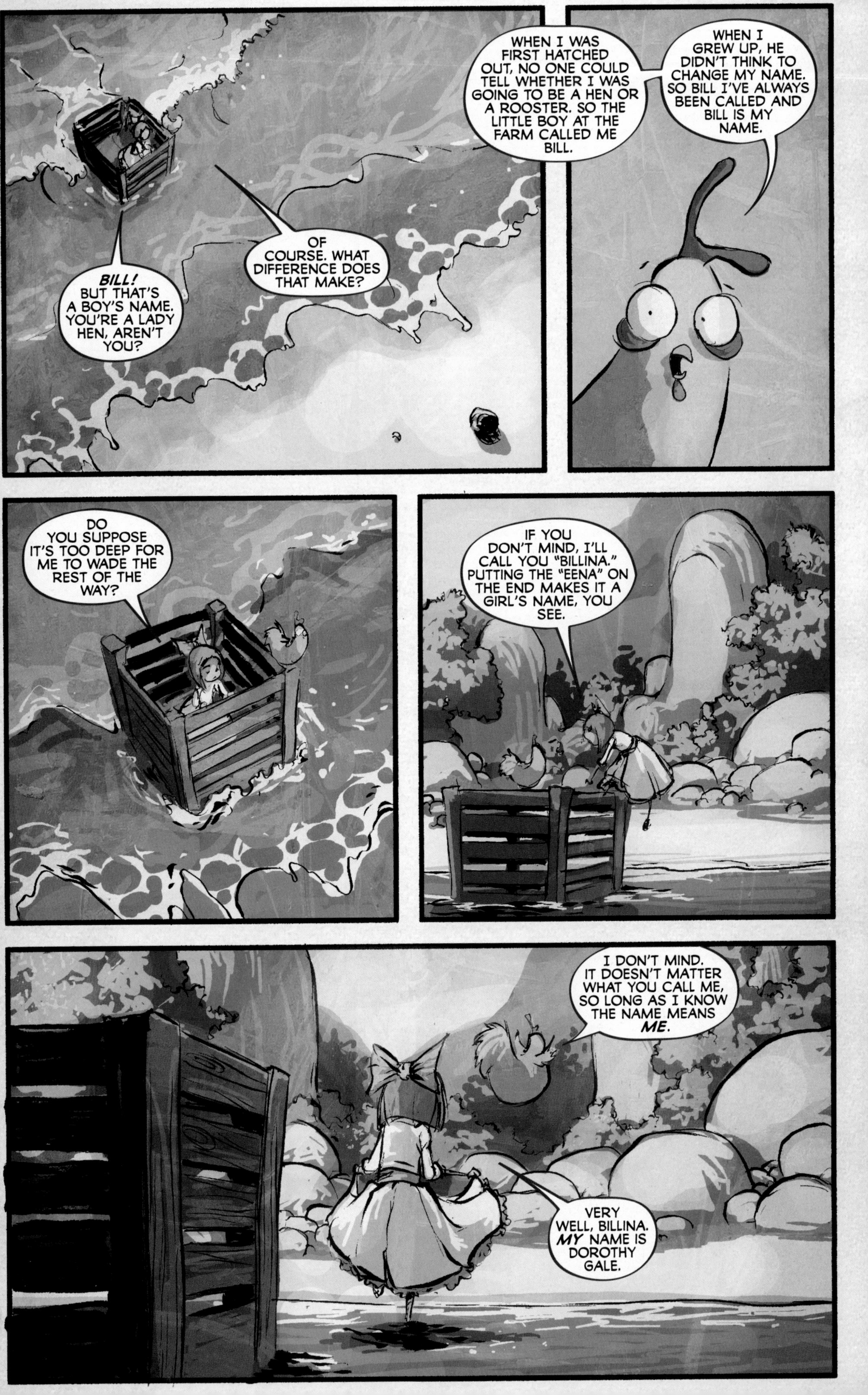
BILL! BUT THAT'S A BOY'S NAME. YOU'RE A LADY HEN, AREN'T YOU?
OF COURSE. WHAT DIFFERENCE DOES THAT MAKE?
WHEN I WAS FIRST HATCHED OUT, NO ONE COULD TELL WHETHER I WAS GOING TO BE A HEN OR A ROOSTER. SO THE LITTLE BOY AT THE FARM CALLED ME BILL.
WHEN I GREW UP, HE DIDN'T THINK TO CHANGE MY NAME. SO BILL I'VE ALWAYS BEEN CALLED AND BILL IS MY NAME.
DO YOU SUPPOSE IT'S TOO DEEP FOR ME TO WADE THE REST OF THE WAY?
IF YOU DON'T MIND, I'LL CALL YOU "BILLINA." PUTTING THE "EENA" ON THE END MAKES IT A GIRL'S NAME, YOU SEE.
I DON'T MIND. IT DOESN'T MATTER WHAT YOU CALL ME, SO LONG AS I KNOW THE NAME MEANS ME.
VERY WELL, BILLINA. MY NAME IS DOROTHY GALE.

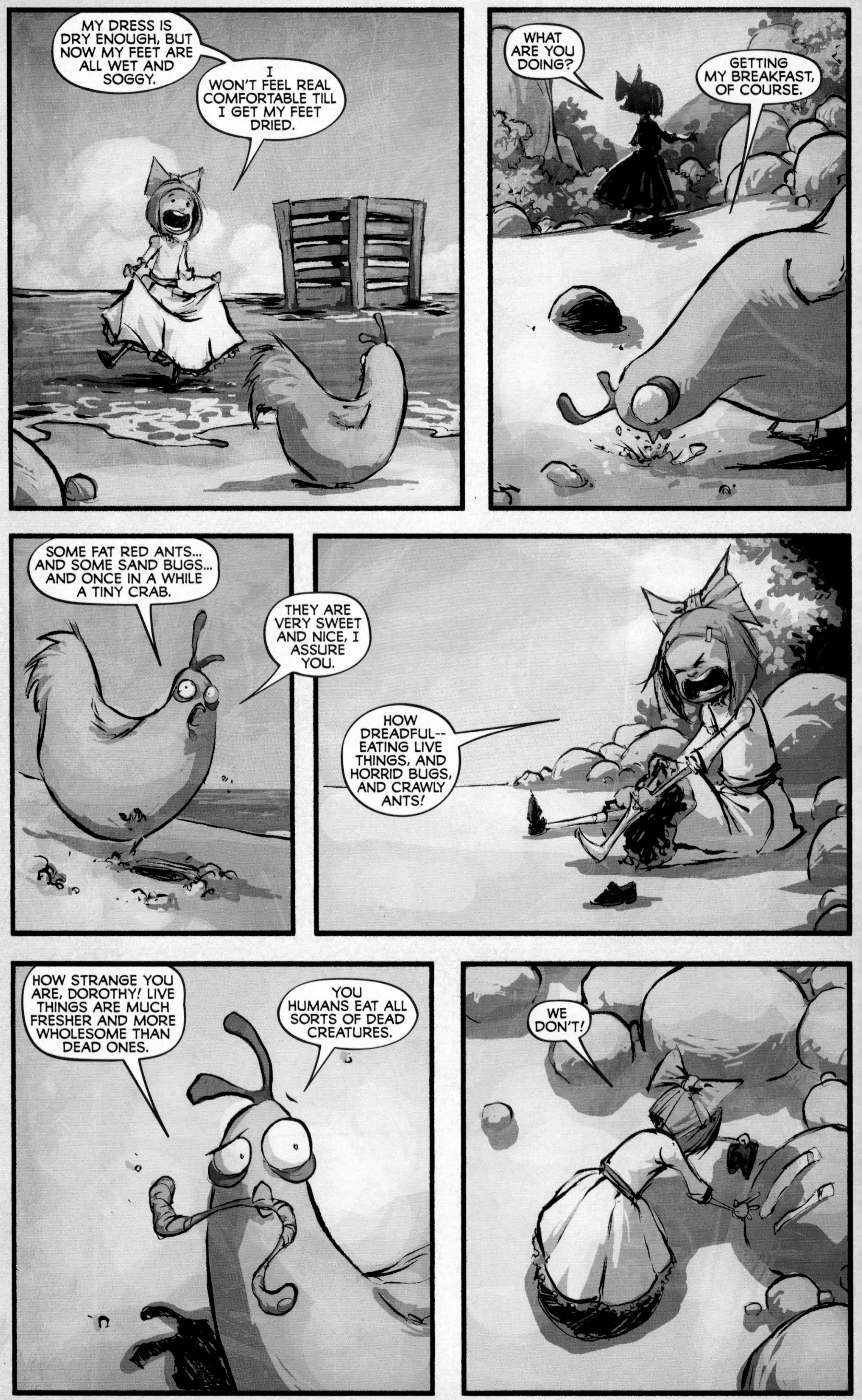
MY DRESS IS DRY ENOUGH, BUT NOW MY FEET ARE ALL WET AND SOGGY.
I WON'T FEEL REAL COMFORTABLE TILL I GET MY FEET DRIED.
WHAT ARE YOU DOING?
GETTING MY BREAKFAST, OF COURSE.
SOME FAT RED ANTS... AND SOME SAND BUGS... AND ONCE IN A WHILE A TINY CRAB.
THEY ARE VERY SWEET AND NICE, I ASSURE YOU.
HOW DREADFUL-- EATING LIVE THINGS, AND HORRID BUGS, AND CRAWLY ANTS!
HOW STRANGE YOU ARE, DOROTHY! LIVE THINGS ARE MUCH FRESHER AND MORE WHOLESOME THAN DEAD ONES.
YOU HUMANS EAT ALL SORTS OF DEAD CREATURES.
WE DON'T!

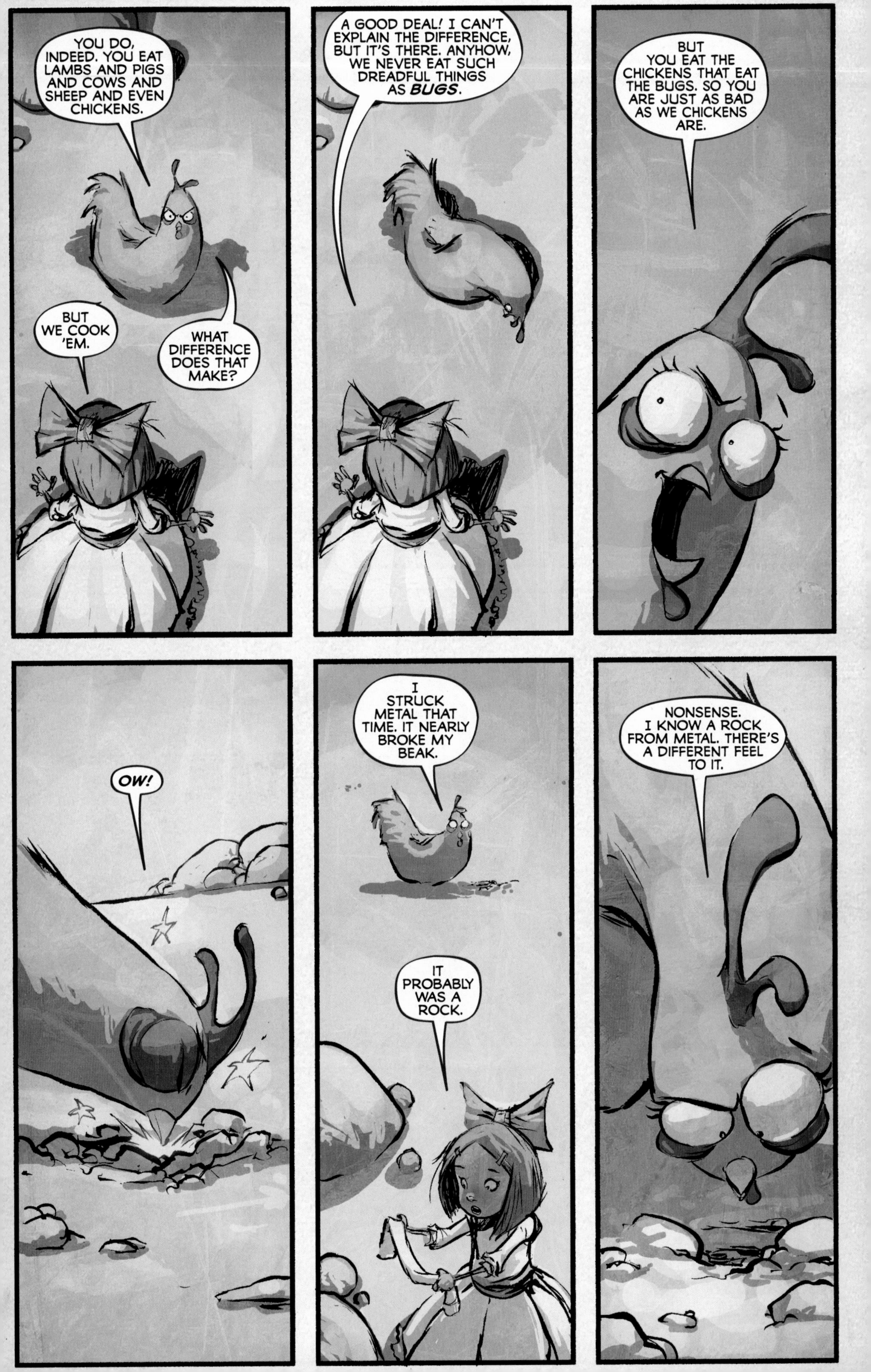
YOU DO, INDEED. YOU EAT LAMBS AND PIGS AND COWS AND SHEEP AND EVEN CHICKENS.
BUT WE COOK 'EM.
WHAT DIFFERENCE DOES THAT MAKE?
A GOOD DEAL! I CAN'T EXPLAIN THE DIFFERENCE, BUT IT'S THERE. ANYHOW, WE NEVER EAT SUCH DREADFUL THINGS AS BUGS.
BUT YOU EAT THE CHICKENS THAT EAT THE BUGS. SO YOU ARE JUST AS BAD AS WE CHICKENS ARE.
OW!
I STRUCK METAL THAT TIME. IT NEARLY BROKE MY BEAK.
IT PROBABLY WAS A ROCK.
NONSENSE. I KNOW A ROCK FROM METAL. THERE'S A DIFFERENT FEEL TO IT.

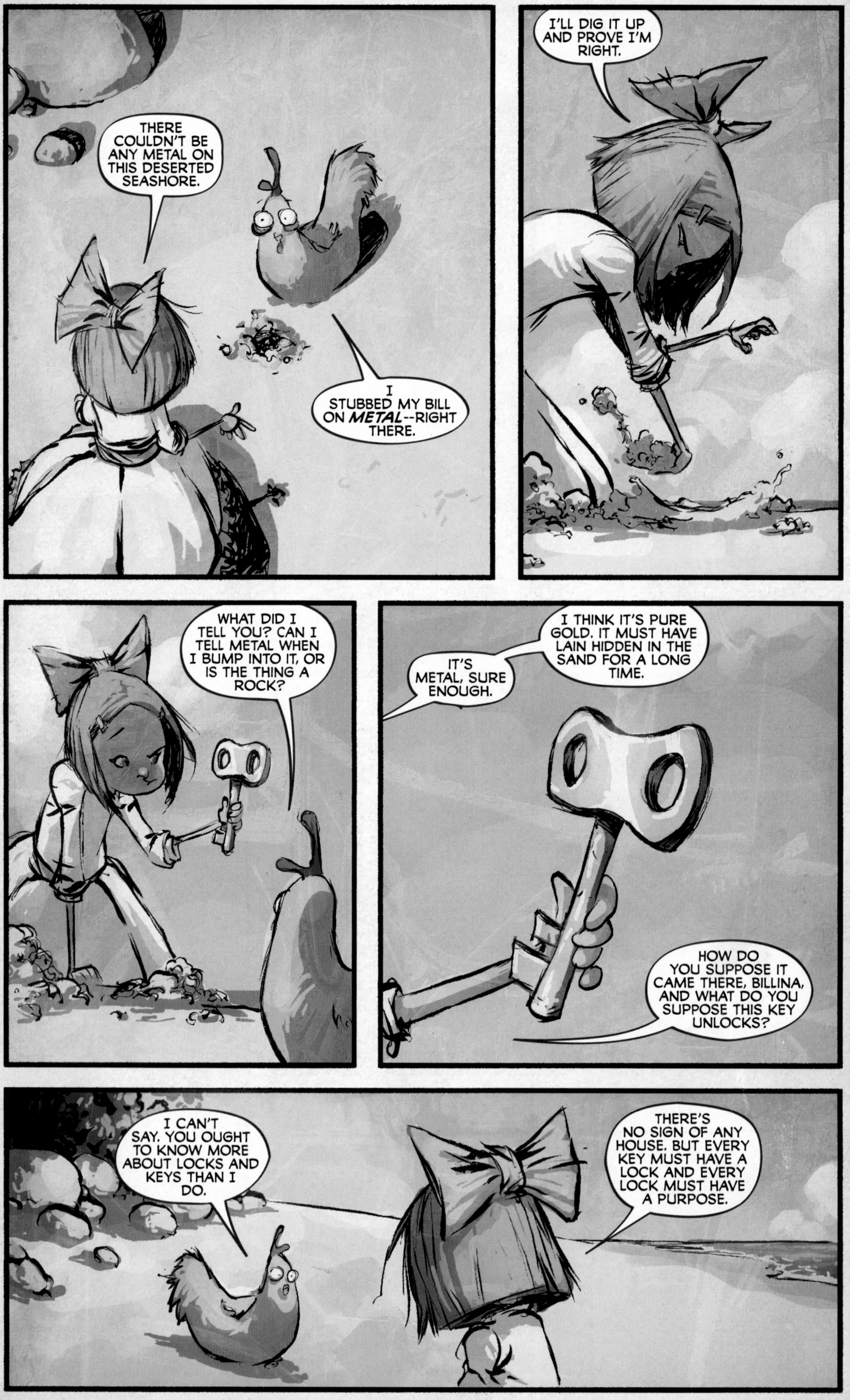
THERE COULDN'T BE ANY METAL ON THIS DESERTED SEASHORE.
I STUBBED MY BILL ON METAL--RIGHT THERE.
I'LL DIG IT UP AND PROVE I'M RIGHT.
WHAT DID I TELL YOU? CAN I TELL METAL WHEN I BUMP INTO IT, OR IS THE THING A ROCK?
IT'S METAL, SURE ENOUGH.
I THINK IT'S PURE GOLD. IT MUST HAVE LAIN HIDDEN IN THE SAND FOR A LONG TIME.
HOW DO YOU SUPPOSE IT CAME THERE, BILLINA, AND WHAT DO YOU SUPPOSE THIS KEY UNLOCKS?
I CAN'T SAY. YOU OUGHT TO KNOW MORE ABOUT LOCKS AND KEYS THAN I DO.
THERE'S NO SIGN OF ANY HOUSE. BUT EVERY KEY MUST HAVE A LOCK AND EVERY LOCK MUST HAVE A PURPOSE.

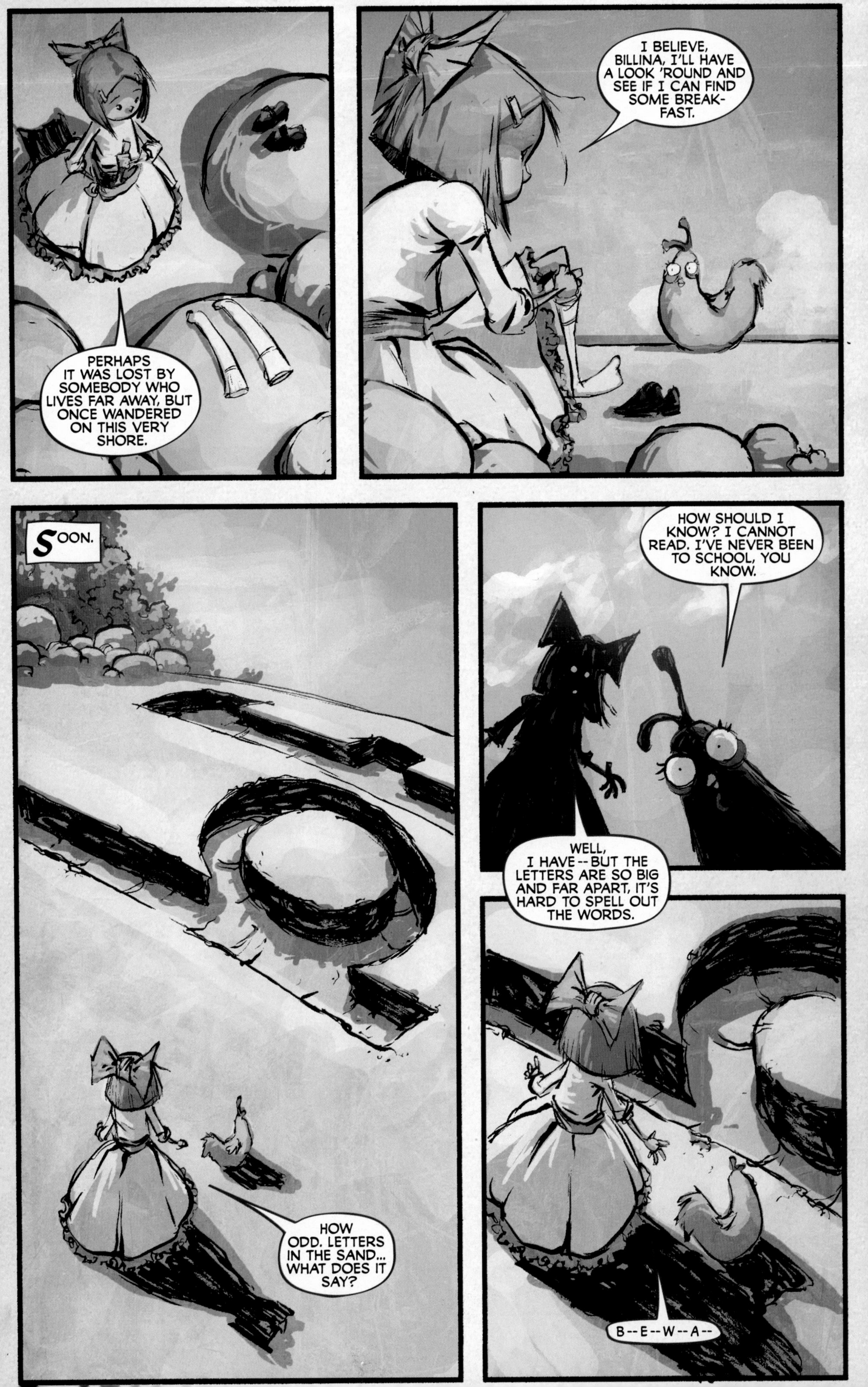
PERHAPS IT WAS LOST BY SOMEBODY WHO LIVES FAR AWAY, BUT ONCE WANDERED ON THIS VERY SHORE.
I BELIEVE, BILLINA, I'LL HAVE A LOOK 'ROUND AND SEE IF I CAN FIND SOME BREAK-FAST.
SOON.
HOW ODD. LETTERS IN THE SAND... WHAT DOES IT SAY?
HOW SHOULD I KNOW? I CANNOT READ. I'VE NEVER BEEN TO SCHOOL, YOU KNOW.
WELL, I HAVE -- BUT THE LETTERS ARE SO BIG AND FAR APART, IT'S HARD TO SPELL OUT THE WORDS.
B--E--W--A--

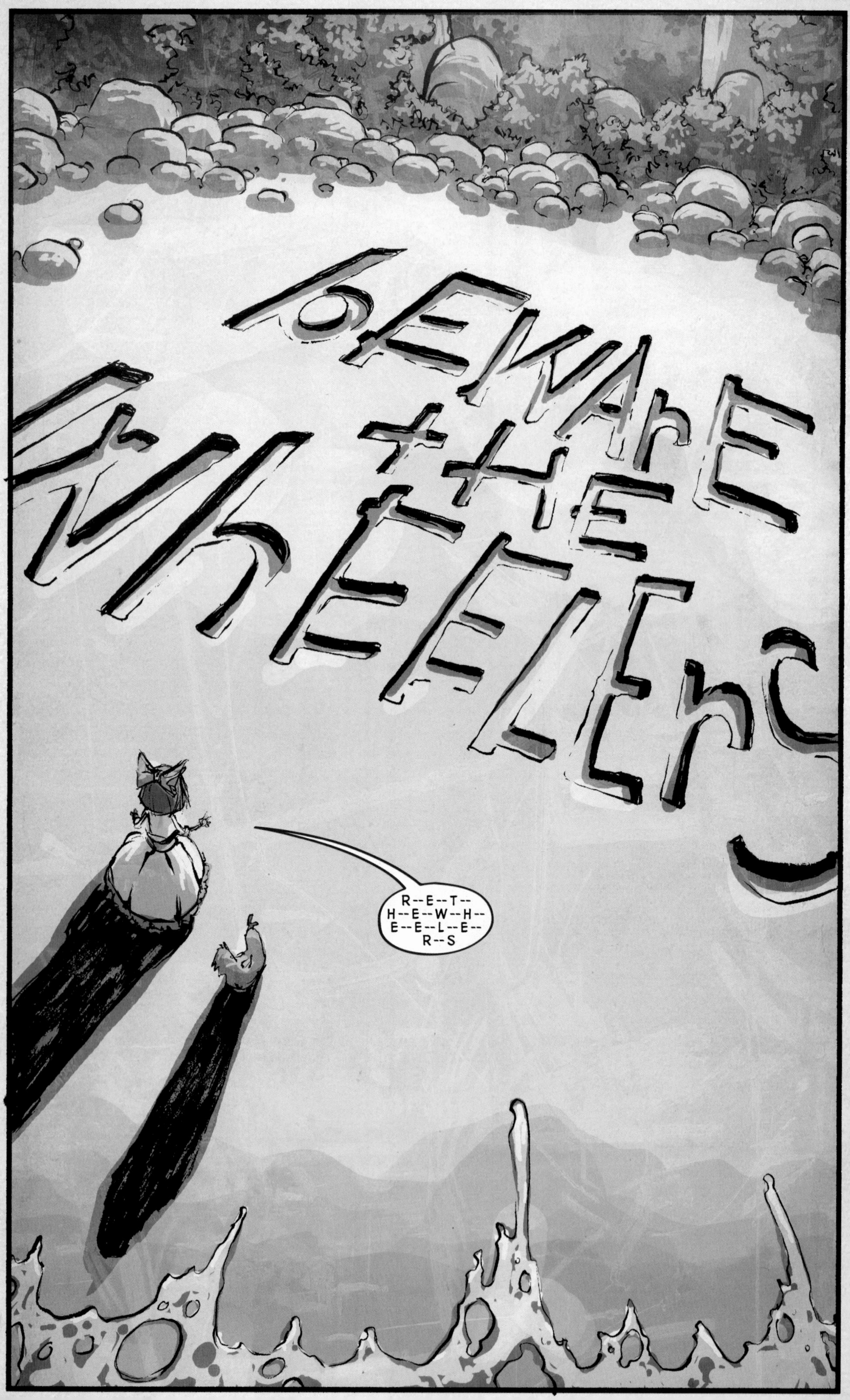
BEWARE THE WHEELERS
R--E--T--H--E--W--H--E--E--L--E--R--S

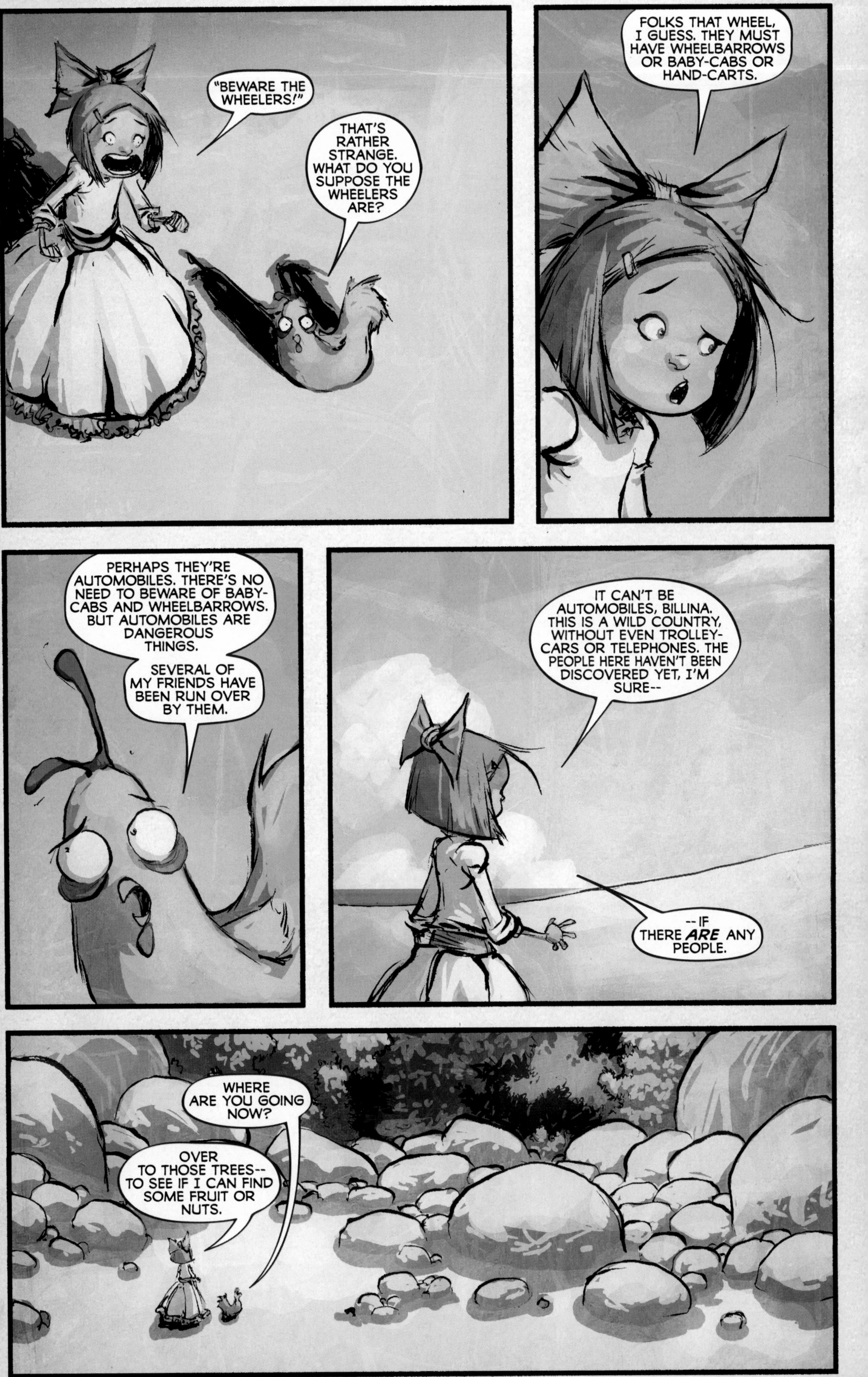
"BEWARE THE WHEELERS!"
THAT'S RATHER STRANGE. WHAT DO YOU SUPPOSE THE WHEELERS ARE?
FOLKS THAT WHEEL, I GUESS. THEY MUST HAVE WHEELBARROWS OR BABY-CABS OR HAND-CARTS.
PERHAPS THEY'RE AUTOMOBILES. THERE'S NO NEED TO BEWARE OF BABY-CABS AND WHEELBARROWS. BUT AUTOMOBILES ARE DANGEROUS THINGS.
SEVERAL OF MY FRIENDS HAVE BEEN RUN OVER BY THEM.
IT CAN'T BE AUTOMOBILES, BILLINA. THIS IS A WILD COUNTRY, WITHOUT EVEN TROLLEY-CARS OR TELEPHONES. THE PEOPLE HERE HAVEN'T BEEN DISCOVERED YET, I'M SURE--
--IF THERE ***ARE*** ANY PEOPLE.
WHERE ARE YOU GOING NOW?
OVER TO THOSE TREES-- TO SEE IF I CAN FIND SOME FRUIT OR NUTS.

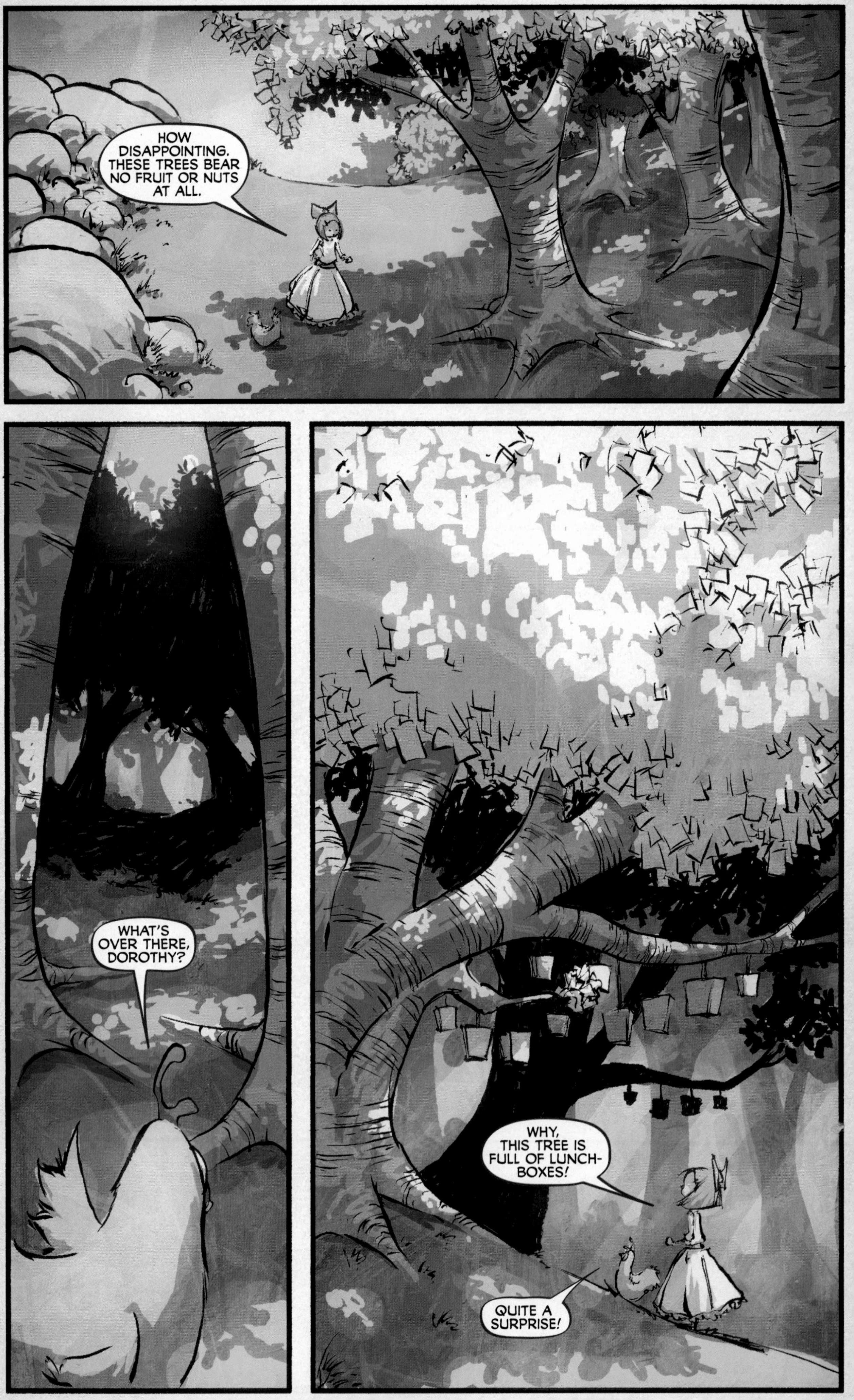
HOW DISAPPOINTING. THESE TREES BEAR NO FRUIT OR NUTS AT ALL.
WHAT'S OVER THERE, DOROTHY?
WHY, THIS TREE IS FULL OF LUNCH-BOXES!
QUITE A SURPRISE!

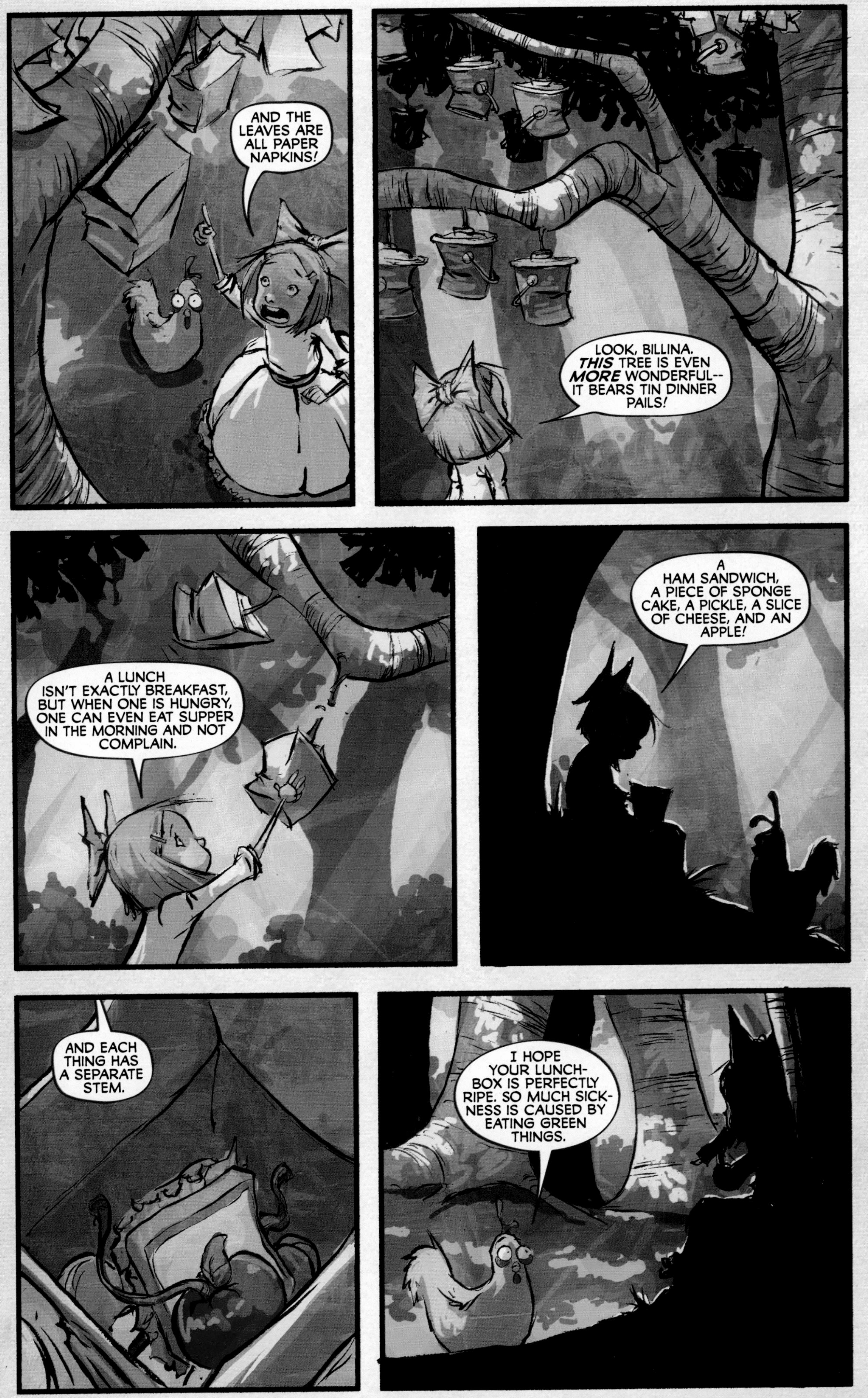
AND THE LEAVES ARE ALL PAPER NAPKINS!
LOOK, BILLINA. *THIS* TREE IS EVEN *MORE* WONDERFUL-- IT BEARS TIN DINNER PAILS!
A LUNCH ISN'T EXACTLY BREAKFAST, BUT WHEN ONE IS HUNGRY, ONE CAN EVEN EAT SUPPER IN THE MORNING AND NOT COMPLAIN.
A HAM SANDWICH, A PIECE OF SPONGE CAKE, A PICKLE, A SLICE OF CHEESE, AND AN APPLE!
AND EACH THING HAS A SEPARATE STEM.
I HOPE YOUR LUNCH-BOX IS PERFECTLY RIPE. SO MUCH SICK-NESS IS CAUSED BY EATING GREEN THINGS.

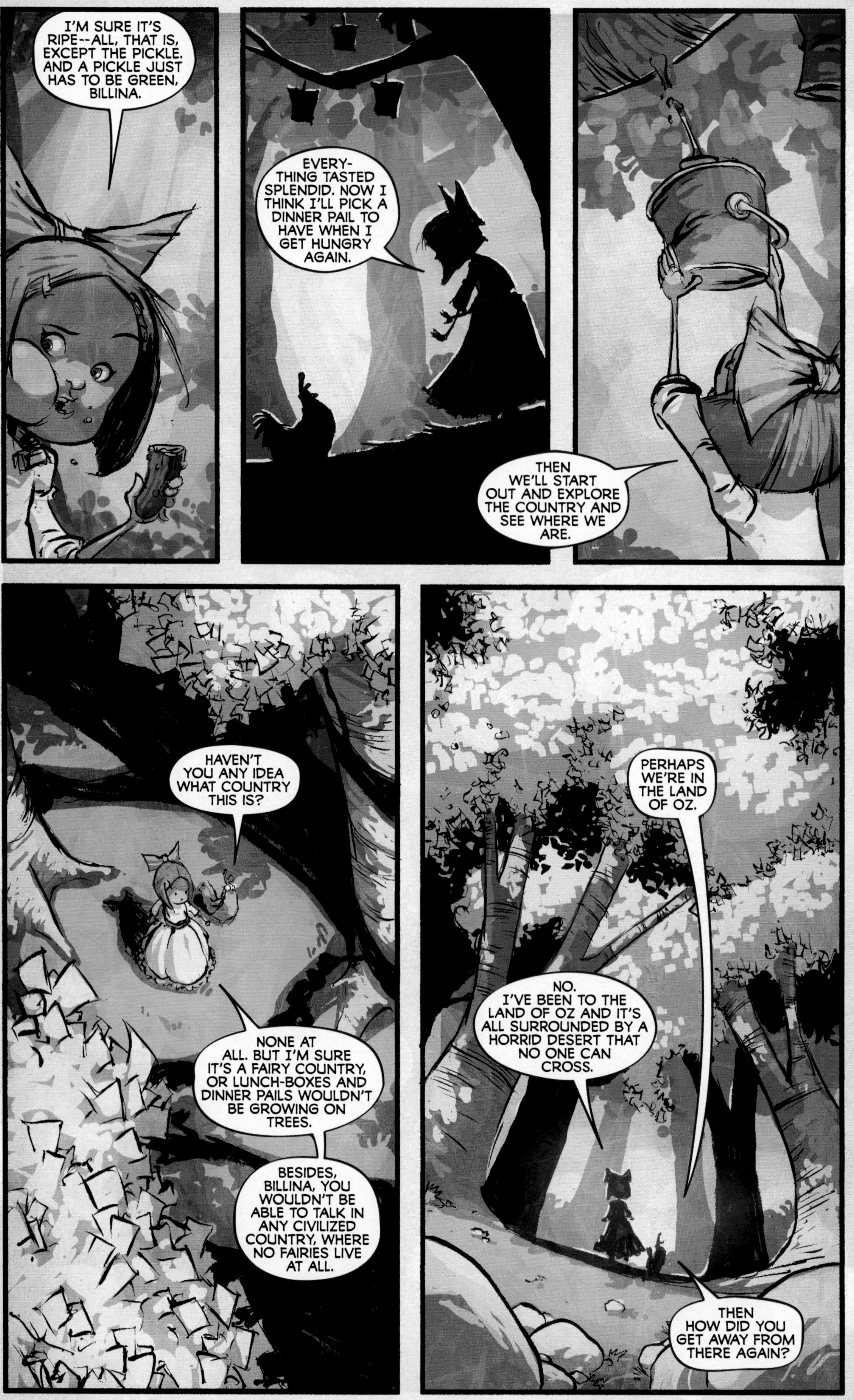

I'M SURE IT'S RIPE--ALL, THAT IS, EXCEPT THE PICKLE. AND A PICKLE JUST HAS TO BE GREEN, BILLINA.
EVERY-THING TASTED SPLENDID. NOW I THINK I'LL PICK A DINNER PAIL TO HAVE WHEN I GET HUNGRY AGAIN.
THEN WE'LL START OUT AND EXPLORE THE COUNTRY AND SEE WHERE WE ARE.
HAVEN'T YOU ANY IDEA WHAT COUNTRY THIS IS?
NONE AT ALL. BUT I'M SURE IT'S A FAIRY COUNTRY, OR LUNCH-BOXES AND DINNER PAILS WOULDN'T BE GROWING ON TREES.
BESIDES, BILLINA, YOU WOULDN'T BE ABLE TO TALK IN ANY CIVILIZED COUNTRY, WHERE NO FAIRIES LIVE AT ALL.
PERHAPS WE'RE IN THE LAND OF OZ.
NO. I'VE BEEN TO THE LAND OF OZ AND IT'S ALL SURROUNDED BY A HORRID DESERT THAT NO ONE CAN CROSS.
THEN HOW DID YOU GET AWAY FROM THERE AGAIN?

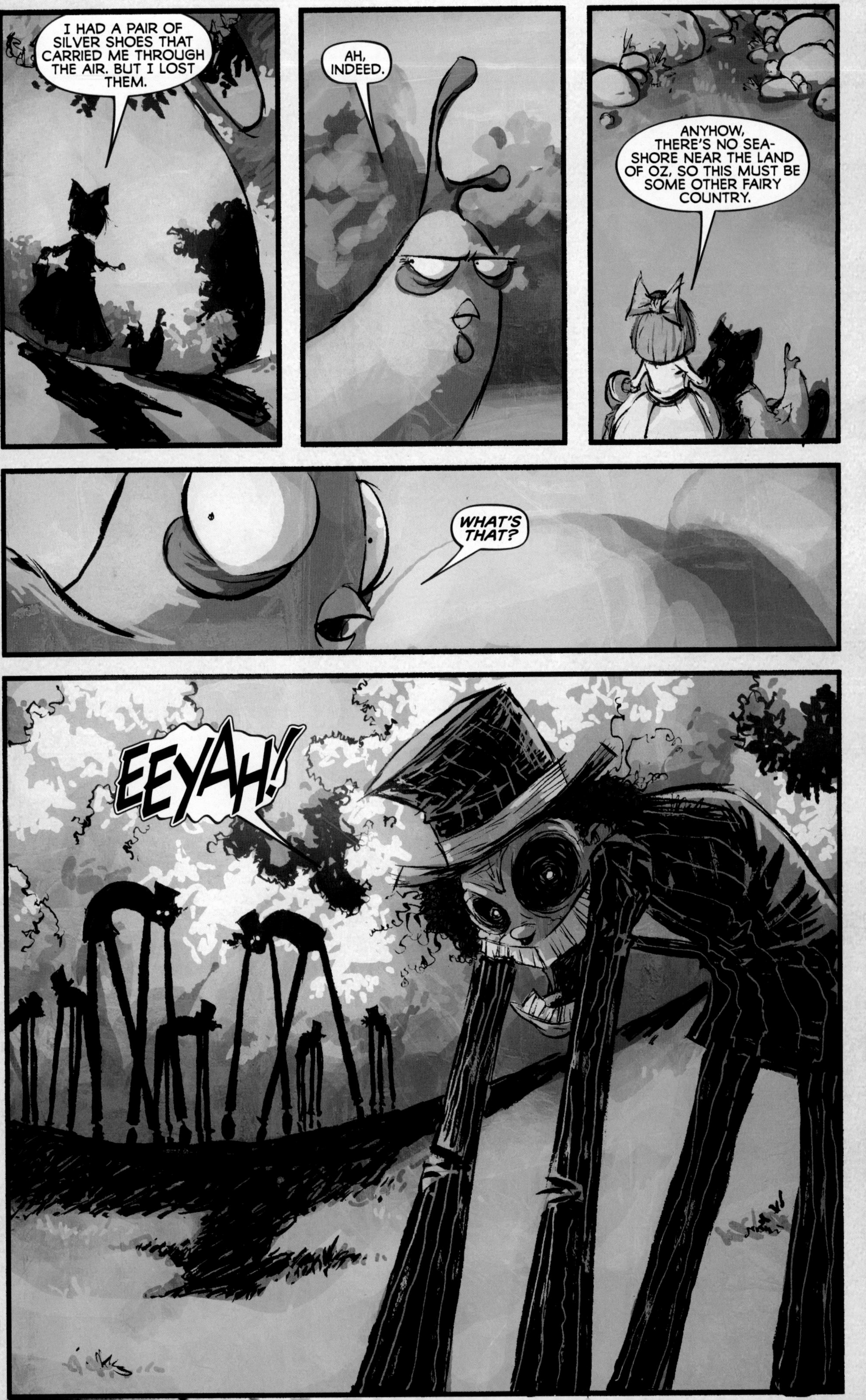
I HAD A PAIR OF SILVER SHOES THAT CARRIED ME THROUGH THE AIR. BUT I LOST THEM.
AH, INDEED.
ANYHOW, THERE'S NO SEA-SHORE NEAR THE LAND OF OZ, SO THIS MUST BE SOME OTHER FAIRY COUNTRY.
WHAT'S THAT?
EEYAH!

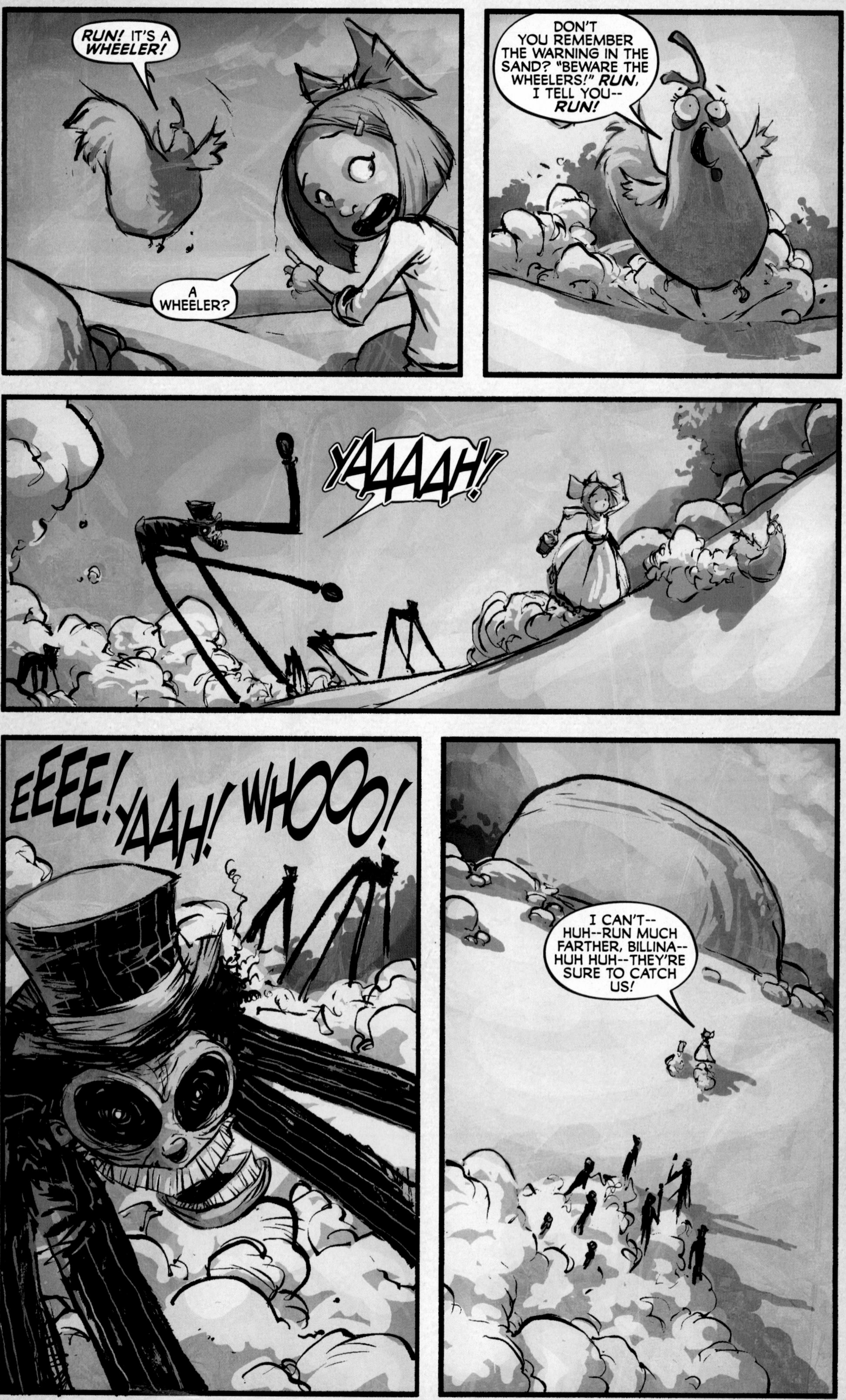
RUN! IT'S A WHEELER!
A WHEELER?
DON'T YOU REMEMBER THE WARNING IN THE SAND? "BEWARE THE WHEELERS!" RUN, I TELL YOU-- RUN!
YAAAAH!
EEEE! YAAH! WHOOO!
I CAN'T-- HUH--RUN MUCH FARTHER, BILLINA-- HUH HUH--THEY'RE SURE TO CATCH US!

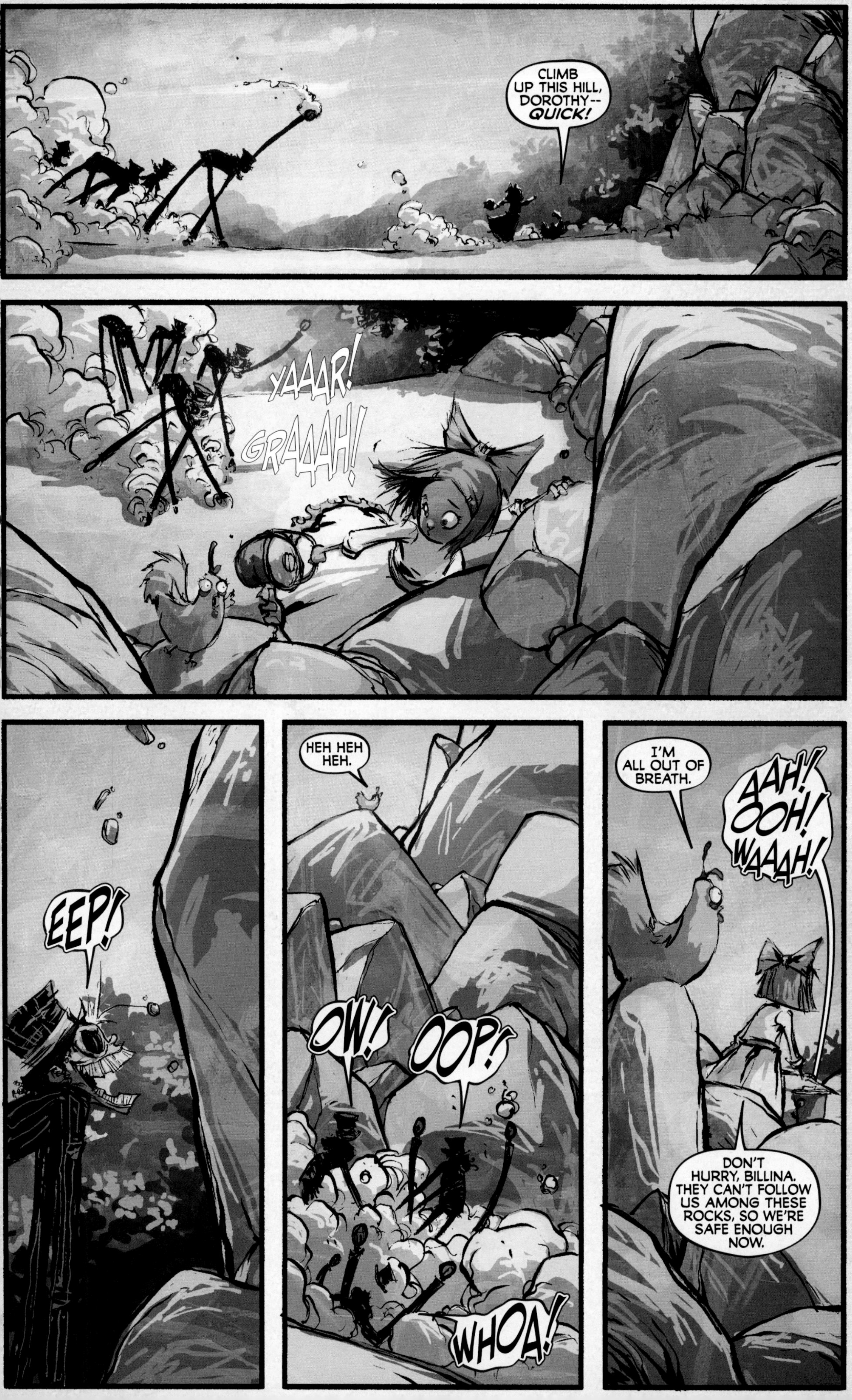

CLIMB UP THIS HILL, DOROTHY-- QUICK!
YAAAR!
GRAAAH!
EEP!
HEH HEH HEH.
OW!
OOP!
WHOA!
I'M ALL OUT OF BREATH.
AAH! OOH! WAAAH!
DON'T HURRY, BILLINA. THEY CAN'T FOLLOW US AMONG THESE ROCKS, SO WE'RE SAFE ENOUGH NOW.

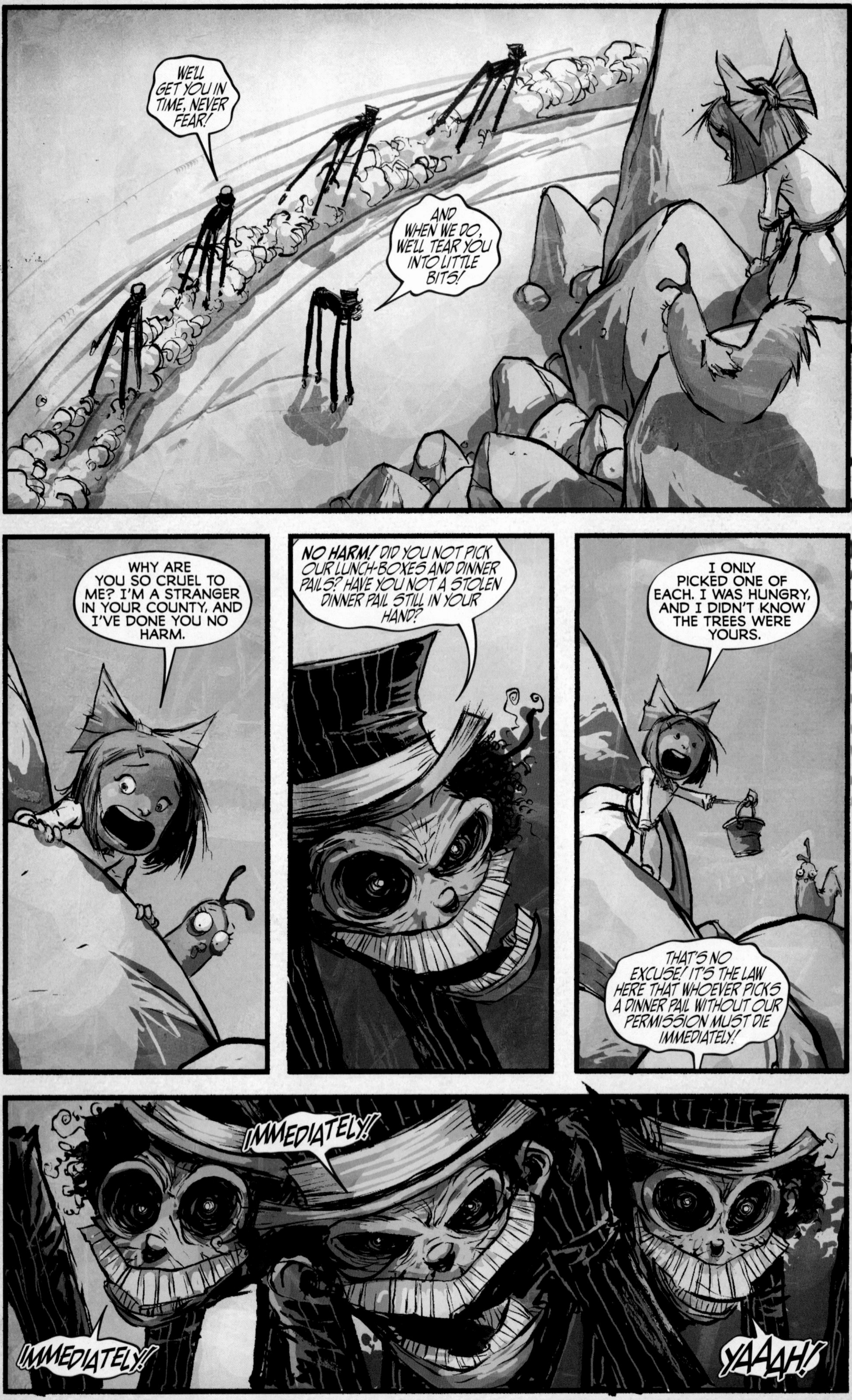

WE'LL GET YOU IN TIME, NEVER FEAR!
AND WHEN WE DO, WE'LL TEAR YOU INTO LITTLE BITS!
WHY ARE YOU SO CRUEL TO ME? I'M A STRANGER IN YOUR COUNTY, AND I'VE DONE YOU NO HARM.
NO HARM! DID YOU NOT PICK OUR LUNCH-BOXES AND DINNER PAILS? HAVE YOU NOT A STOLEN DINNER PAIL STILL IN YOUR HAND?
I ONLY PICKED ONE OF EACH. I WAS HUNGRY, AND I DIDN'T KNOW THE TREES WERE YOURS.
THAT'S NO EXCUSE! IT'S THE LAW HERE THAT WHOEVER PICKS A DINNER PAIL WITHOUT OUR PERMISSION MUST DIE IMMEDIATELY!
IMMEDIATELY!
IMMEDIATELY!
YAAAH!

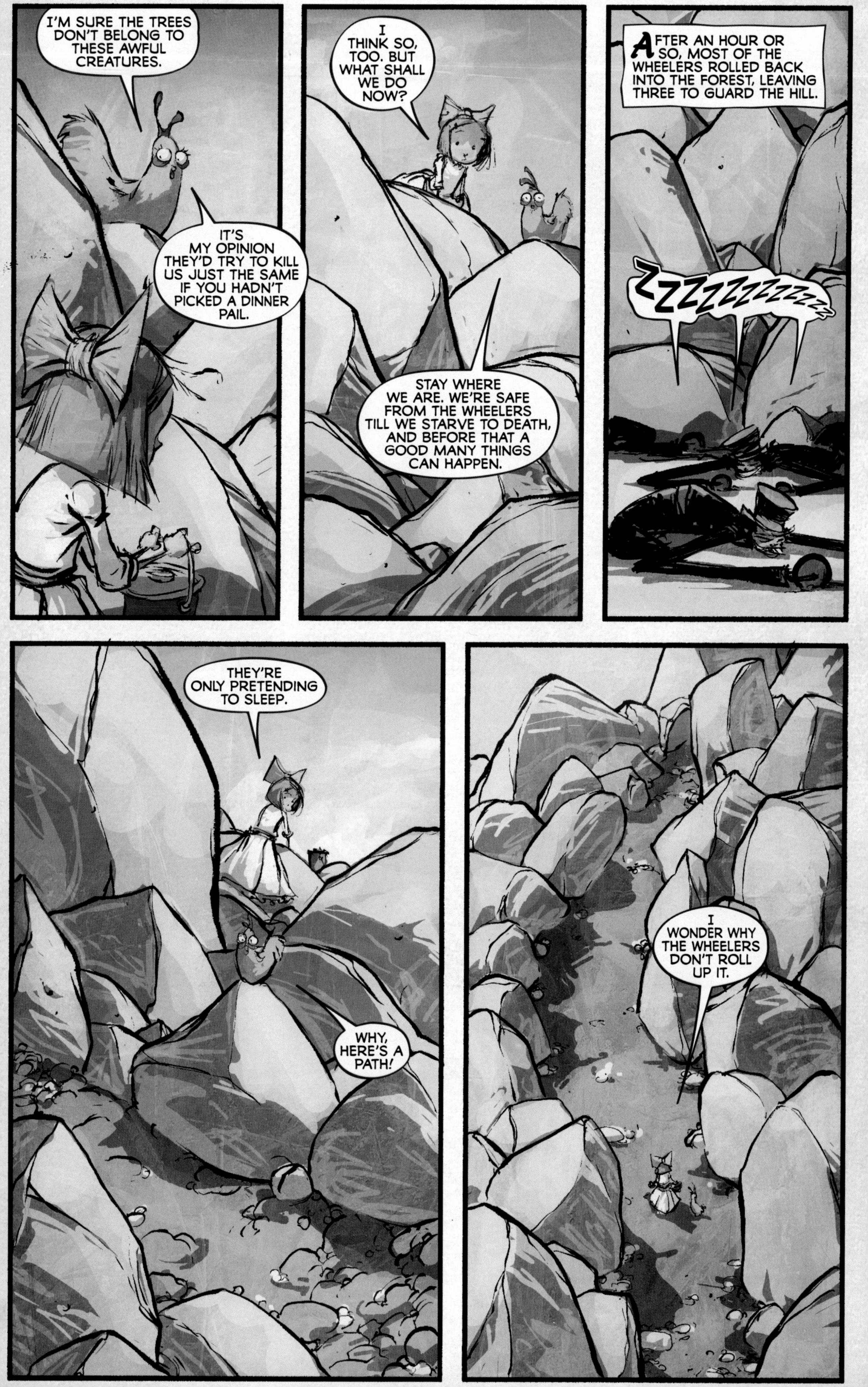
I'M SURE THE TREES DON'T BELONG TO THESE AWFUL CREATURES.
IT'S MY OPINION THEY'D TRY TO KILL US JUST THE SAME IF YOU HADN'T PICKED A DINNER PAIL.
I THINK SO, TOO. BUT WHAT SHALL WE DO NOW?
STAY WHERE WE ARE. WE'RE SAFE FROM THE WHEELERS TILL WE STARVE TO DEATH, AND BEFORE THAT A GOOD MANY THINGS CAN HAPPEN.
AFTER AN HOUR OR SO, MOST OF THE WHEELERS ROLLED BACK INTO THE FOREST, LEAVING THREE TO GUARD THE HILL.
ZZZZZZZZZZZZZ
THEY'RE ONLY PRETENDING TO SLEEP.
WHY, HERE'S A PATH!
I WONDER WHY THE WHEELERS DON'T ROLL UP IT.

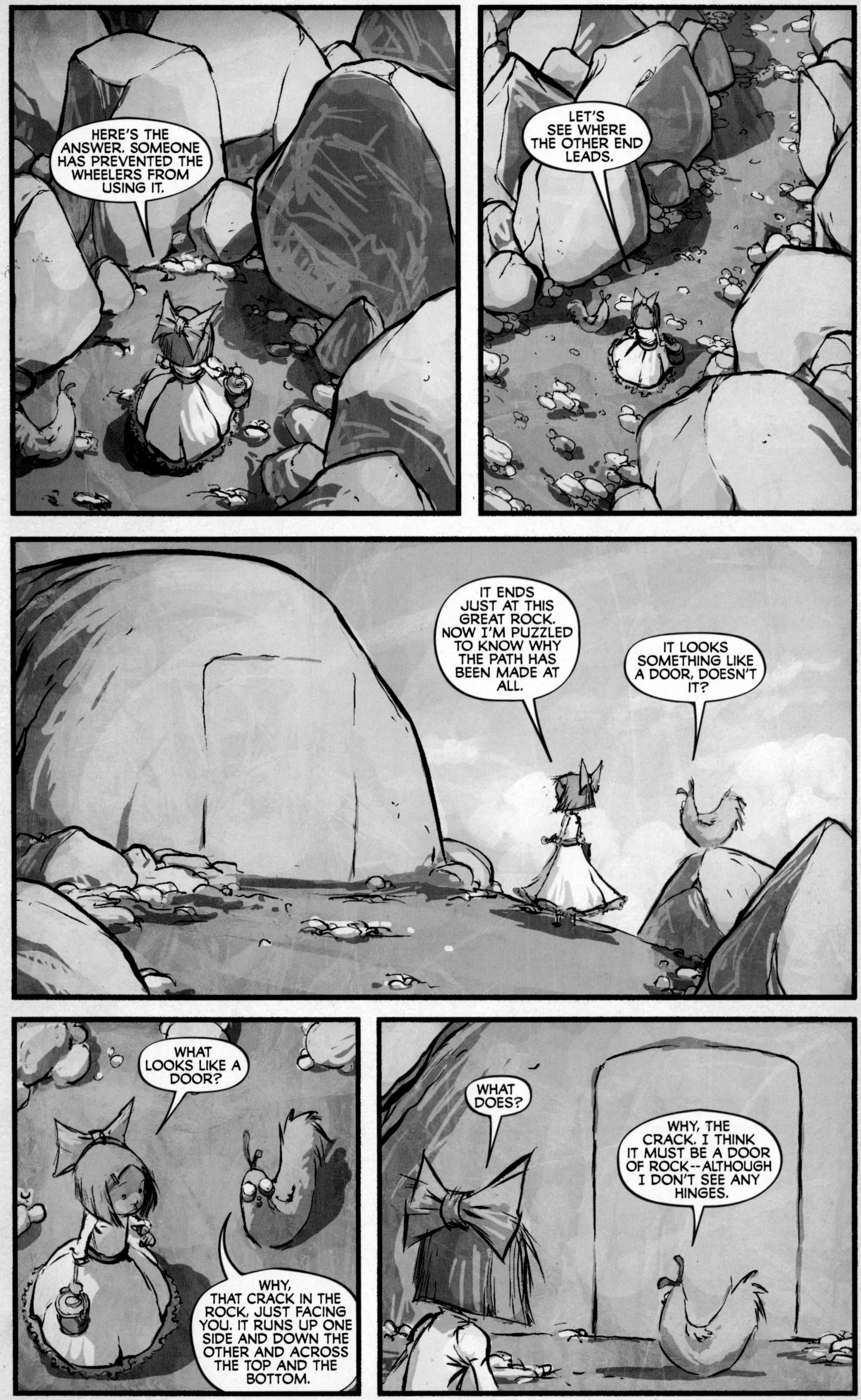
HERE'S THE ANSWER. SOMEONE HAS PREVENTED THE WHEELERS FROM USING IT.
LET'S SEE WHERE THE OTHER END LEADS.
IT ENDS JUST AT THIS GREAT ROCK. NOW I'M PUZZLED TO KNOW WHY THE PATH HAS BEEN MADE AT ALL.
IT LOOKS SOMETHING LIKE A DOOR, DOESN'T IT?
WHAT LOOKS LIKE A DOOR?
WHY, THAT CRACK IN THE ROCK, JUST FACING YOU. IT RUNS UP ONE SIDE AND DOWN THE OTHER AND ACROSS THE TOP AND THE BOTTOM.
WHAT DOES?
WHY, THE CRACK. I THINK IT MUST BE A DOOR OF ROCK--ALTHOUGH I DON'T SEE ANY HINGES.

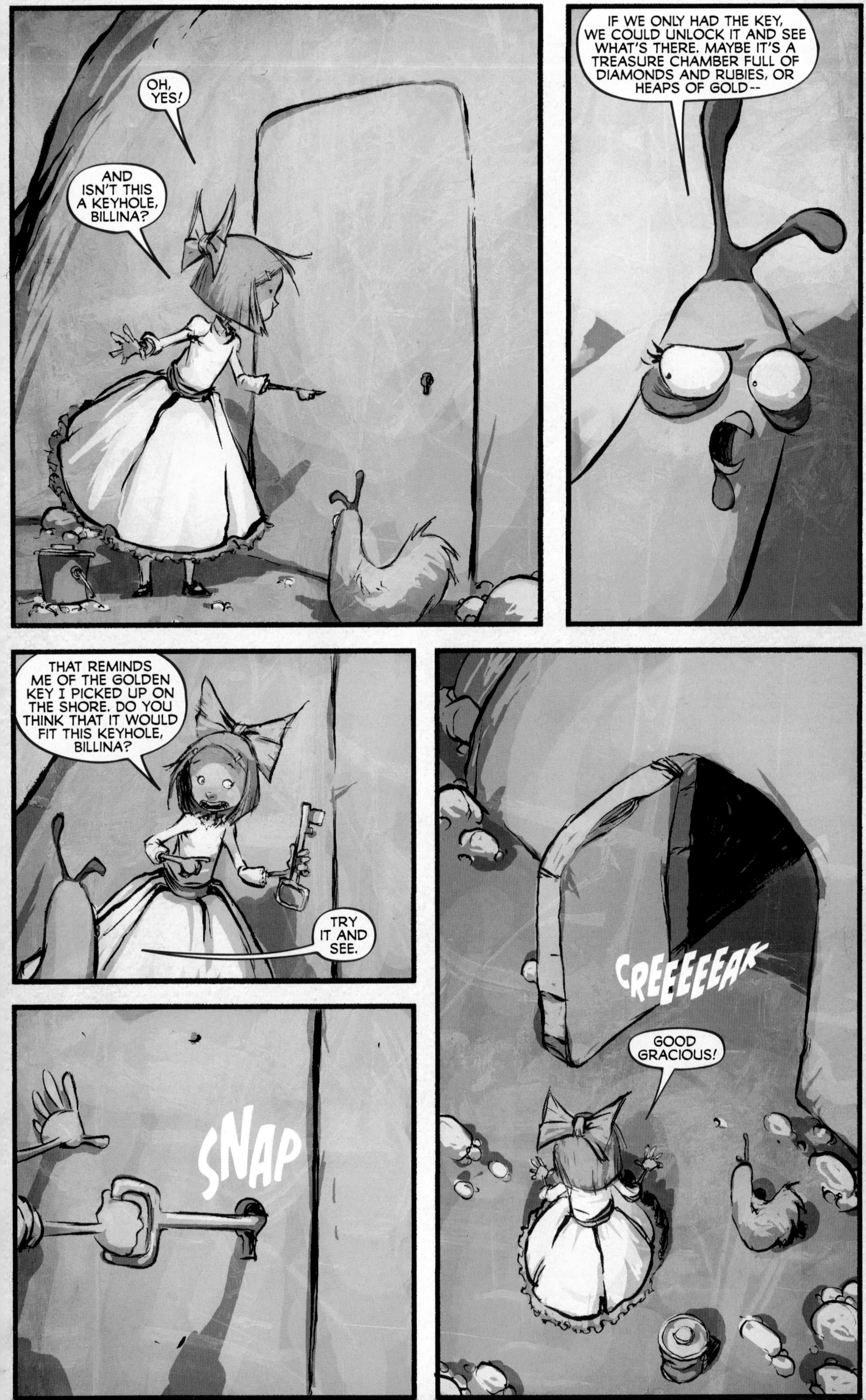
OH, YES!
AND ISN'T THIS A KEYHOLE, BILLINA?
IF WE ONLY HAD THE KEY, WE COULD UNLOCK IT AND SEE WHAT'S THERE. MAYBE IT'S A TREASURE CHAMBER FULL OF DIAMONDS AND RUBIES, OR HEAPS OF GOLD--
THAT REMINDS ME OF THE GOLDEN KEY I PICKED UP ON THE SHORE. DO YOU THINK THAT IT WOULD FIT THIS KEYHOLE, BILLINA?
TRY IT AND SEE.
SNAP
CREEEEEAK
GOOD GRACIOUS!

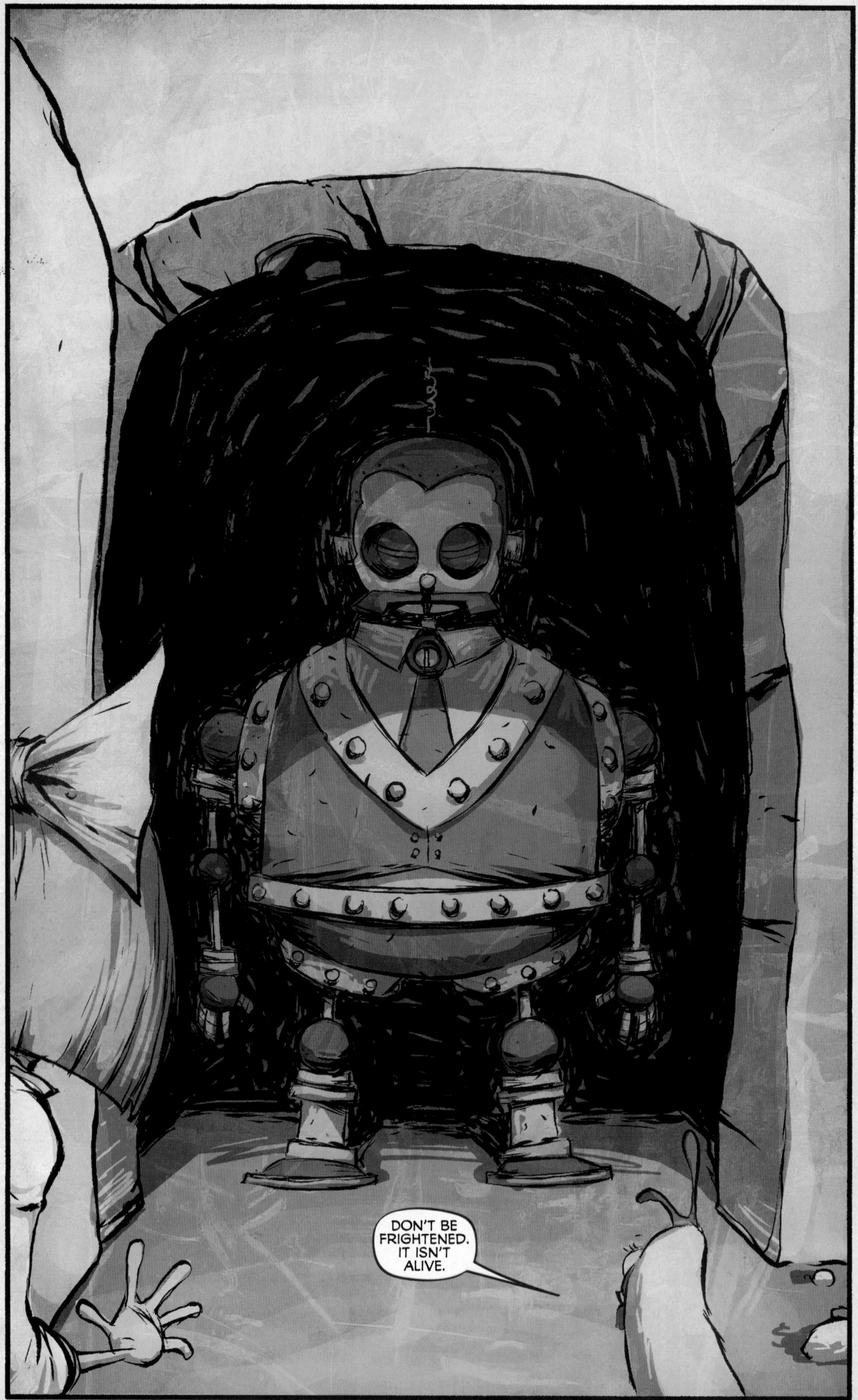
DON'T BE FRIGHTENED. IT ISN'T ALIVE.

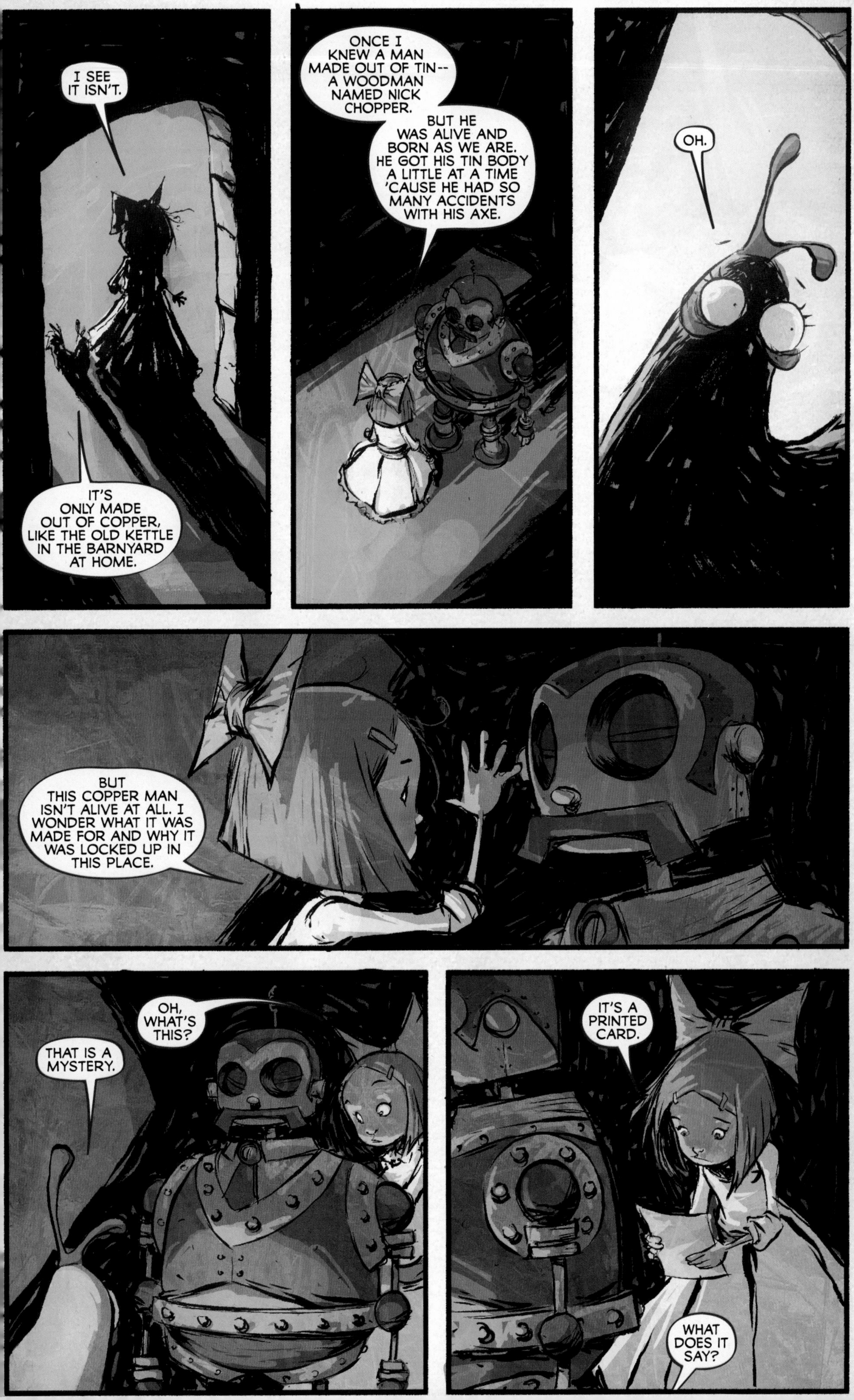
I SEE IT ISN'T.
IT'S ONLY MADE OUT OF COPPER, LIKE THE OLD KETTLE IN THE BARNYARD AT HOME.
ONCE I KNEW A MAN MADE OUT OF TIN-- A WOODMAN NAMED NICK CHOPPER.
BUT HE WAS ALIVE AND BORN AS WE ARE. HE GOT HIS TIN BODY A LITTLE AT A TIME 'CAUSE HE HAD SO MANY ACCIDENTS WITH HIS AXE.
OH.
BUT THIS COPPER MAN ISN'T ALIVE AT ALL. I WONDER WHAT IT WAS MADE FOR AND WHY IT WAS LOCKED UP IN THIS PLACE.
THAT IS A MYSTERY.
OH, WHAT'S THIS?
IT'S A PRINTED CARD.
WHAT DOES IT SAY?

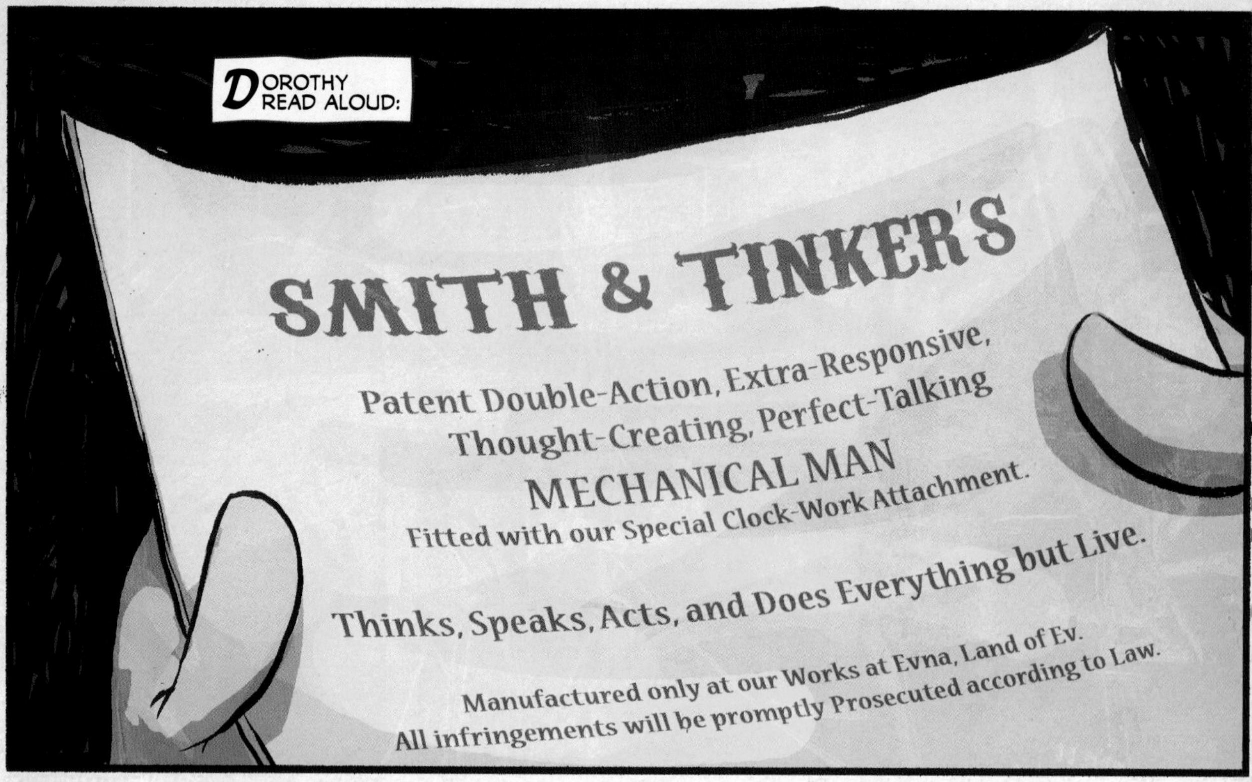
DOROTHY READ ALOUD:
SMITH & TINKER'S
Patent Double-Action, Extra-Responsive, Thought-Creating, Perfect-Talking
MECHANICAL MAN
Fitted with our Special Clock-Work Attachment.
Thinks, Speaks, Acts, and Does Everything but Live.
Manufactured only at our Works at Evna, Land of Ev.
All infringements will be promptly Prosecuted according to Law.

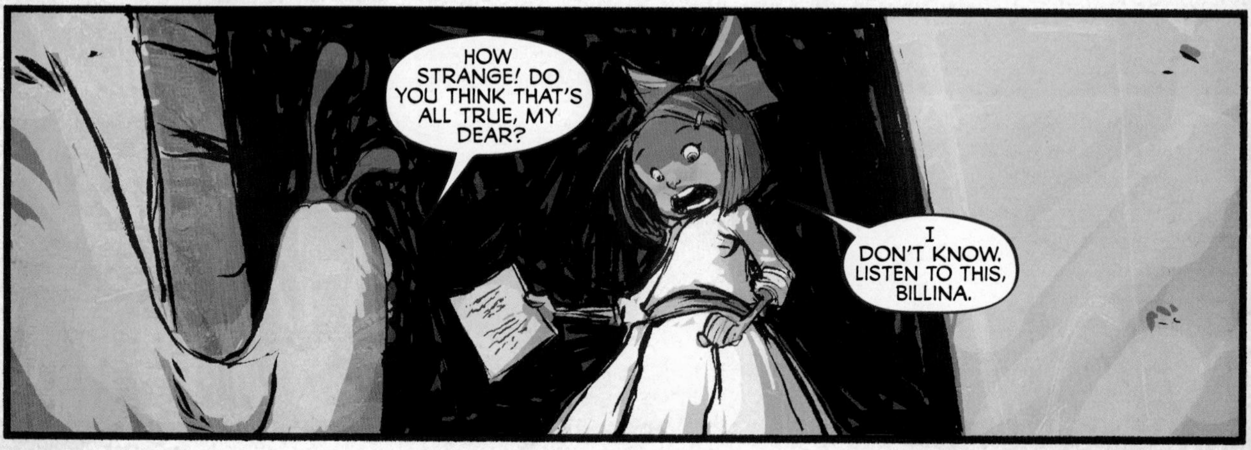
HOW STRANGE! DO YOU THINK THAT'S ALL TRUE, MY DEAR?
I DON'T KNOW. LISTEN TO THIS, BILLINA.

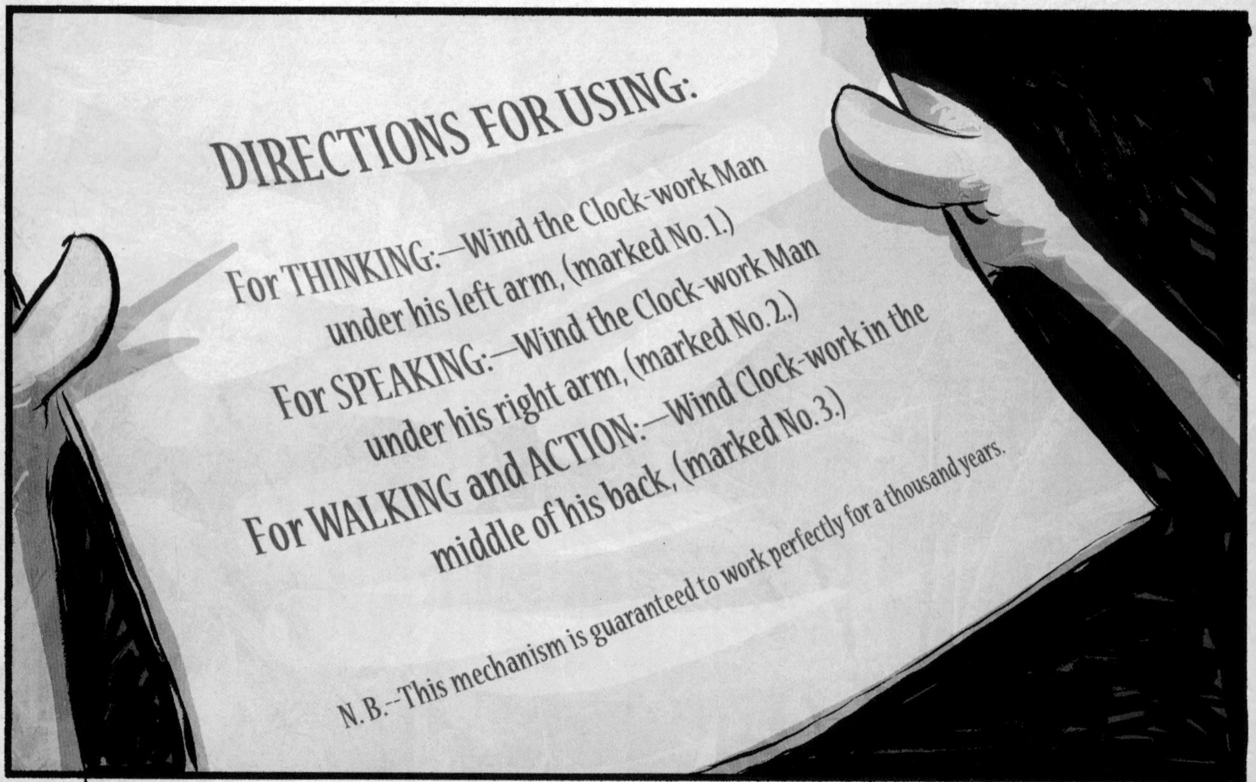
DIRECTIONS FOR USING:
For THINKING:—Wind the Clock-work Man under his left arm, (marked No.1.)
For SPEAKING:—Wind the Clock-work Man under his right arm, (marked No.2.)
For WALKING and ACTION:—Wind Clock-work in the middle of his back, (marked No.3.)
N. B.–This mechanism is guaranteed to work perfectly for a thousand years.

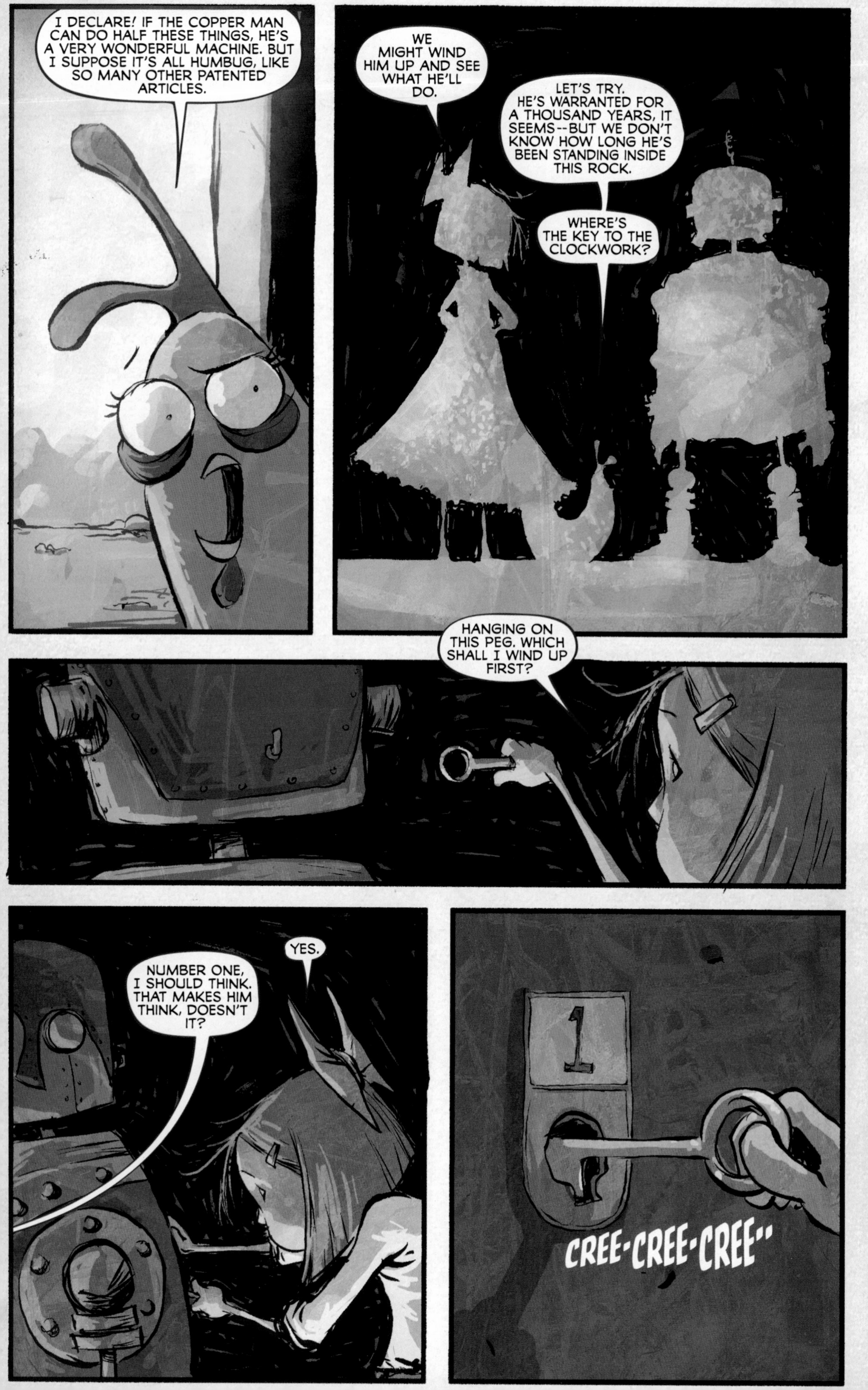
I DECLARE! IF THE COPPER MAN CAN DO HALF THESE THINGS, HE'S A VERY WONDERFUL MACHINE. BUT I SUPPOSE IT'S ALL HUMBUG, LIKE SO MANY OTHER PATENTED ARTICLES.
WE MIGHT WIND HIM UP AND SEE WHAT HE'LL DO.
LET'S TRY. HE'S WARRANTED FOR A THOUSAND YEARS, IT SEEMS--BUT WE DON'T KNOW HOW LONG HE'S BEEN STANDING INSIDE THIS ROCK.
WHERE'S THE KEY TO THE CLOCKWORK?
HANGING ON THIS PEG. WHICH SHALL I WIND UP FIRST?
NUMBER ONE, I SHOULD THINK. THAT MAKES HIM THINK, DOESN'T IT?
YES.
1
CREE-CREE-CREE--

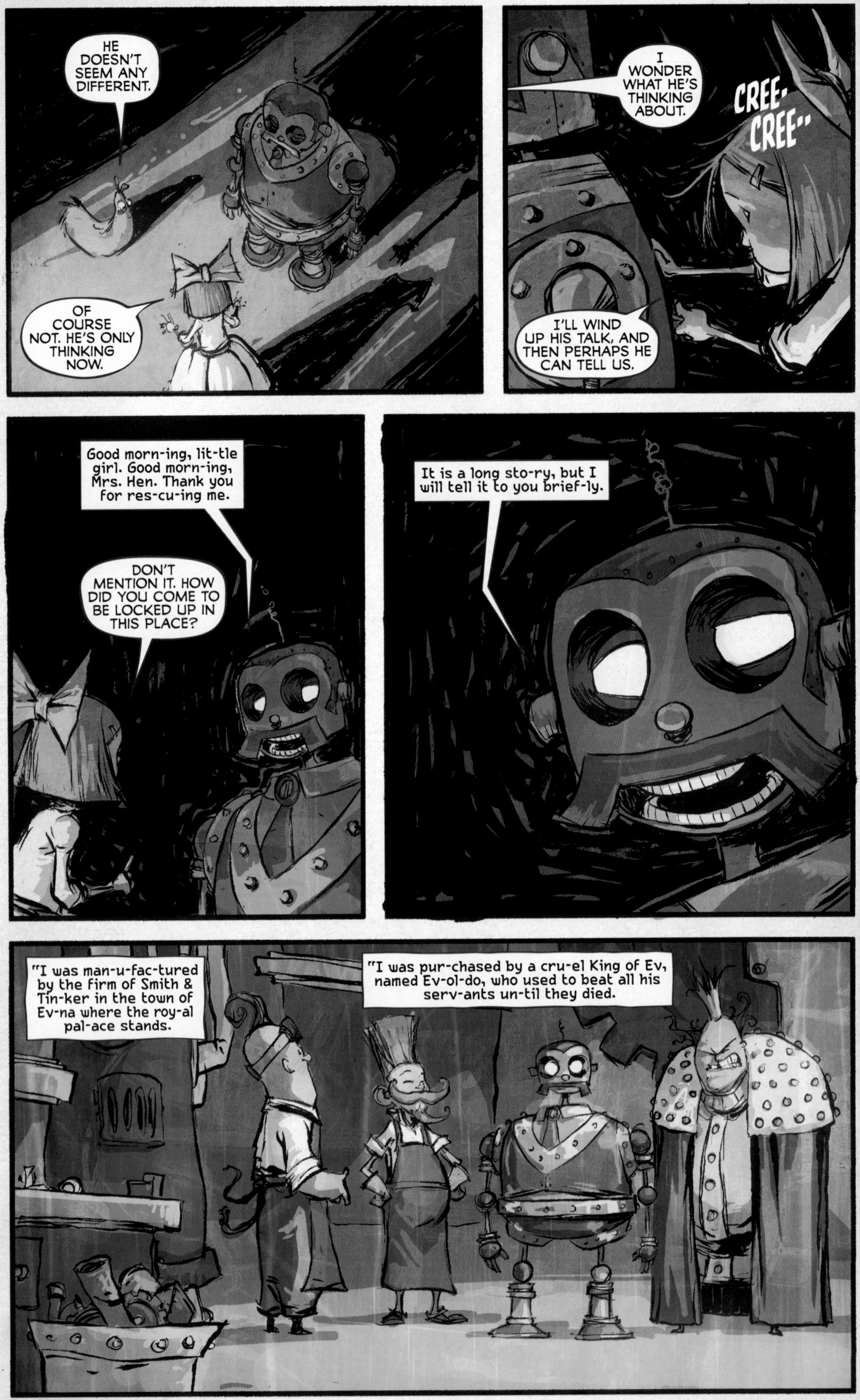
HE DOESN'T SEEM ANY DIFFERENT.
OF COURSE NOT. HE'S ONLY THINKING NOW.
I WONDER WHAT HE'S THINKING ABOUT.
CREE-CREE--
I'LL WIND UP HIS TALK, AND THEN PERHAPS HE CAN TELL US.
Good morn-ing, lit-tle girl. Good morn-ing, Mrs. Hen. Thank you for res-cu-ing me.
DON'T MENTION IT. HOW DID YOU COME TO BE LOCKED UP IN THIS PLACE?
It is a long sto-ry, but I will tell it to you brief-ly.
"I was man-u-fac-tured by the firm of Smith & Tin-ker in the town of Ev-na where the roy-al pal-ace stands.
"I was pur-chased by a cru-el King of Ev, named Ev-ol-do, who used to beat all his serv-ants un-til they died.

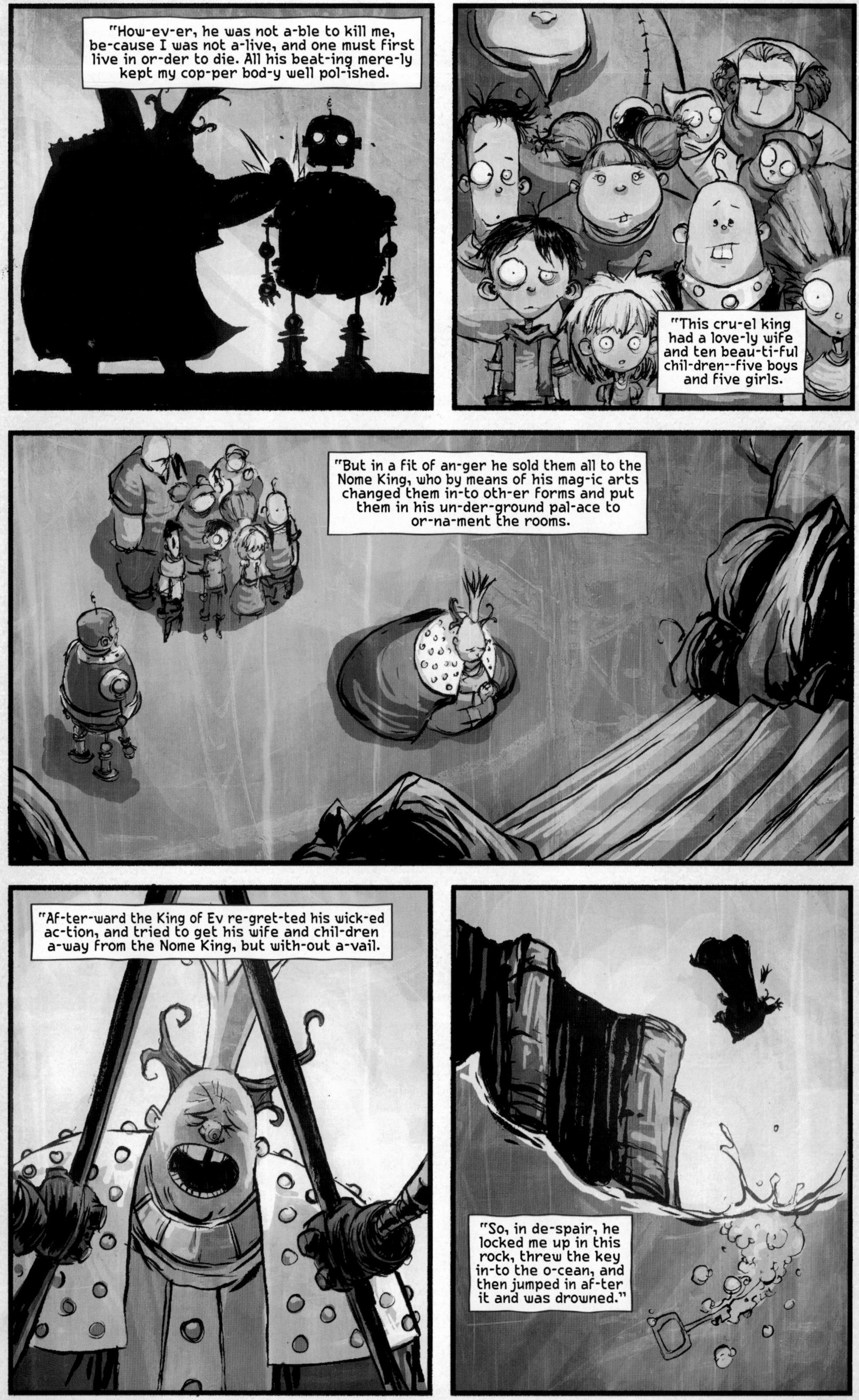
"How-ev-er, he was not a-ble to kill me, be-cause I was not a-live, and one must first live in or-der to die. All his beat-ing mere-ly kept my cop-per bod-y well pol-ished.
"This cru-el king had a love-ly wife and ten beau-ti-ful chil-dren--five boys and five girls.
"But in a fit of an-ger he sold them all to the Nome King, who by means of his mag-ic arts changed them in-to oth-er forms and put them in his un-der-ground pal-ace to or-na-ment the rooms.
"Af-ter-ward the King of Ev re-gret-ted his wick-ed ac-tion, and tried to get his wife and chil-dren a-way from the Nome King, but with-out a-vail.
"So, in de-spair, he locked me up in this rock, threw the key in-to the o-cean, and then jumped in af-ter it and was drowned."

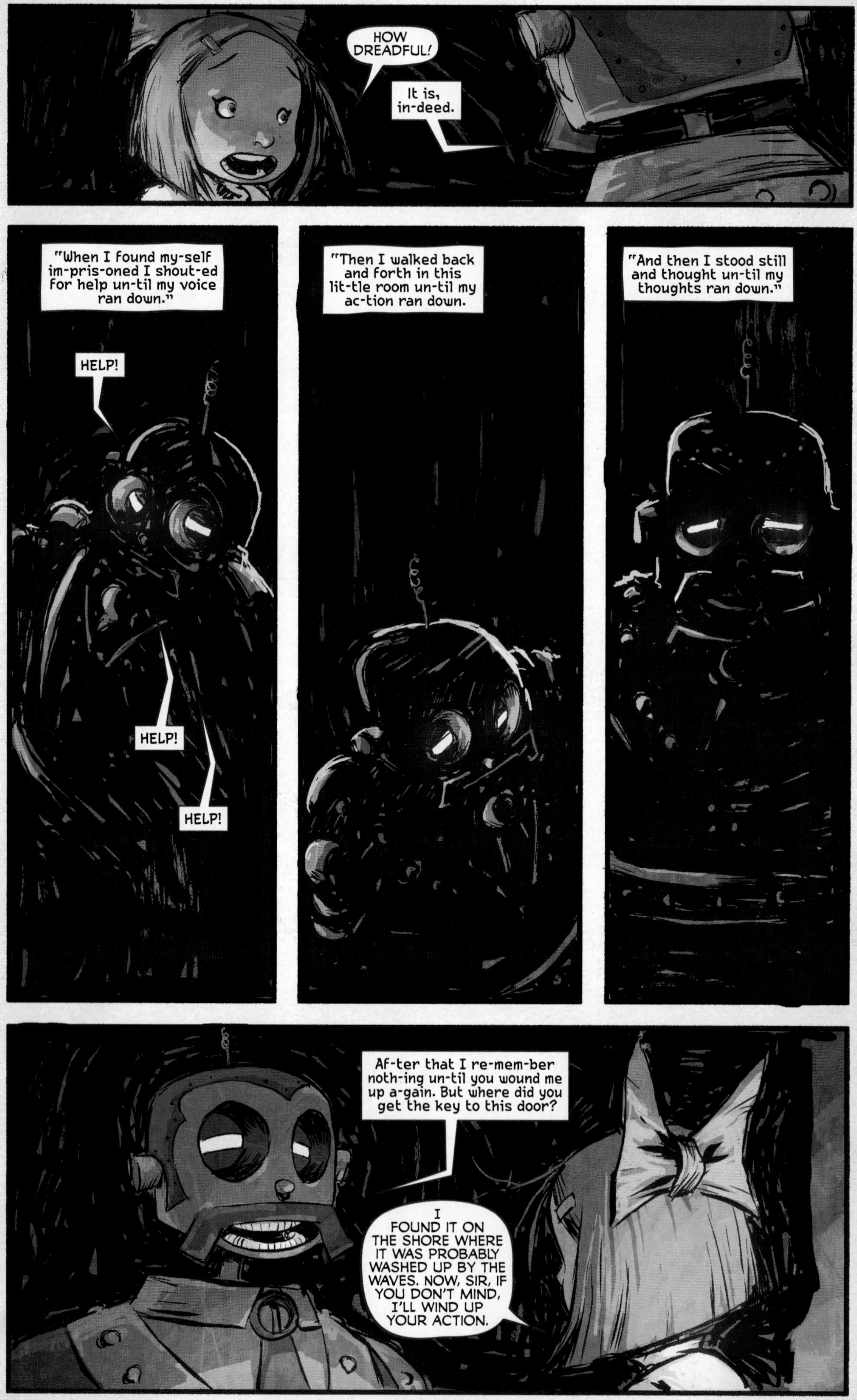
HOW DREADFUL!
It is, in-deed.
"When I found my-self im-pris-oned I shout-ed for help un-til my voice ran down."
HELP!
HELP!
HELP!
"Then I walked back and forth in this lit-tle room un-til my ac-tion ran down.
"And then I stood still and thought un-til my thoughts ran down."
Af-ter that I re-mem-ber noth-ing un-til you wound me up a-gain. But where did you get the key to this door?
I FOUND IT ON THE SHORE WHERE IT WAS PROBABLY WASHED UP BY THE WAVES. NOW, SIR, IF YOU DON'T MIND, I'LL WIND UP YOUR ACTION.

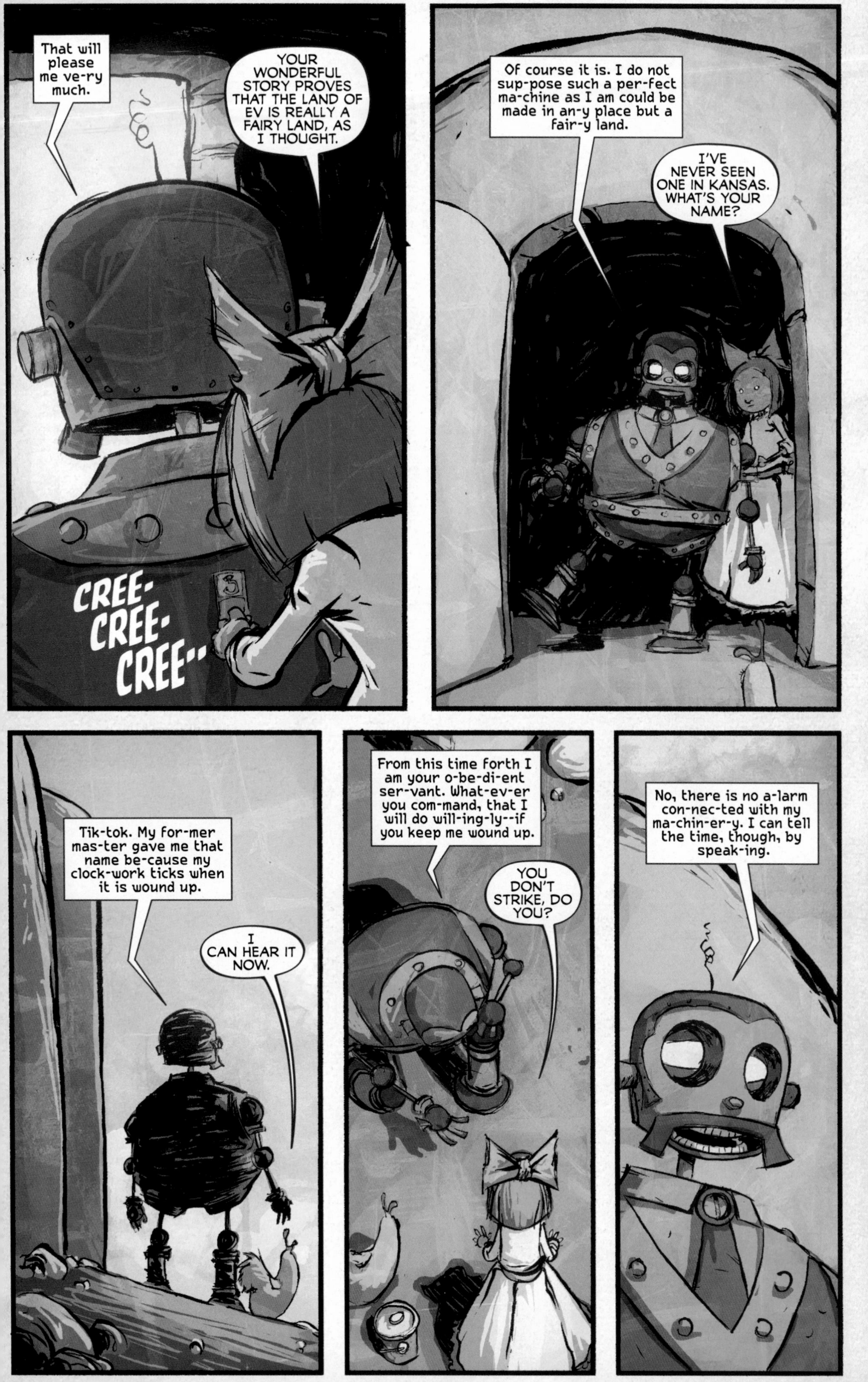
That will please me ve-ry much.
YOUR WONDERFUL STORY PROVES THAT THE LAND OF EV IS REALLY A FAIRY LAND, AS I THOUGHT.
CREE-CREE-CREE--
Of course it is. I do not sup-pose such a per-fect ma-chine as I am could be made in an-y place but a fair-y land.
I'VE NEVER SEEN ONE IN KANSAS. WHAT'S YOUR NAME?
Tik-tok. My for-mer mas-ter gave me that name be-cause my clock-work ticks when it is wound up.
I CAN HEAR IT NOW.
From this time forth I am your o-be-di-ent ser-vant. What-ev-er you com-mand, that I will do will-ing-ly--if you keep me wound up.
YOU DON'T STRIKE, DO YOU?
No, there is no a-larm con-nec-ted with my ma-chin-er-y. I can tell the time, though, by speak-ing.

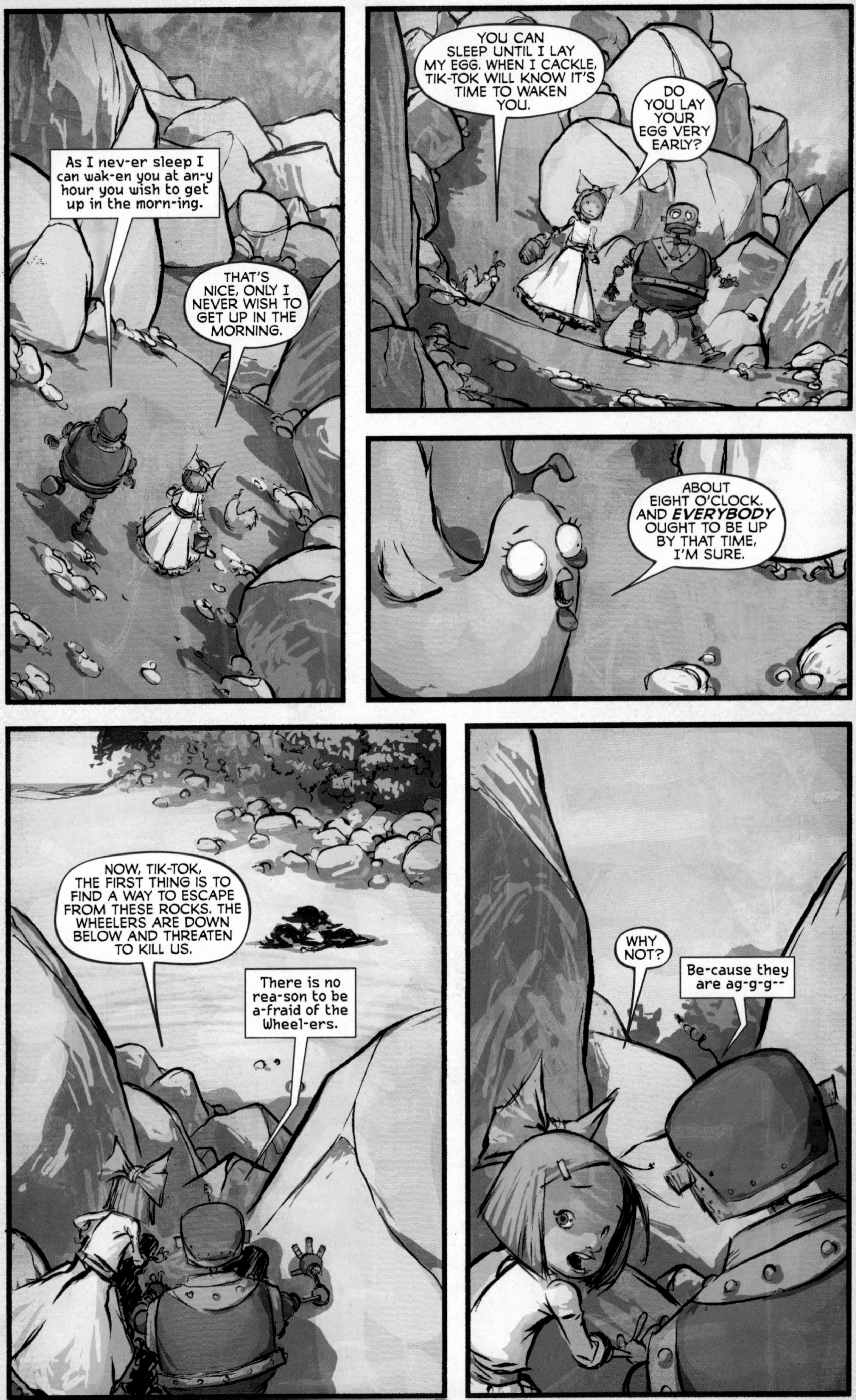
As I nev-er sleep I can wak-en you at an-y hour you wish to get up in the morn-ing.
THAT'S NICE, ONLY I NEVER WISH TO GET UP IN THE MORNING.
YOU CAN SLEEP UNTIL I LAY MY EGG. WHEN I CACKLE, TIK-TOK WILL KNOW IT'S TIME TO WAKEN YOU.
DO YOU LAY YOUR EGG VERY EARLY?
ABOUT EIGHT O'CLOCK. AND EVERYBODY OUGHT TO BE UP BY THAT TIME, I'M SURE.
NOW, TIK-TOK, THE FIRST THING IS TO FIND A WAY TO ESCAPE FROM THESE ROCKS. THE WHEELERS ARE DOWN BELOW AND THREATEN TO KILL US.
There is no rea-son to be a-fraid of the Wheel-ers.
WHY NOT?
Be-cause they are ag-g-g--

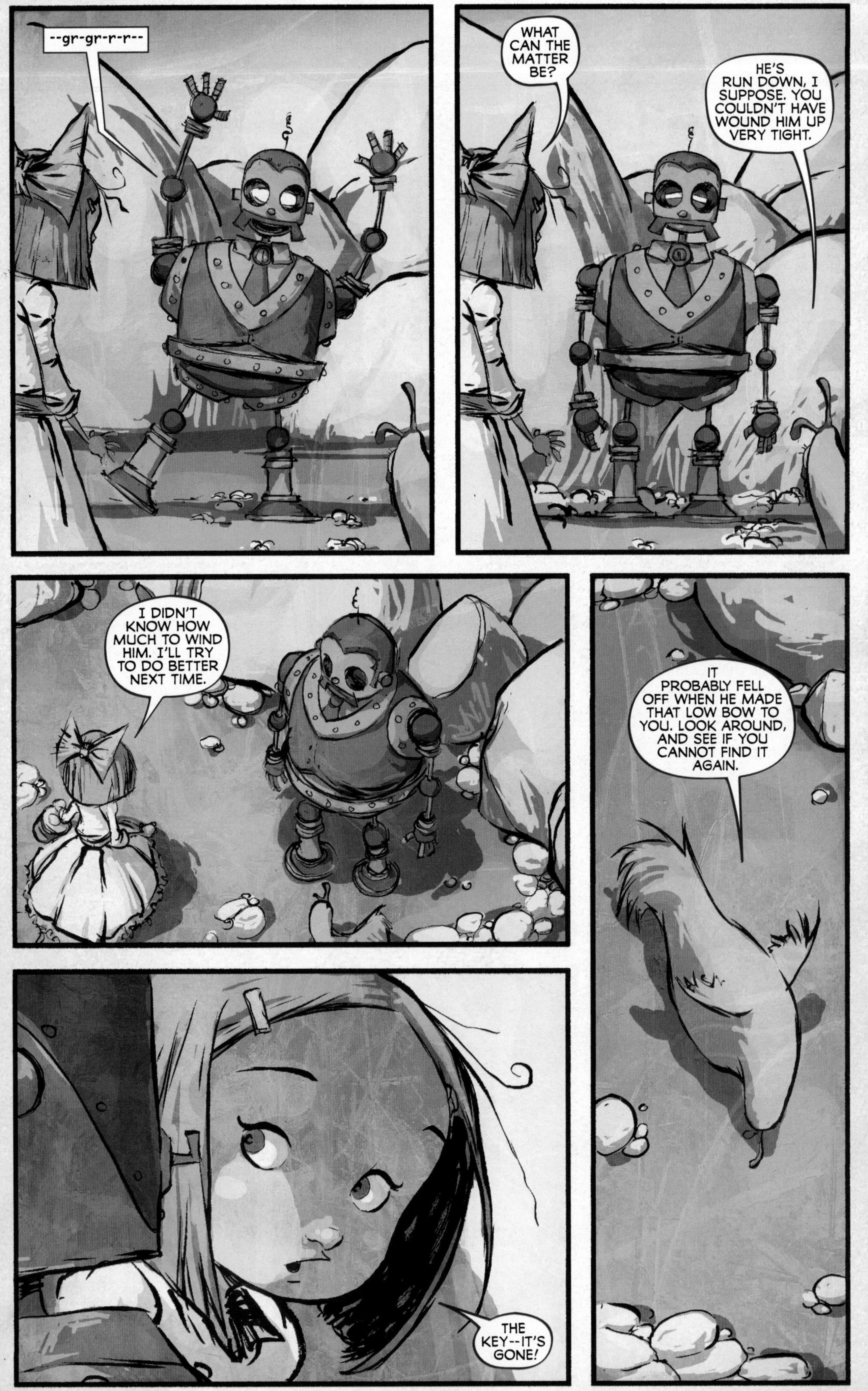
--gr-gr-r-r--
WHAT CAN THE MATTER BE?
HE'S RUN DOWN, I SUPPOSE. YOU COULDN'T HAVE WOUND HIM UP VERY TIGHT.
I DIDN'T KNOW HOW MUCH TO WIND HIM. I'LL TRY TO DO BETTER NEXT TIME.
IT PROBABLY FELL OFF WHEN HE MADE THAT LOW BOW TO YOU. LOOK AROUND, AND SEE IF YOU CANNOT FIND IT AGAIN.
THE KEY--IT'S GONE!

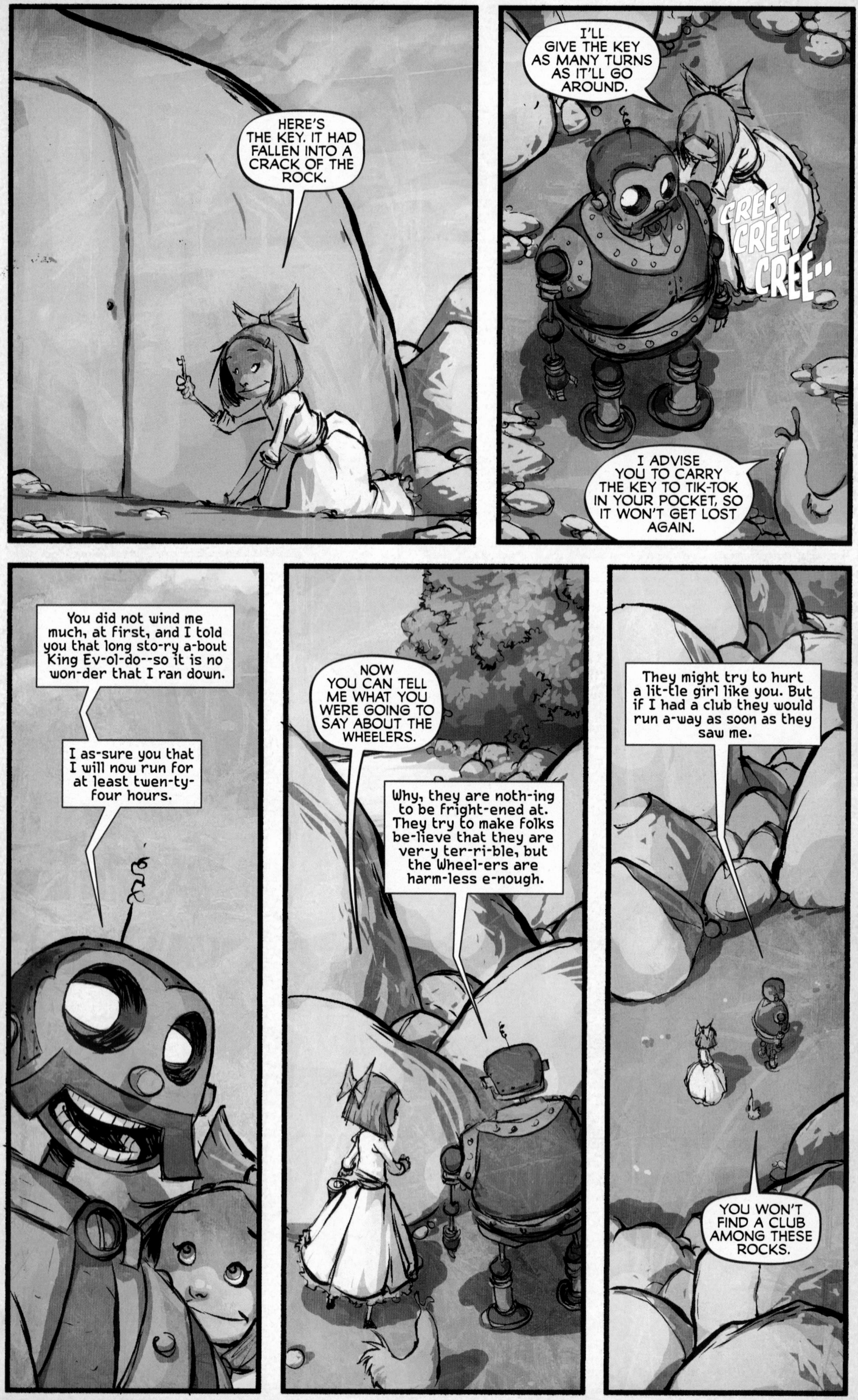
HERE'S THE KEY. IT HAD FALLEN INTO A CRACK OF THE ROCK.
I'LL GIVE THE KEY AS MANY TURNS AS IT'LL GO AROUND.
CREE-CREE-CREE..
I ADVISE YOU TO CARRY THE KEY TO TIK-TOK IN YOUR POCKET, SO IT WON'T GET LOST AGAIN.
You did not wind me much, at first, and I told you that long sto-ry a-bout King Ev-ol-do--so it is no won-der that I ran down.
I as-sure you that I will now run for at least twen-ty-four hours.
NOW YOU CAN TELL ME WHAT YOU WERE GOING TO SAY ABOUT THE WHEELERS.
Why, they are noth-ing to be fright-ened at. They try to make folks be-lieve that they are ver-y ter-ri-ble, but the Wheel-ers are harm-less e-nough.
They might try to hurt a lit-tle girl like you. But if I had a club they would run a-way as soon as they saw me.
YOU WON'T FIND A CLUB AMONG THESE ROCKS.

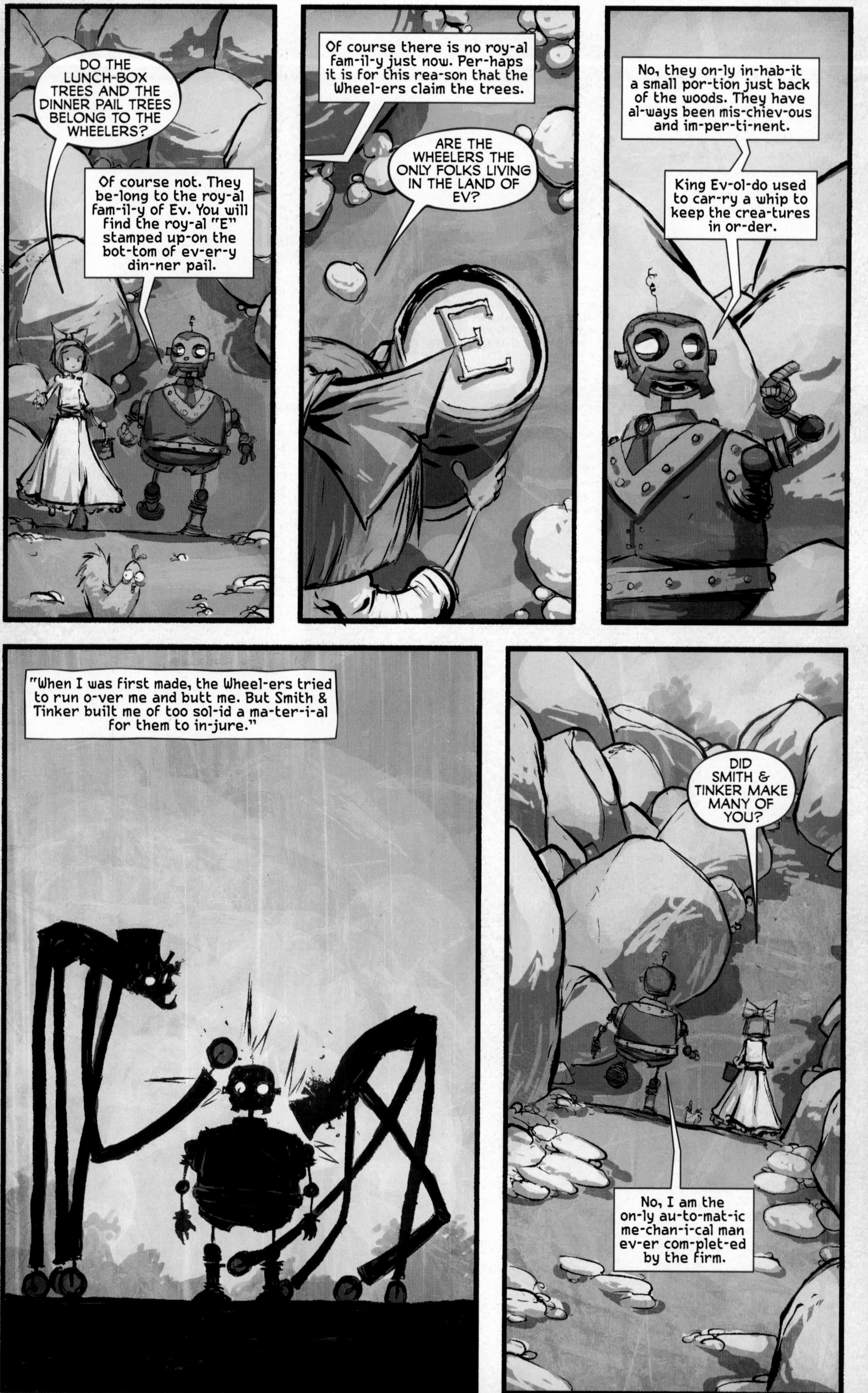
DO THE LUNCH-BOX TREES AND THE DINNER PAIL TREES BELONG TO THE WHEELERS?
Of course not. They be-long to the roy-al fam-il-y of Ev. You will find the roy-al "E" stamped up-on the bot-tom of ev-er-y din-ner pail.
Of course there is no roy-al fam-il-y just now. Per-haps it is for this rea-son that the Wheel-ers claim the trees.
E
ARE THE WHEELERS THE ONLY FOLKS LIVING IN THE LAND OF EV?
No, they on-ly in-hab-it a small por-tion just back of the woods. They have al-ways been mis-chiev-ous and im-per-ti-nent.
King Ev-ol-do used to car-ry a whip to keep the crea-tures in or-der.
"When I was first made, the Wheel-ers tried to run o-ver me and butt me. But Smith & Tinker built me of too sol-id a ma-ter-i-al for them to in-jure."
DID SMITH & TINKER MAKE MANY OF YOU?
No, I am the on-ly au-to-mat-ic me-chan-i-cal man ev-er com-plet-ed by the firm.

"They were ver-y won-der-ful in-ven-tors, were my mak-ers. Mis-ter Smith was an art-ist, as well as an in-vent-or.

"He paint-ed a pic-ture of a riv-er which was so nat-ur-al that, as he was reach-ing to paint some flow-ers on the op-po-site bank, he fell in and was drowned.

"Mis-ter Tin-ker made a lad-der so tall that he could rest the end of it a-gainst the moon while he picked stars to set in the points of the king's crown.

"But Mis-ter Tin-ker found the moon such a love-ly place that he de-cid-ed to live there, so he pulled up the lad-der af-ter him, and we have nev-er seen him since."

THEY MUST HAVE BEEN A GREAT LOSS TO THIS COUNTRY.

They are a great loss to me. For if I should get out of or-der I do not know of an-y one a-ble to re-pair me. You have no i-de-a how full of ma-chin-er-y I am.

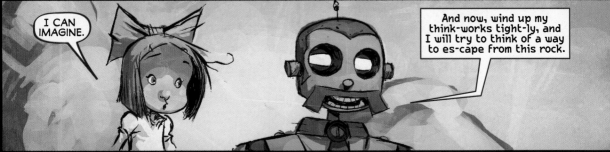

I CAN IMAGINE.

And now, wind up my think-works tight-ly, and I will try to think of a way to es-cape from this rock.

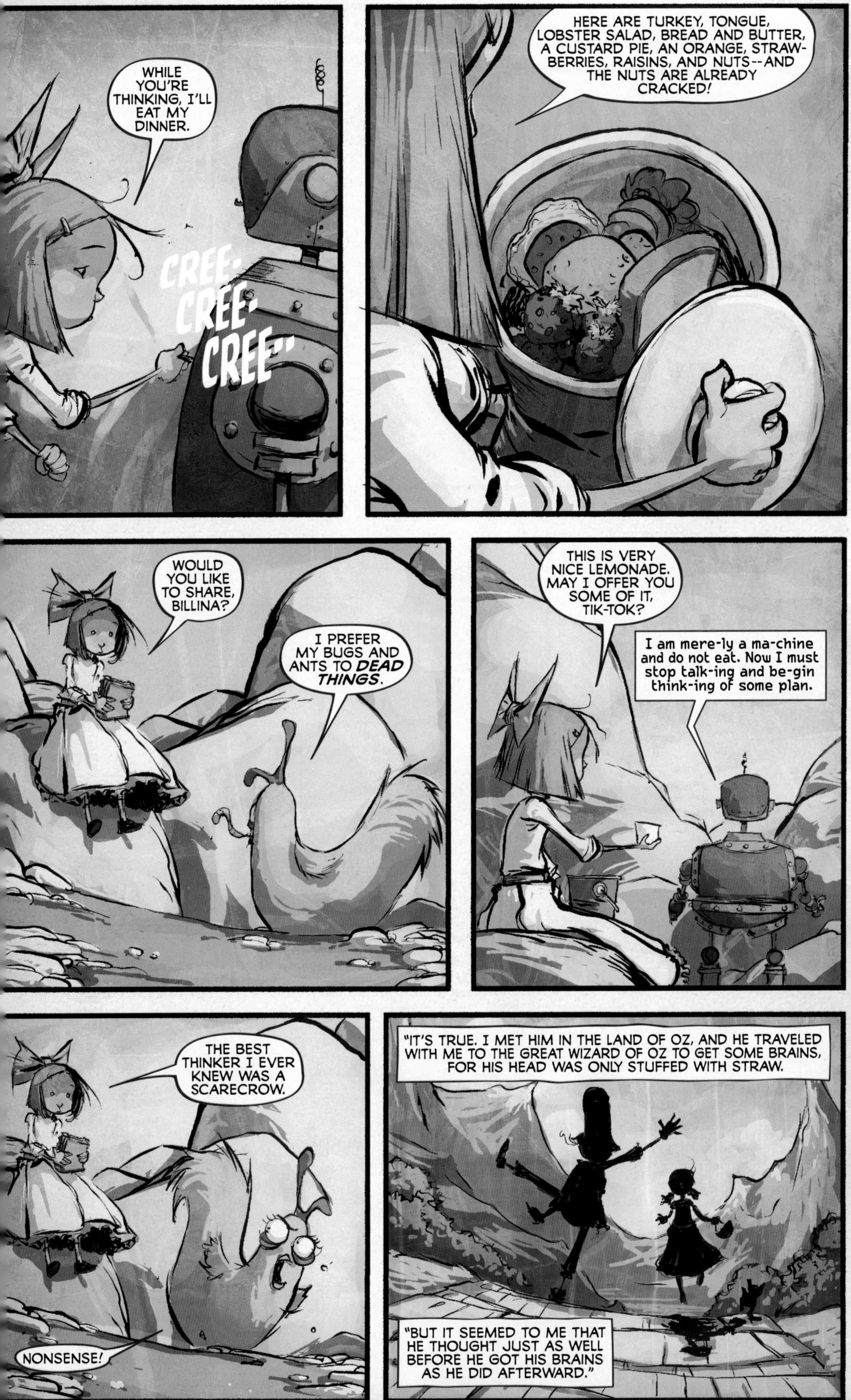
WHILE YOU'RE THINKING, I'LL EAT MY DINNER.
CREE- CREE- CREE-.
HERE ARE TURKEY, TONGUE, LOBSTER SALAD, BREAD AND BUTTER, A CUSTARD PIE, AN ORANGE, STRAW-BERRIES, RAISINS, AND NUTS--AND THE NUTS ARE ALREADY CRACKED!
WOULD YOU LIKE TO SHARE, BILLINA?
I PREFER MY BUGS AND ANTS TO *DEAD THINGS*.
THIS IS VERY NICE LEMONADE. MAY I OFFER YOU SOME OF IT, TIK-TOK?
I am mere-ly a ma-chine and do not eat. Now I must stop talk-ing and be-gin think-ing of some plan.
THE BEST THINKER I EVER KNEW WAS A SCARECROW.
NONSENSE!
"IT'S TRUE. I MET HIM IN THE LAND OF OZ, AND HE TRAVELED WITH ME TO THE GREAT WIZARD OF OZ TO GET SOME BRAINS, FOR HIS HEAD WAS ONLY STUFFED WITH STRAW.
"BUT IT SEEMED TO ME THAT HE THOUGHT JUST AS WELL BEFORE HE GOT HIS BRAINS AS HE DID AFTERWARD."

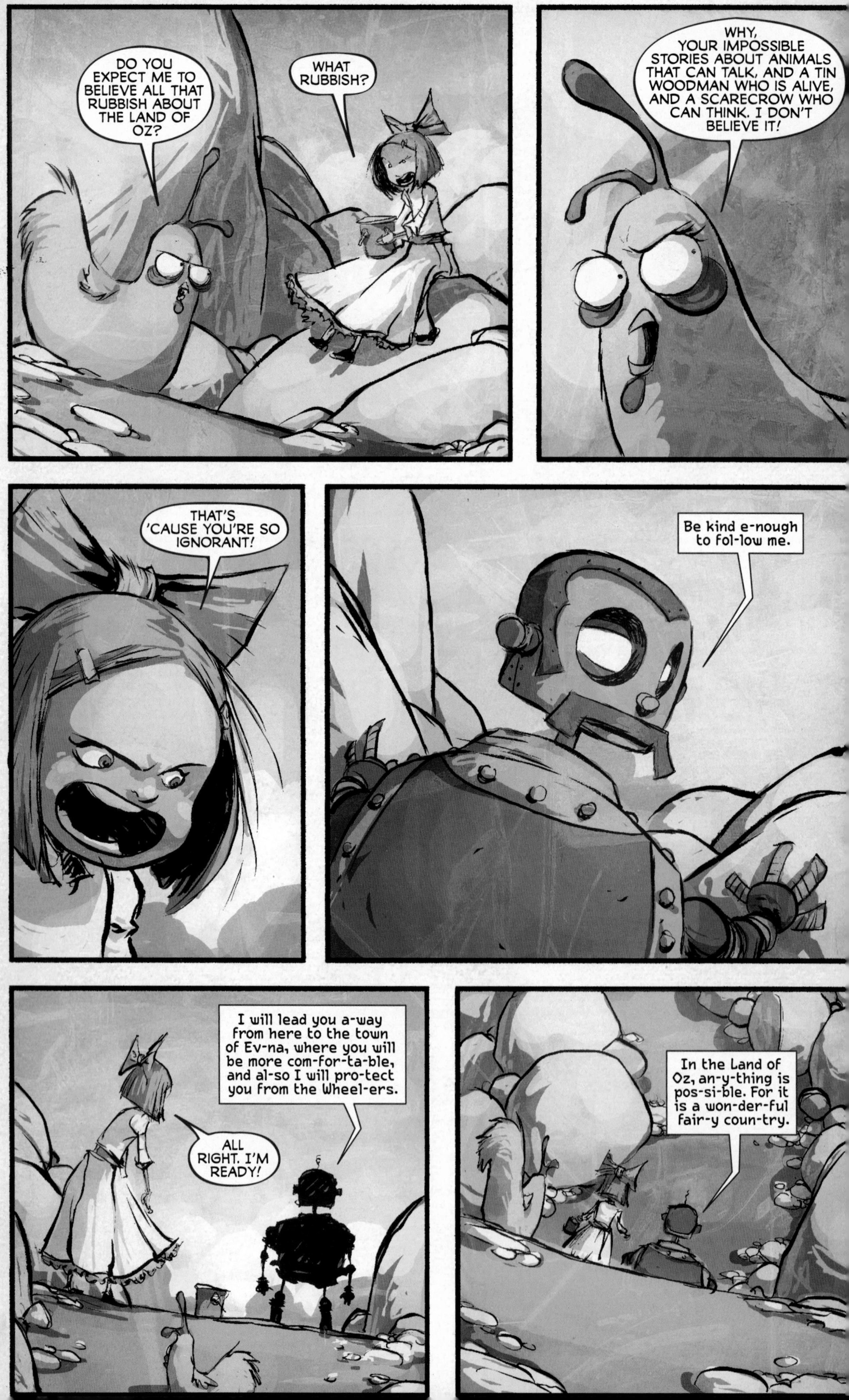
DO YOU EXPECT ME TO BELIEVE ALL THAT RUBBISH ABOUT THE LAND OF OZ?
WHAT RUBBISH?
WHY, YOUR IMPOSSIBLE STORIES ABOUT ANIMALS THAT CAN TALK, AND A TIN WOODMAN WHO IS ALIVE, AND A SCARECROW WHO CAN THINK. I DON'T BELIEVE IT!
THAT'S 'CAUSE YOU'RE SO IGNORANT!
Be kind e-nough to fol-low me.
I will lead you a-way from here to the town of Ev-na, where you will be more com-for-ta-ble, and al-so I will pro-tect you from the Wheel-ers.
ALL RIGHT. I'M READY!
In the Land of Oz, an-y-thing is pos-si-ble. For it is a won-der-ful fair-y coun-try.

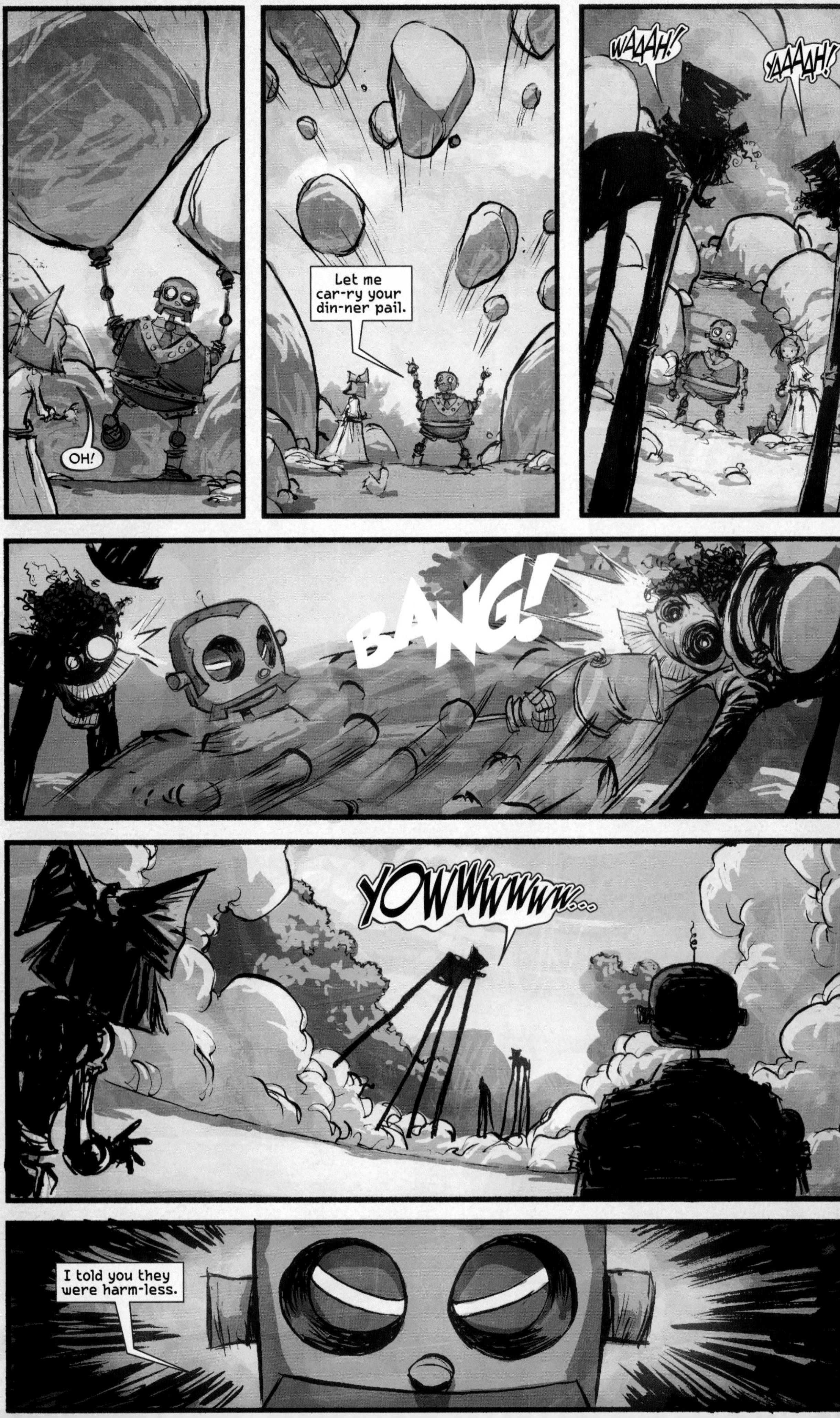
OH!
Let me car-ry your din-ner pail.
WAAAH!
YAAAAH!
BANG!
YOWWWWWW...
I told you they were harm-less.

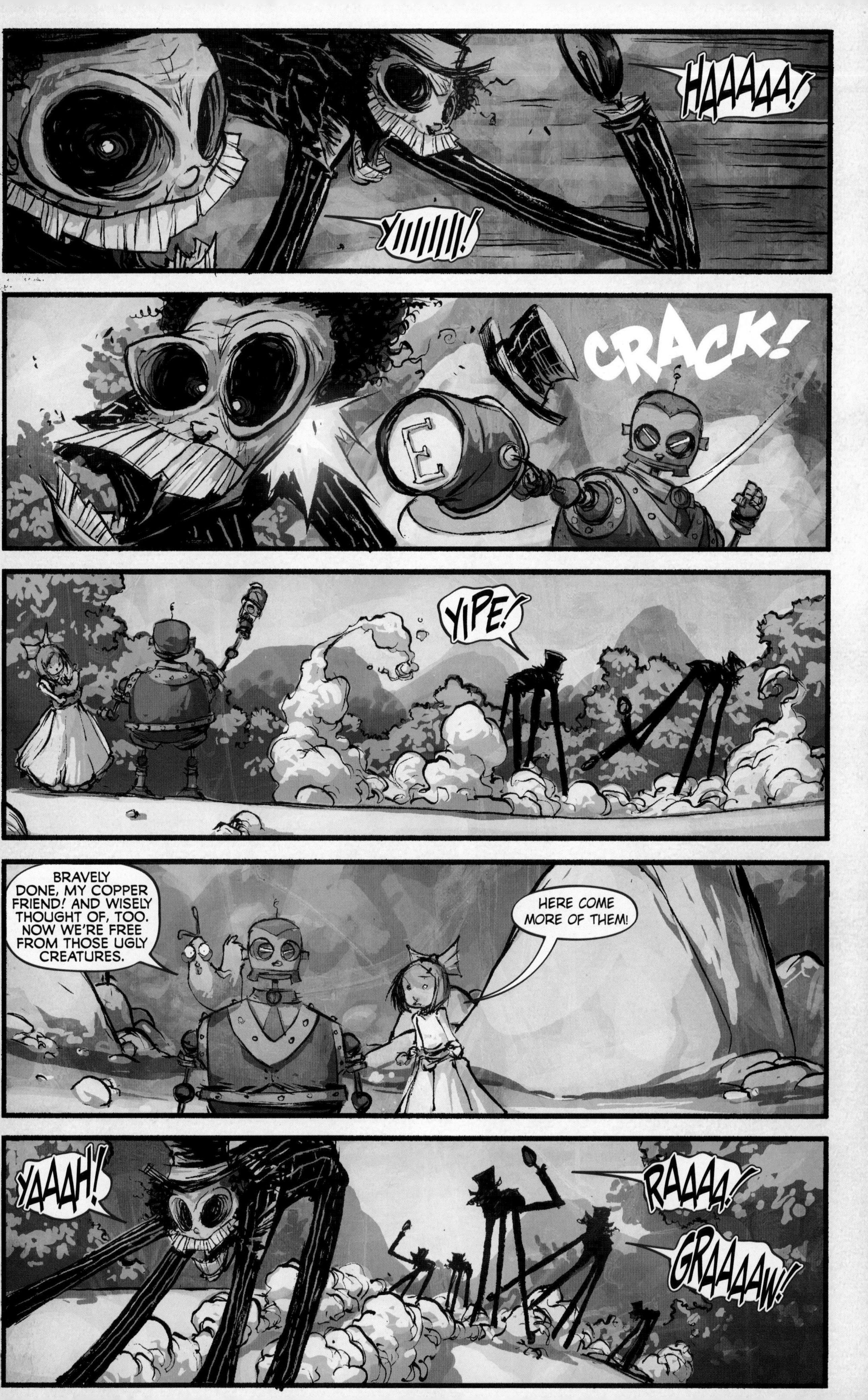
HAAAAA!
YIIIIIII!
CRACK!
YIPE!
BRAVELY DONE, MY COPPER FRIEND! AND WISELY THOUGHT OF, TOO. NOW WE'RE FREE FROM THOSE UGLY CREATURES.
HERE COME MORE OF THEM!
YAAAH!
RAAAA!
GRAAAAW!

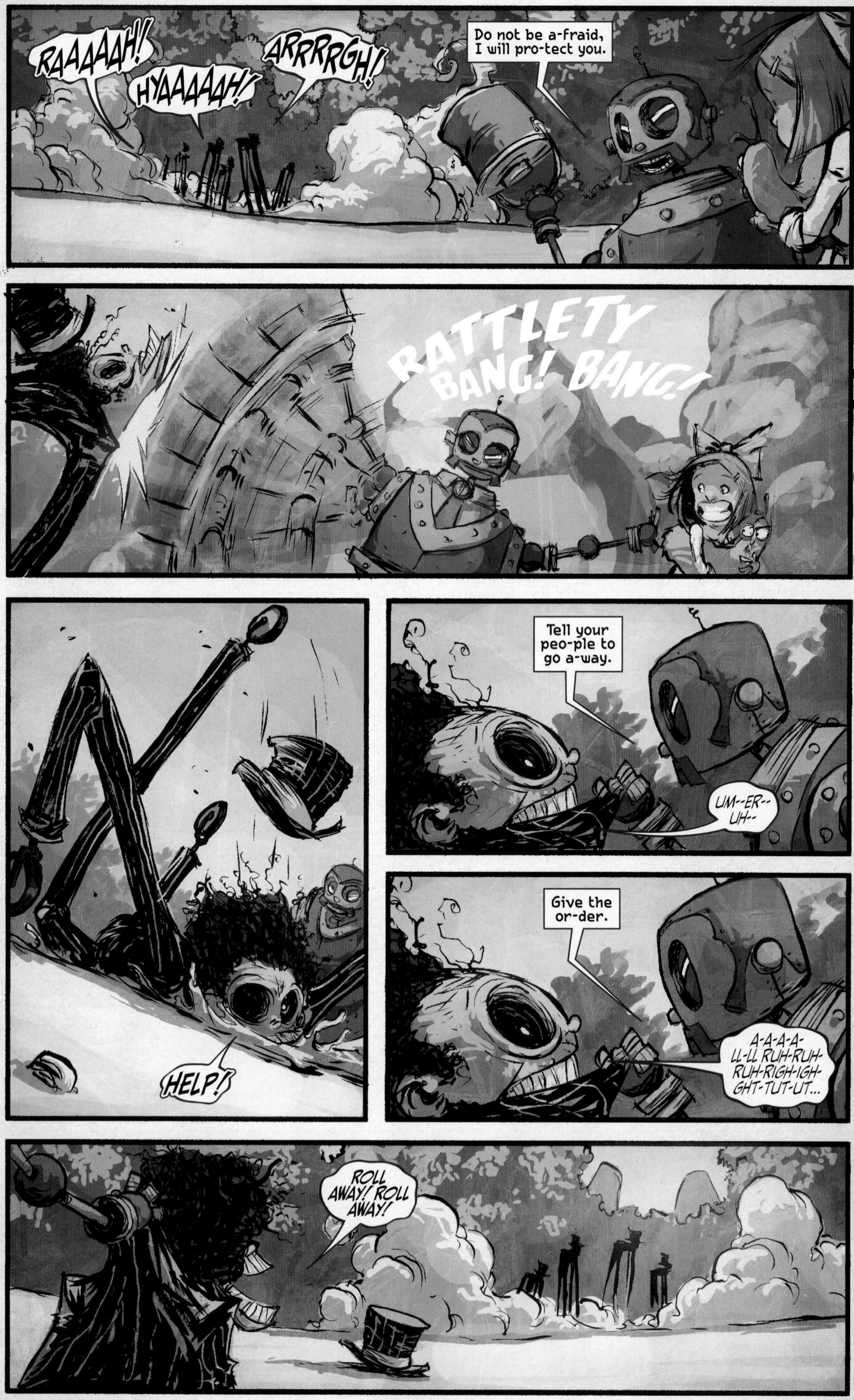
RAAAAAH!
HYAAAAAH!
ARRRRGH!
Do not be a-fraid, I will pro-tect you.
RATTLETY BANG! BANG!
HELP!
Tell your peo-ple to go a-way.
UM--ER-- UH--
Give the or-der.
A-A-A-A-LL-LL RUH-RUH-RUH-RIGH-IGH-GHT-TUT-UT...
ROLL AWAY! ROLL AWAY!

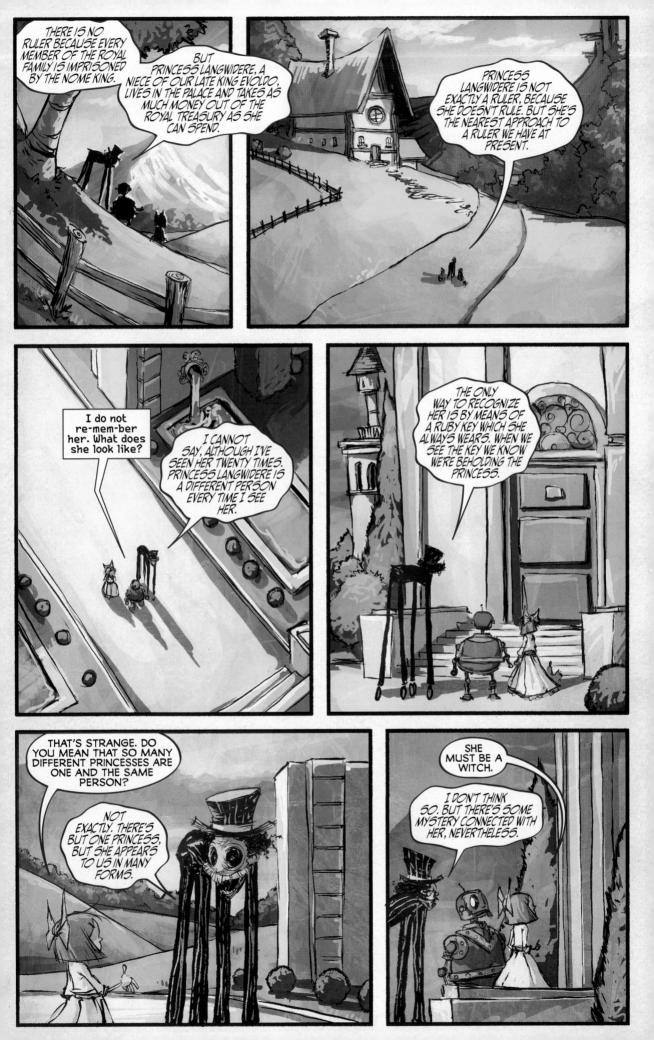

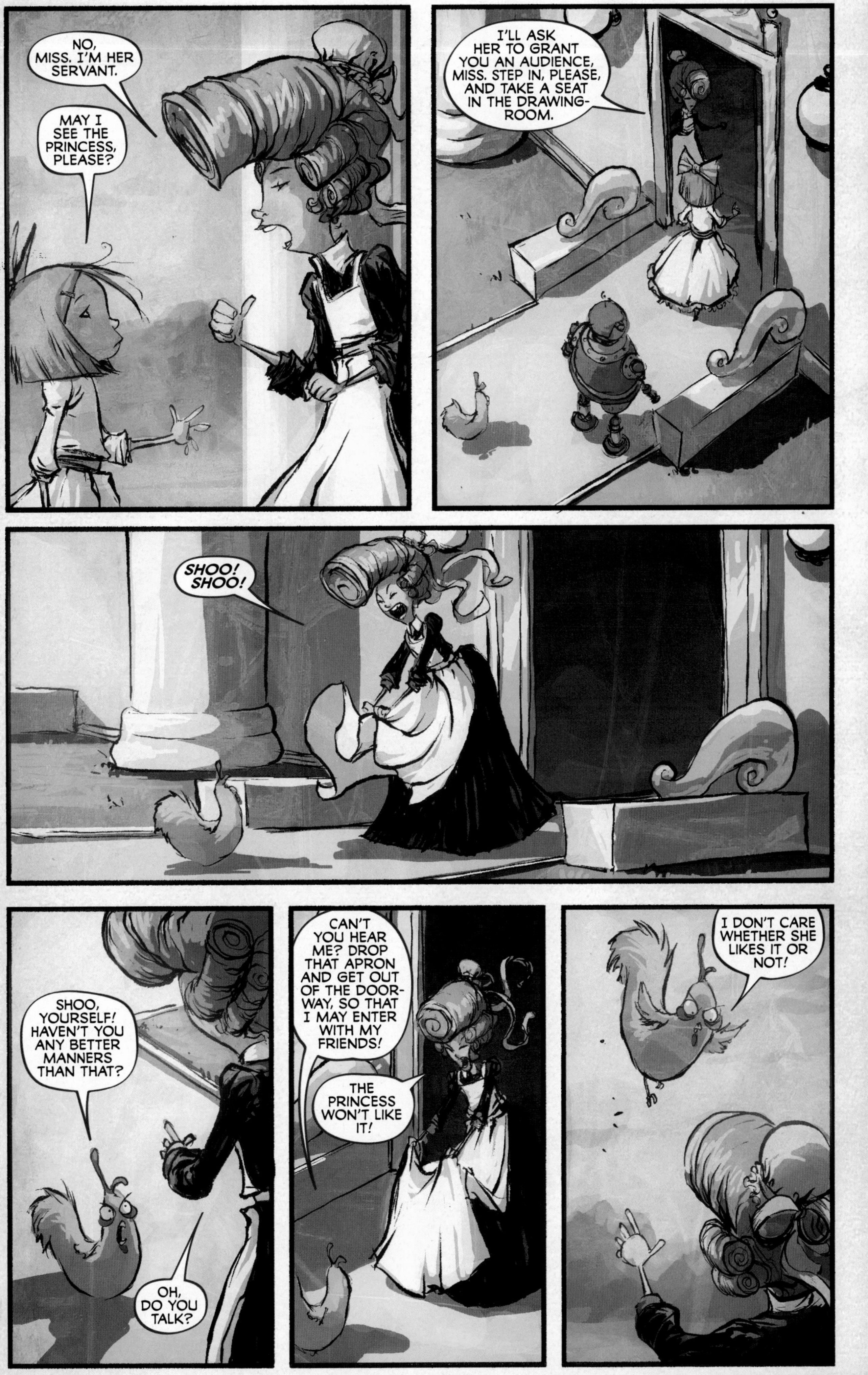
NO, MISS. I'M HER SERVANT.
MAY I SEE THE PRINCESS, PLEASE?
I'LL ASK HER TO GRANT YOU AN AUDIENCE, MISS. STEP IN, PLEASE, AND TAKE A SEAT IN THE DRAWING-ROOM.
SHOO! SHOO!
SHOO, YOURSELF! HAVEN'T YOU ANY BETTER MANNERS THAN THAT?
OH, DO YOU TALK?
CAN'T YOU HEAR ME? DROP THAT APRON AND GET OUT OF THE DOORWAY, SO THAT I MAY ENTER WITH MY FRIENDS!
THE PRINCESS WON'T LIKE IT!
I DON'T CARE WHETHER SHE LIKES IT OR NOT!

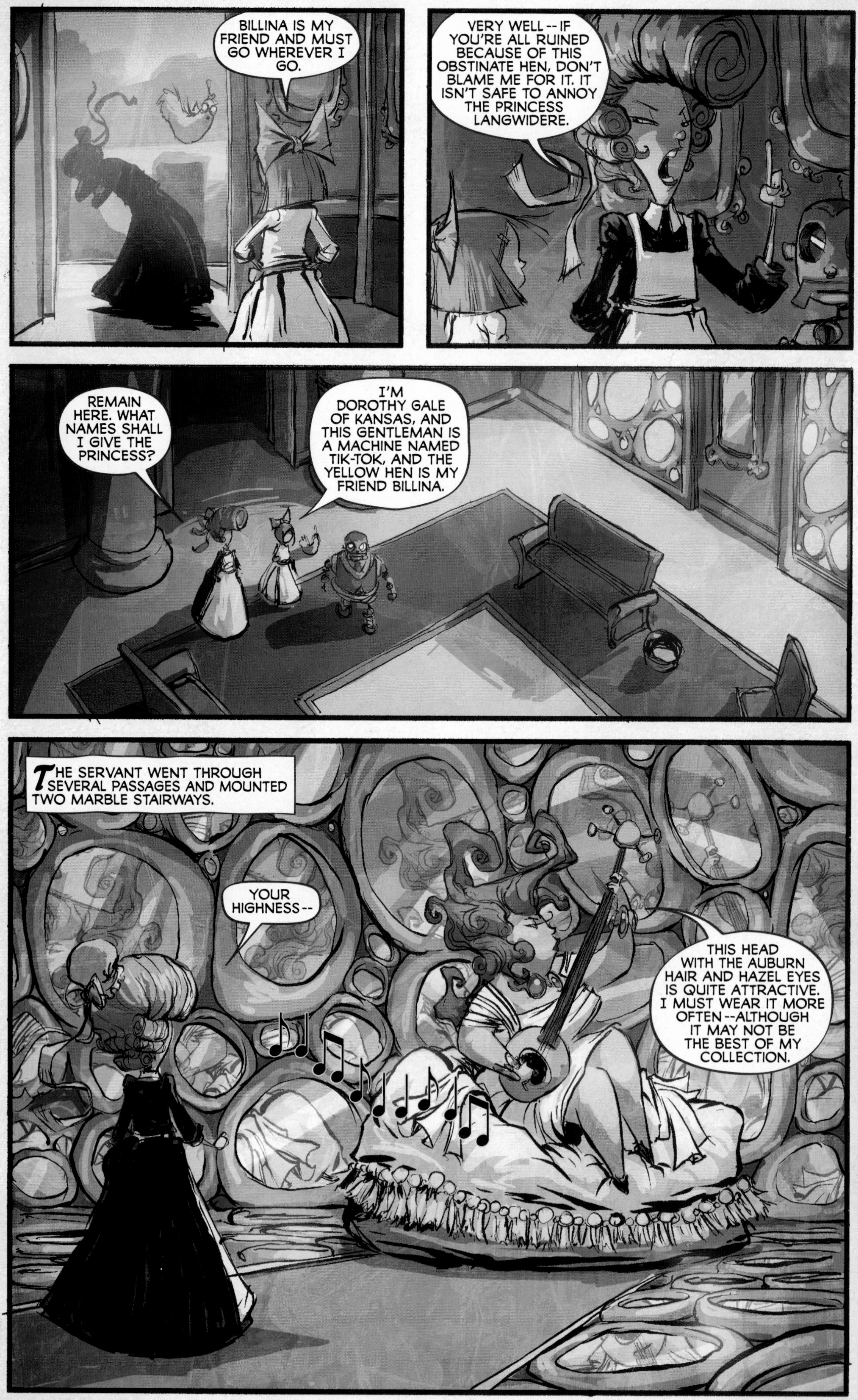
BILLINA IS MY FRIEND AND MUST GO WHEREVER I GO.
VERY WELL--IF YOU'RE ALL RUINED BECAUSE OF THIS OBSTINATE HEN, DON'T BLAME ME FOR IT. IT ISN'T SAFE TO ANNOY THE PRINCESS LANGWIDERE.
REMAIN HERE. WHAT NAMES SHALL I GIVE THE PRINCESS?
I'M DOROTHY GALE OF KANSAS, AND THIS GENTLEMAN IS A MACHINE NAMED TIK-TOK, AND THE YELLOW HEN IS MY FRIEND BILLINA.
THE SERVANT WENT THROUGH SEVERAL PASSAGES AND MOUNTED TWO MARBLE STAIRWAYS.
YOUR HIGHNESS--
THIS HEAD WITH THE AUBURN HAIR AND HAZEL EYES IS QUITE ATTRACTIVE. I MUST WEAR IT MORE OFTEN--ALTHOUGH IT MAY NOT BE THE BEST OF MY COLLECTION.

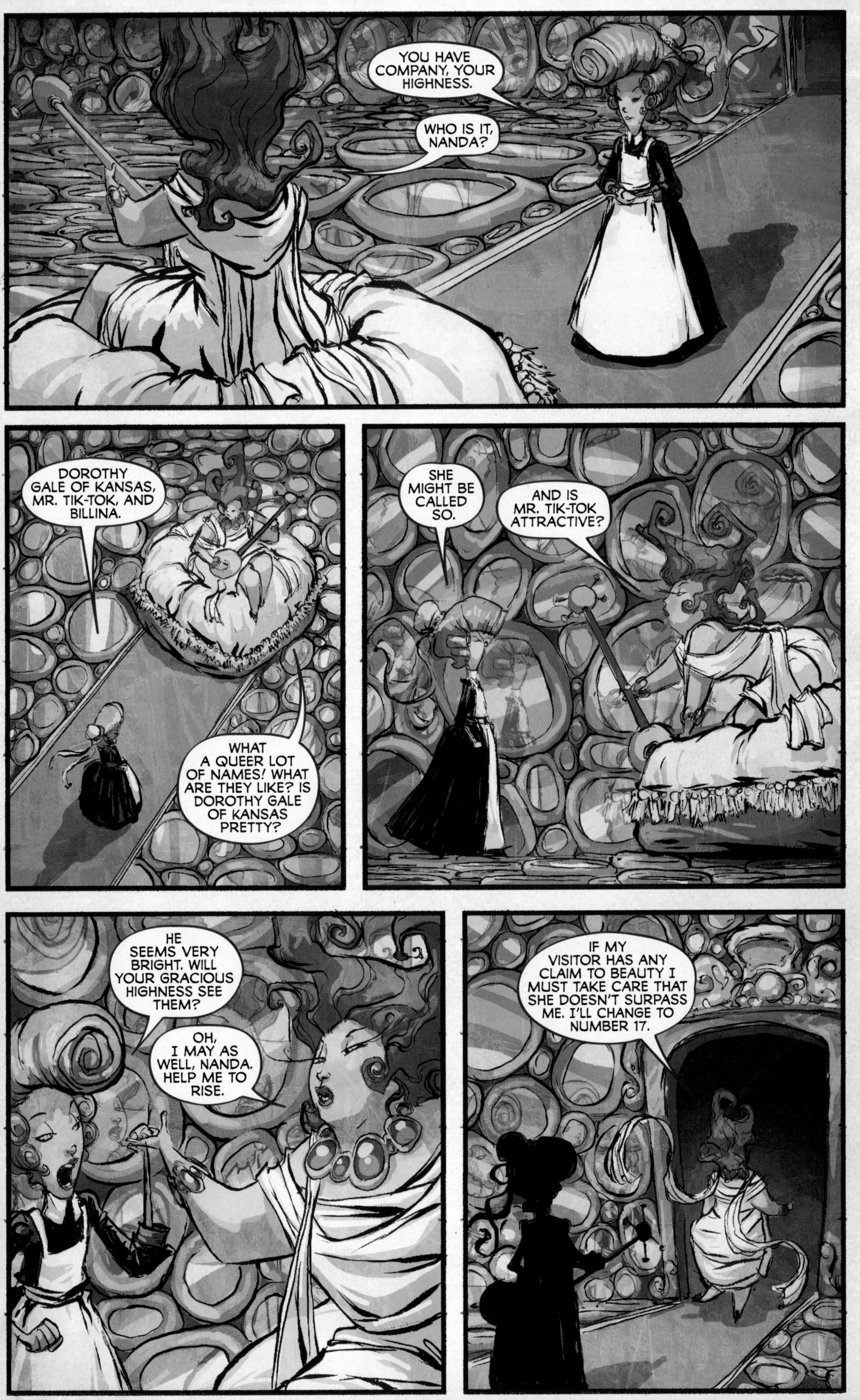
YOU HAVE COMPANY, YOUR HIGHNESS.
WHO IS IT, NANDA?
DOROTHY GALE OF KANSAS, MR. TIK-TOK, AND BILLINA.
WHAT A QUEER LOT OF NAMES! WHAT ARE THEY LIKE? IS DOROTHY GALE OF KANSAS PRETTY?
SHE MIGHT BE CALLED SO.
AND IS MR. TIK-TOK ATTRACTIVE?
HE SEEMS VERY BRIGHT. WILL YOUR GRACIOUS HIGHNESS SEE THEM?
OH, I MAY AS WELL, NANDA. HELP ME TO RISE.
IF MY VISITOR HAS ANY CLAIM TO BEAUTY I MUST TAKE CARE THAT SHE DOESN'T SURPASS ME. I'LL CHANGE TO NUMBER 17.

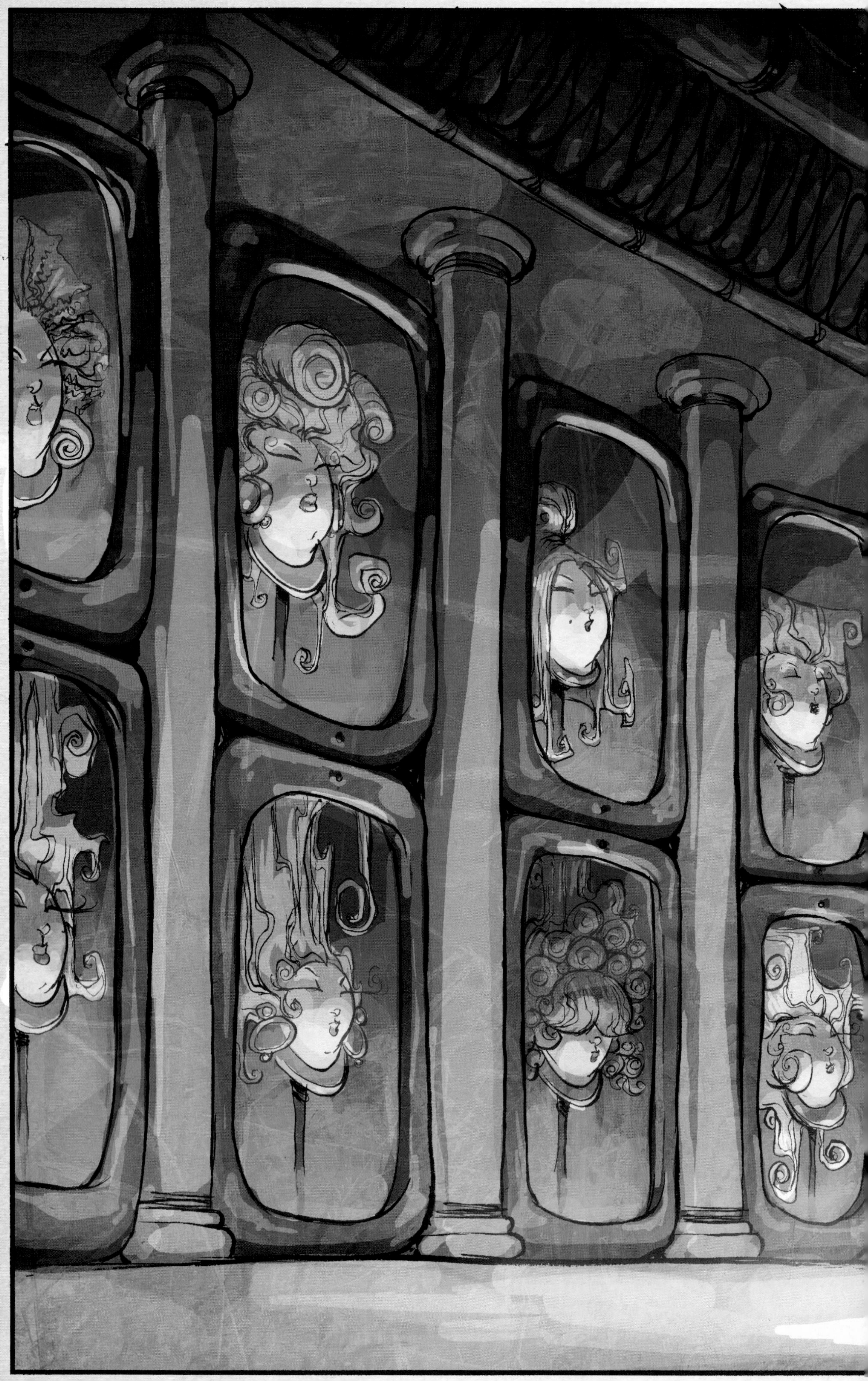

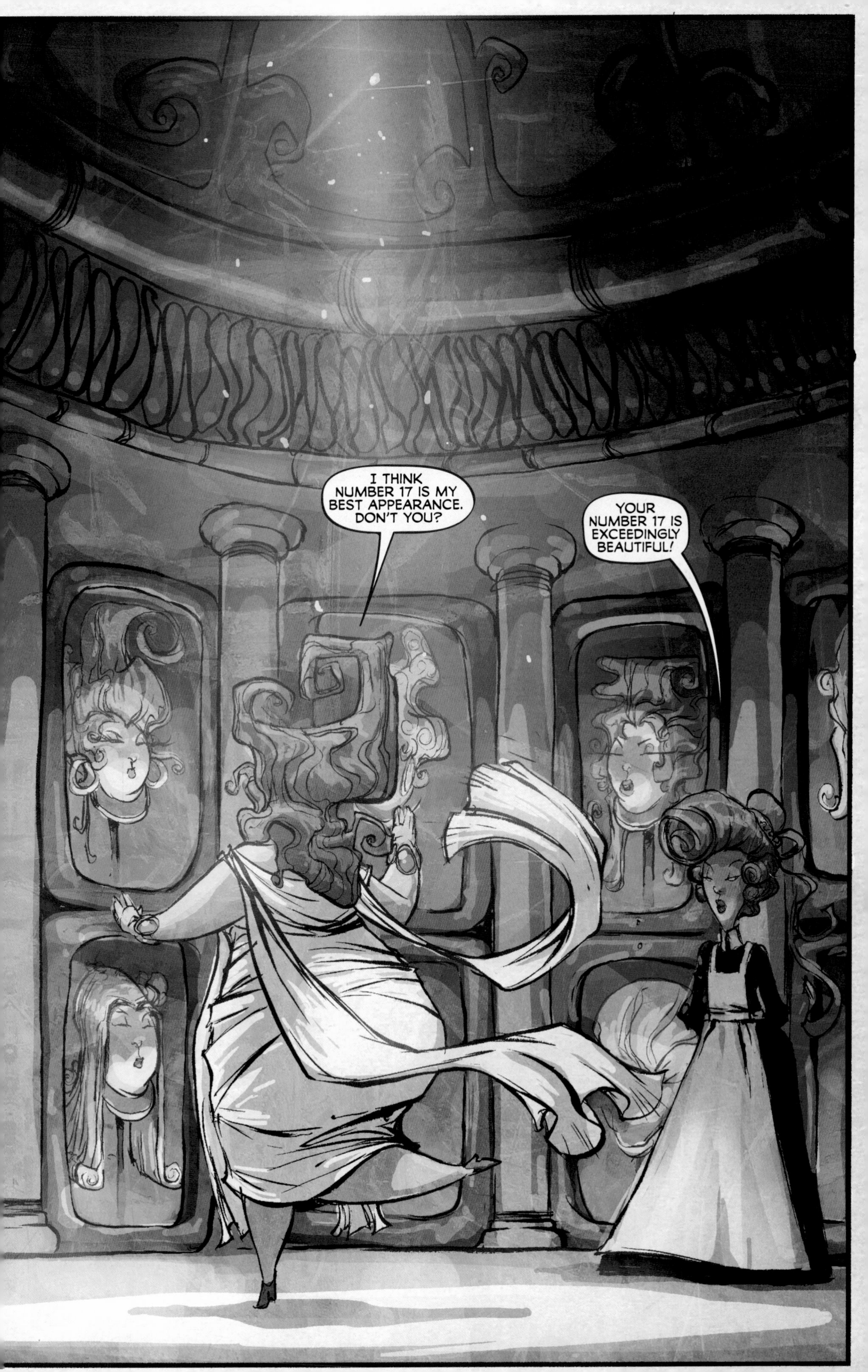
I THINK NUMBER 17 IS MY BEST APPEARANCE. DON'T YOU?
YOUR NUMBER 17 IS EXCEEDINGLY BEAUTIFUL!

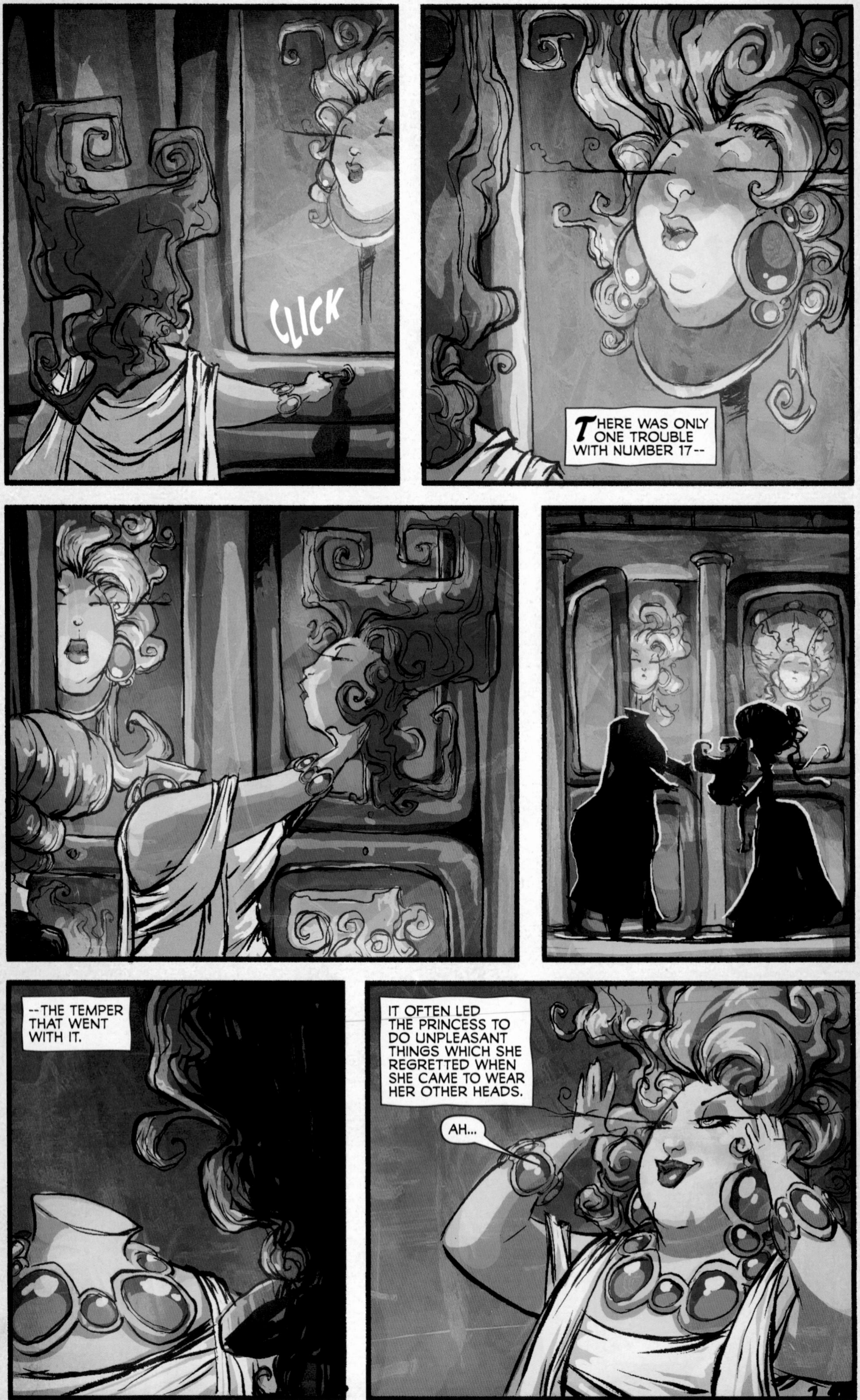
CLICK
THERE WAS ONLY ONE TROUBLE WITH NUMBER 17--
--THE TEMPER THAT WENT WITH IT.
IT OFTEN LED THE PRINCESS TO DO UNPLEASANT THINGS WHICH SHE REGRETTED WHEN SHE CAME TO WEAR HER OTHER HEADS.
AH...

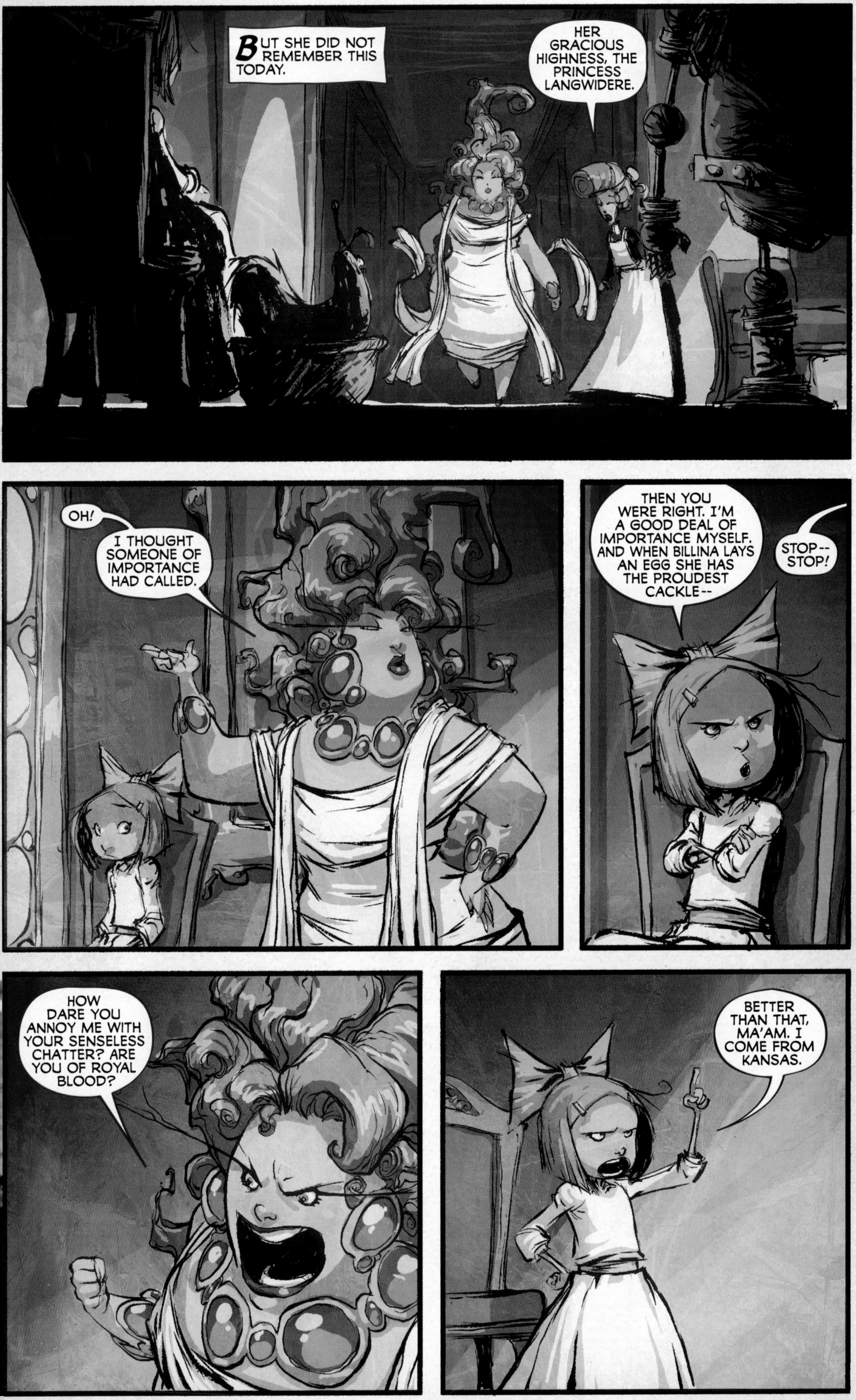
BUT SHE DID NOT REMEMBER THIS TODAY.
HER GRACIOUS HIGHNESS, THE PRINCESS LANGWIDERE.
OH!
I THOUGHT SOMEONE OF IMPORTANCE HAD CALLED.
THEN YOU WERE RIGHT. I'M A GOOD DEAL OF IMPORTANCE MYSELF. AND WHEN BILLINA LAYS AN EGG SHE HAS THE PROUDEST CACKLE--
STOP-- STOP!
HOW DARE YOU ANNOY ME WITH YOUR SENSELESS CHATTER? ARE YOU OF ROYAL BLOOD?
BETTER THAN THAT, MA'AM. I COME FROM KANSAS.

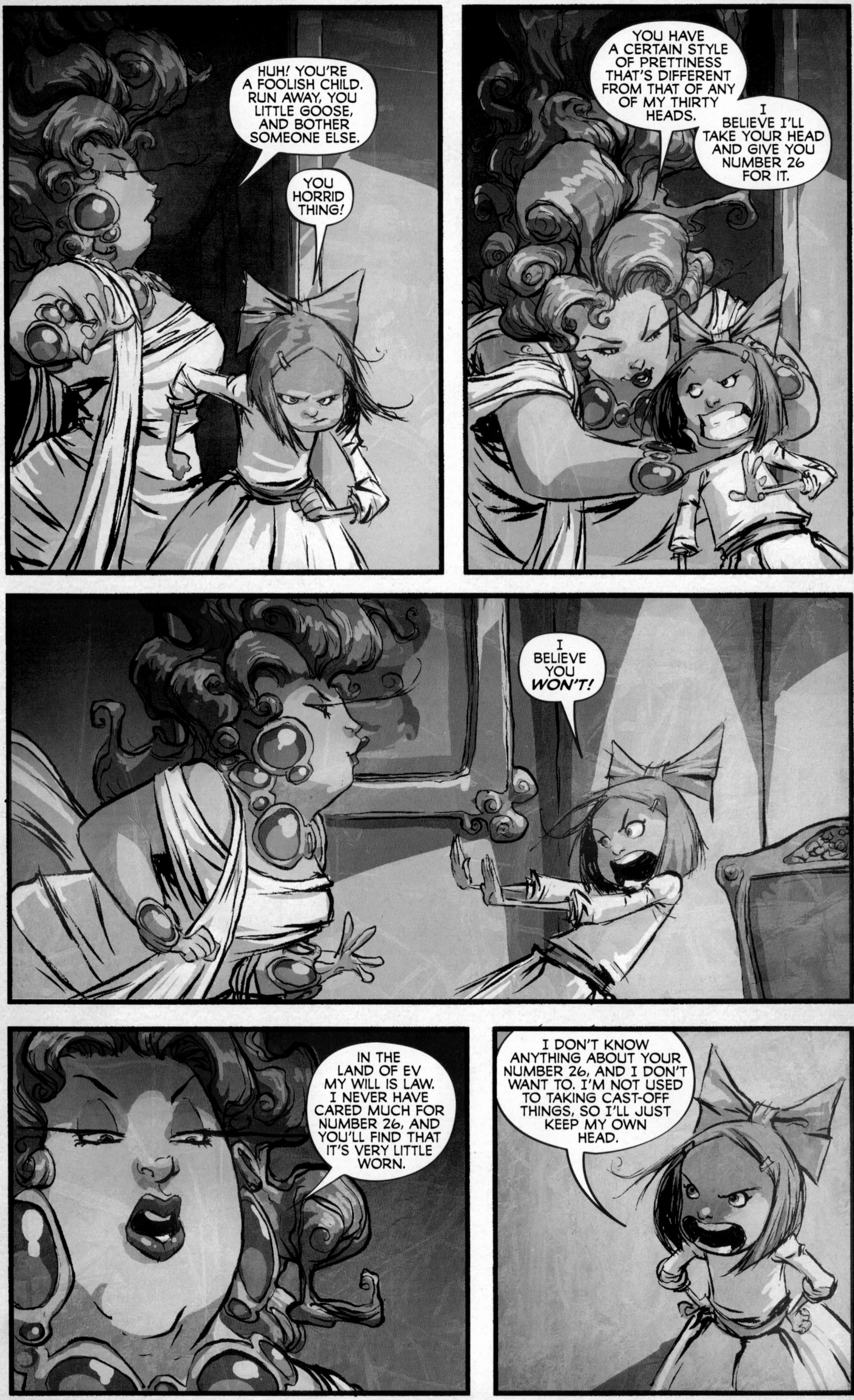
HUH! YOU'RE A FOOLISH CHILD. RUN AWAY, YOU LITTLE GOOSE, AND BOTHER SOMEONE ELSE.
YOU HORRID THING!
YOU HAVE A CERTAIN STYLE OF PRETTINESS THAT'S DIFFERENT FROM THAT OF ANY OF MY THIRTY HEADS.
I BELIEVE I'LL TAKE YOUR HEAD AND GIVE YOU NUMBER 26 FOR IT.
I BELIEVE YOU *WON'T!*
IN THE LAND OF EV MY WILL IS LAW. I NEVER HAVE CARED MUCH FOR NUMBER 26, AND YOU'LL FIND THAT IT'S VERY LITTLE WORN.
I DON'T KNOW ANYTHING ABOUT YOUR NUMBER 26, AND I DON'T WANT TO. I'M NOT USED TO TAKING CAST-OFF THINGS, SO I'LL JUST KEEP MY OWN HEAD.

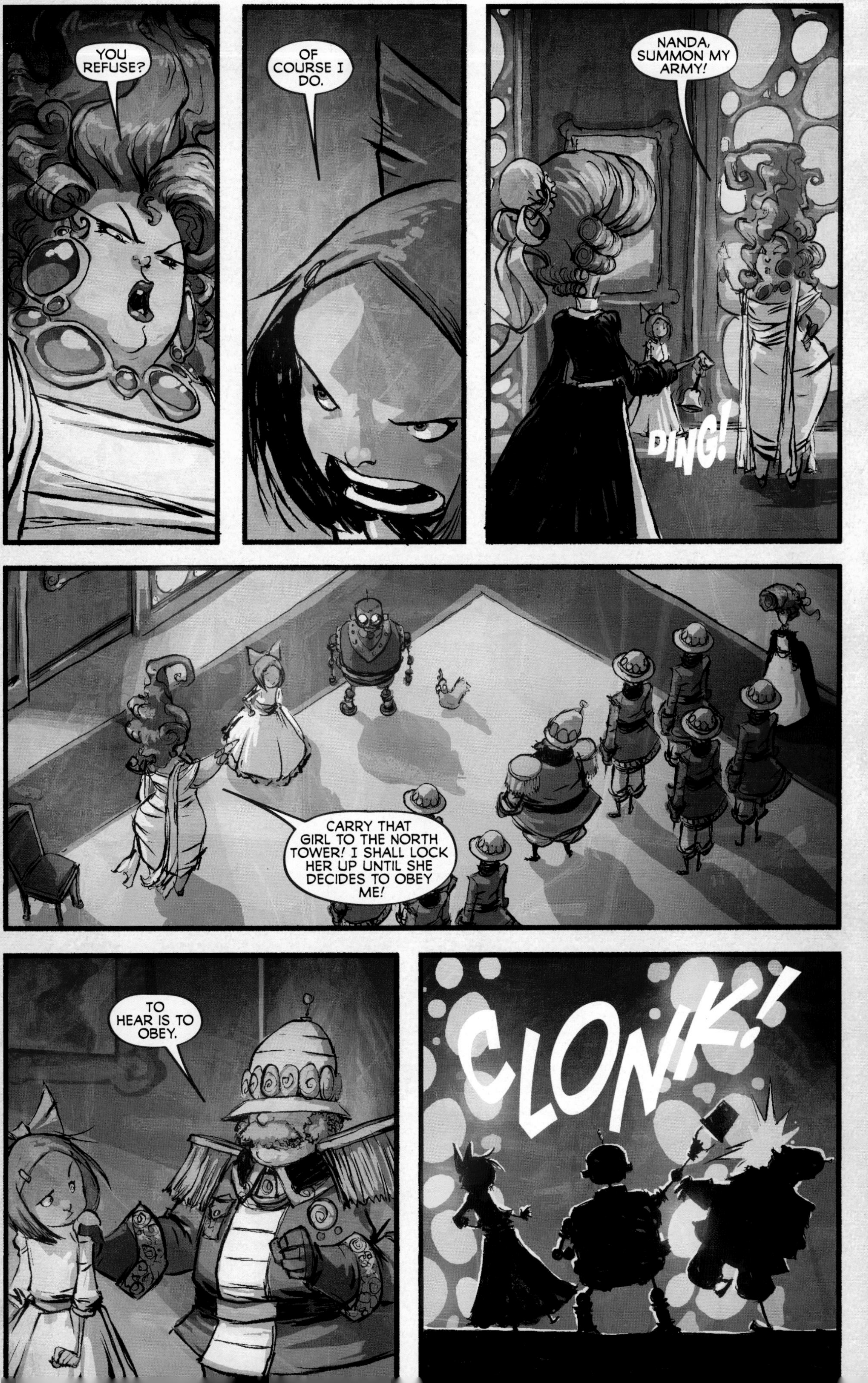
YOU REFUSE?
OF COURSE I DO.
NANDA, SUMMON MY ARMY!
DING!
CARRY THAT GIRL TO THE NORTH TOWER! I SHALL LOCK HER UP UNTIL SHE DECIDES TO OBEY ME!
TO HEAR IS TO OBEY.
CLONK!

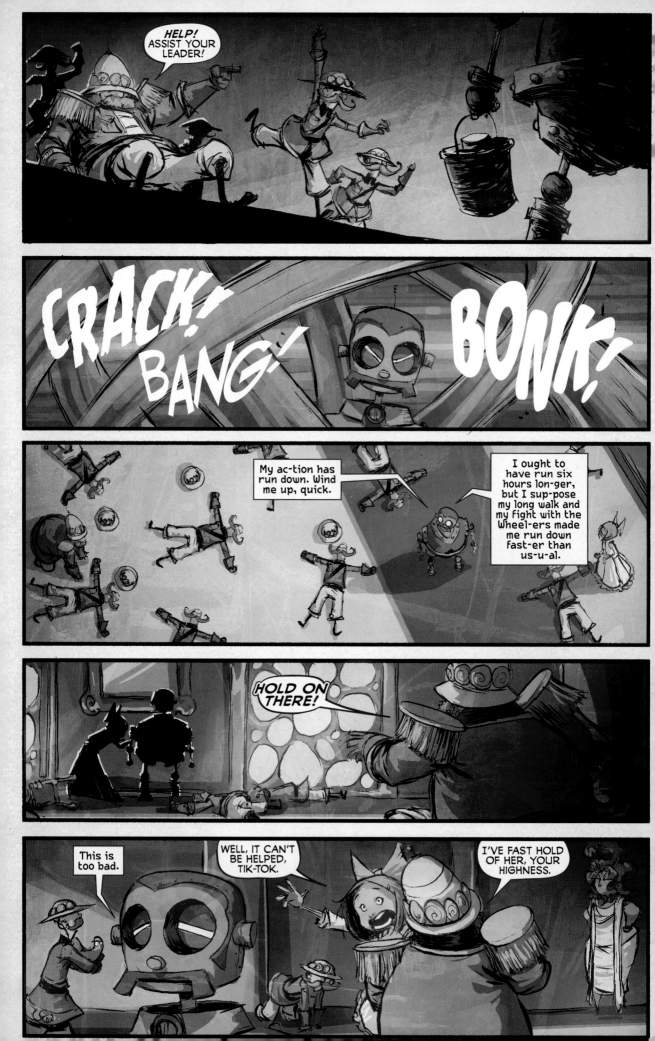

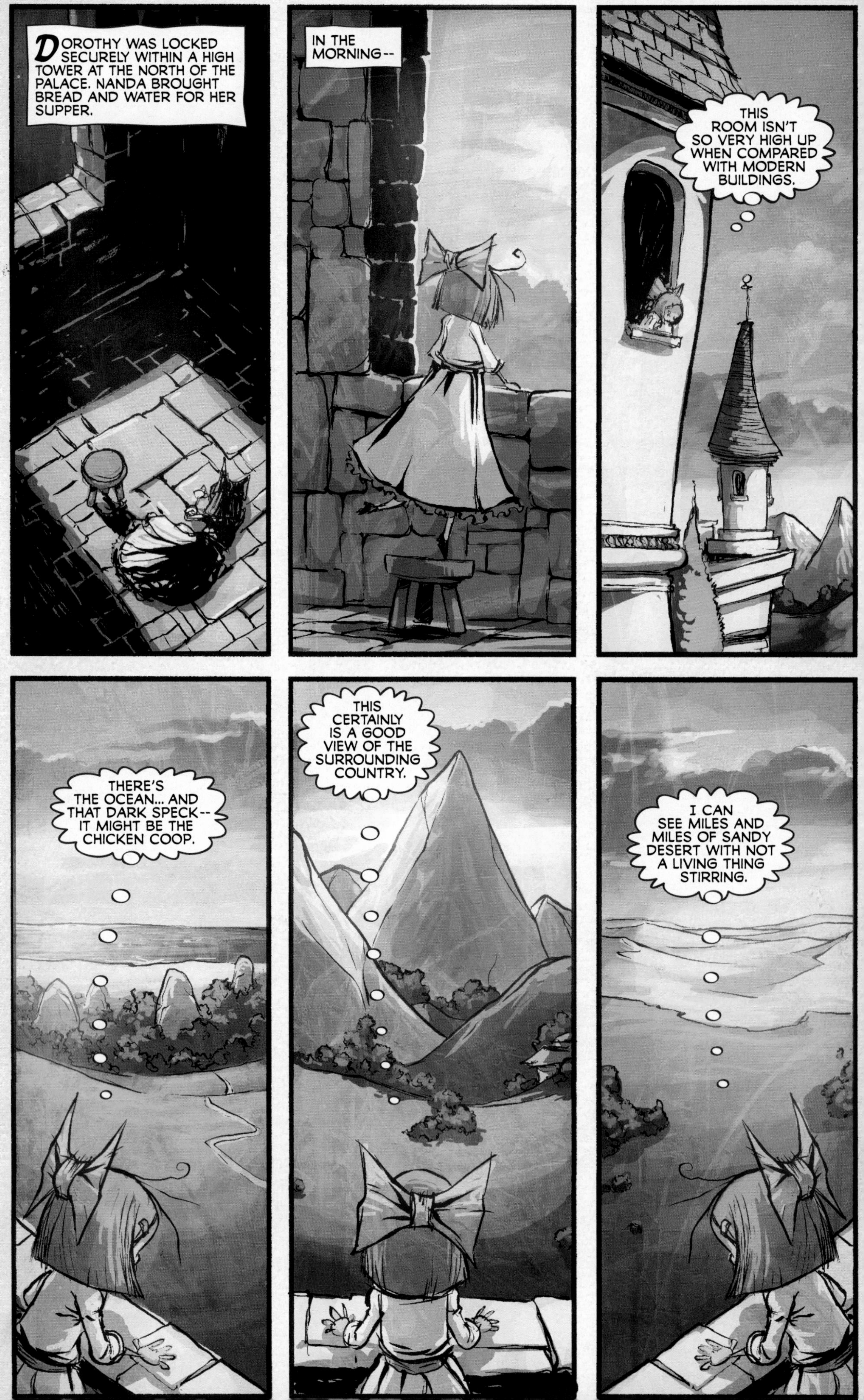
DOROTHY WAS LOCKED SECURELY WITHIN A HIGH TOWER AT THE NORTH OF THE PALACE. NANDA BROUGHT BREAD AND WATER FOR HER SUPPER.
IN THE MORNING--
THIS ROOM ISN'T SO VERY HIGH UP WHEN COMPARED WITH MODERN BUILDINGS.
THERE'S THE OCEAN... AND THAT DARK SPECK-- IT MIGHT BE THE CHICKEN COOP.
THIS CERTAINLY IS A GOOD VIEW OF THE SURROUNDING COUNTRY.
I CAN SEE MILES AND MILES OF SANDY DESERT WITH NOT A LIVING THING STIRRING.

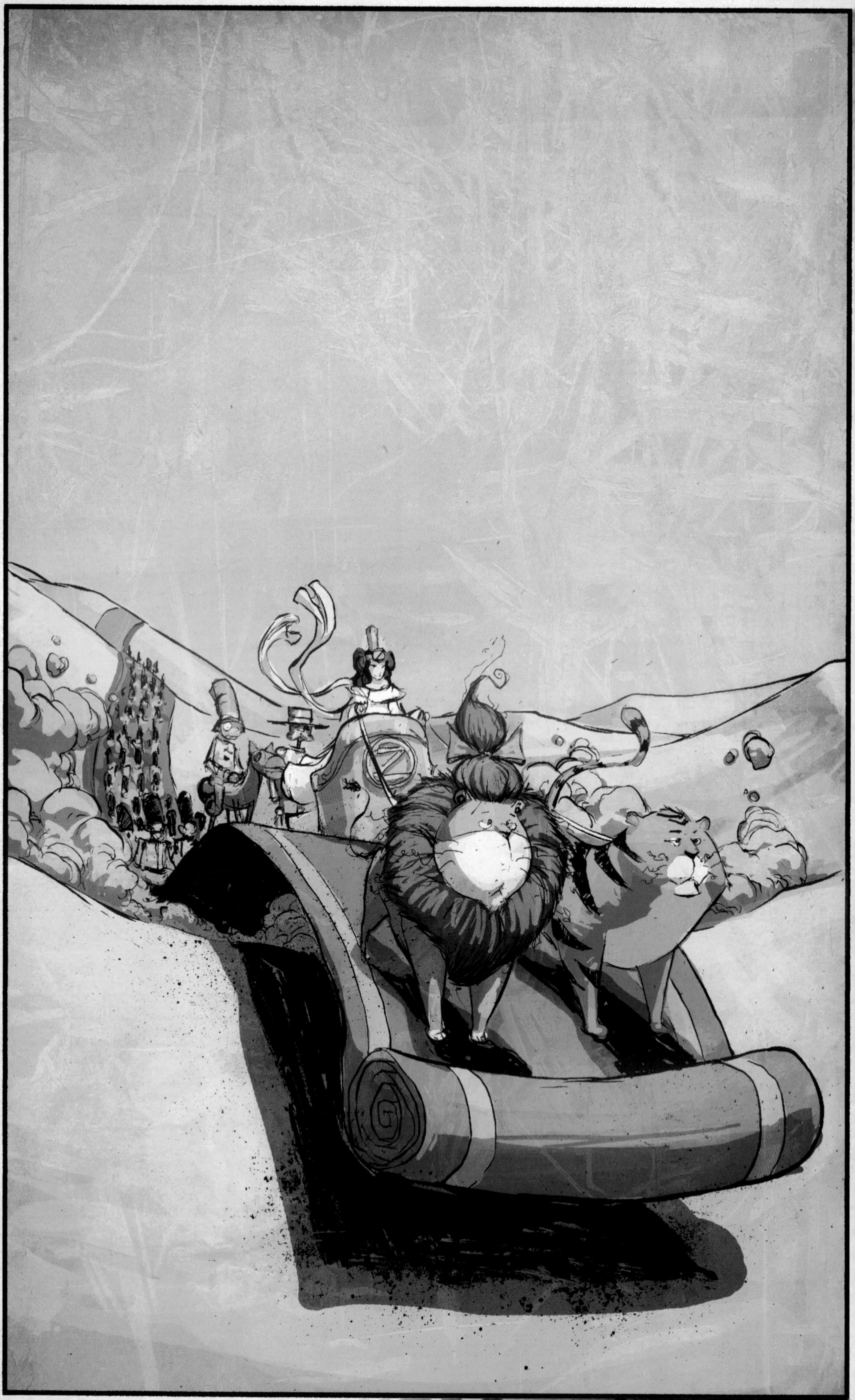

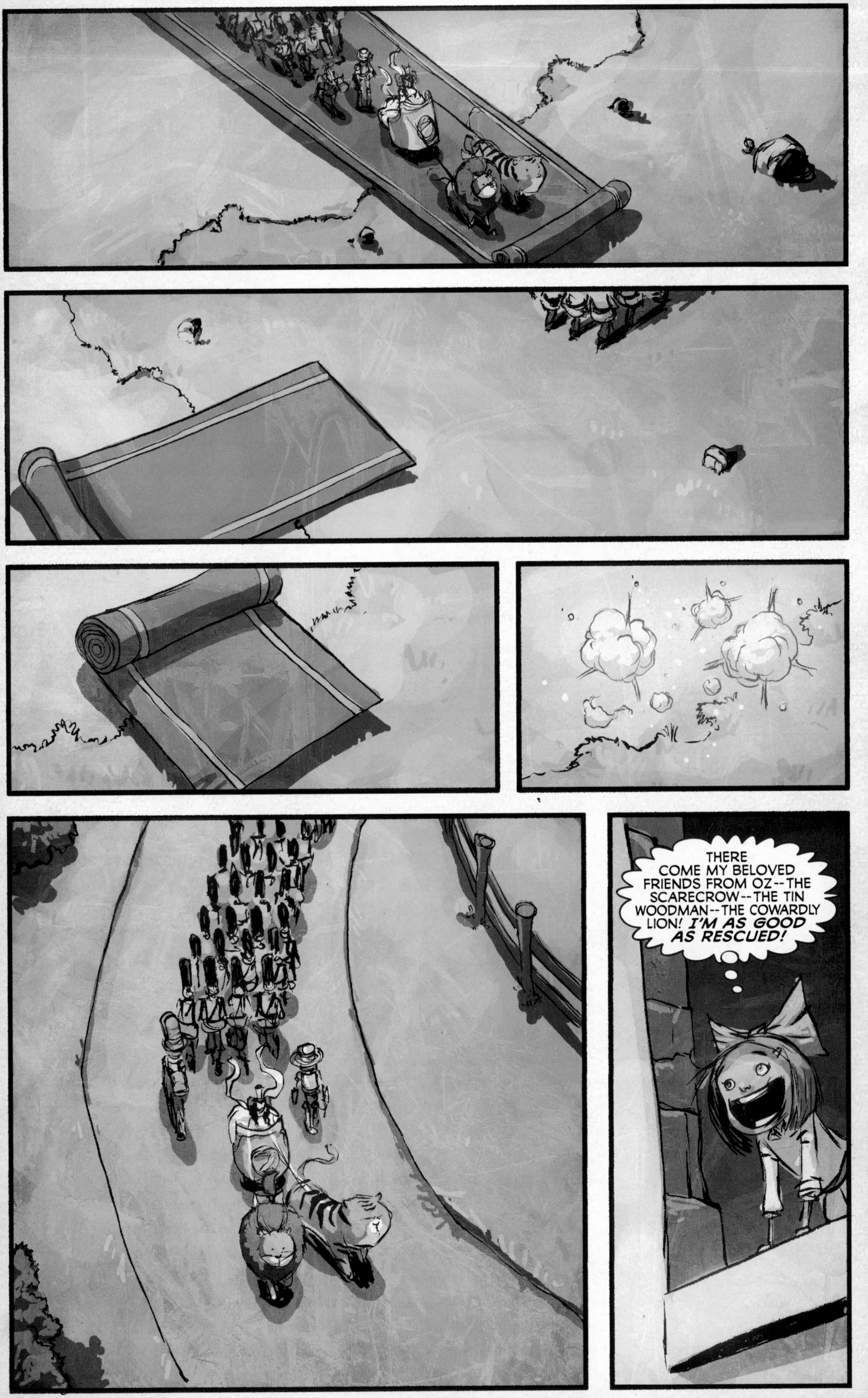
THERE COME MY BELOVED FRIENDS FROM OZ--THE SCARECROW--THE TIN WOODMAN--THE COWARDLY LION! *I'M AS GOOD AS RESCUED!*

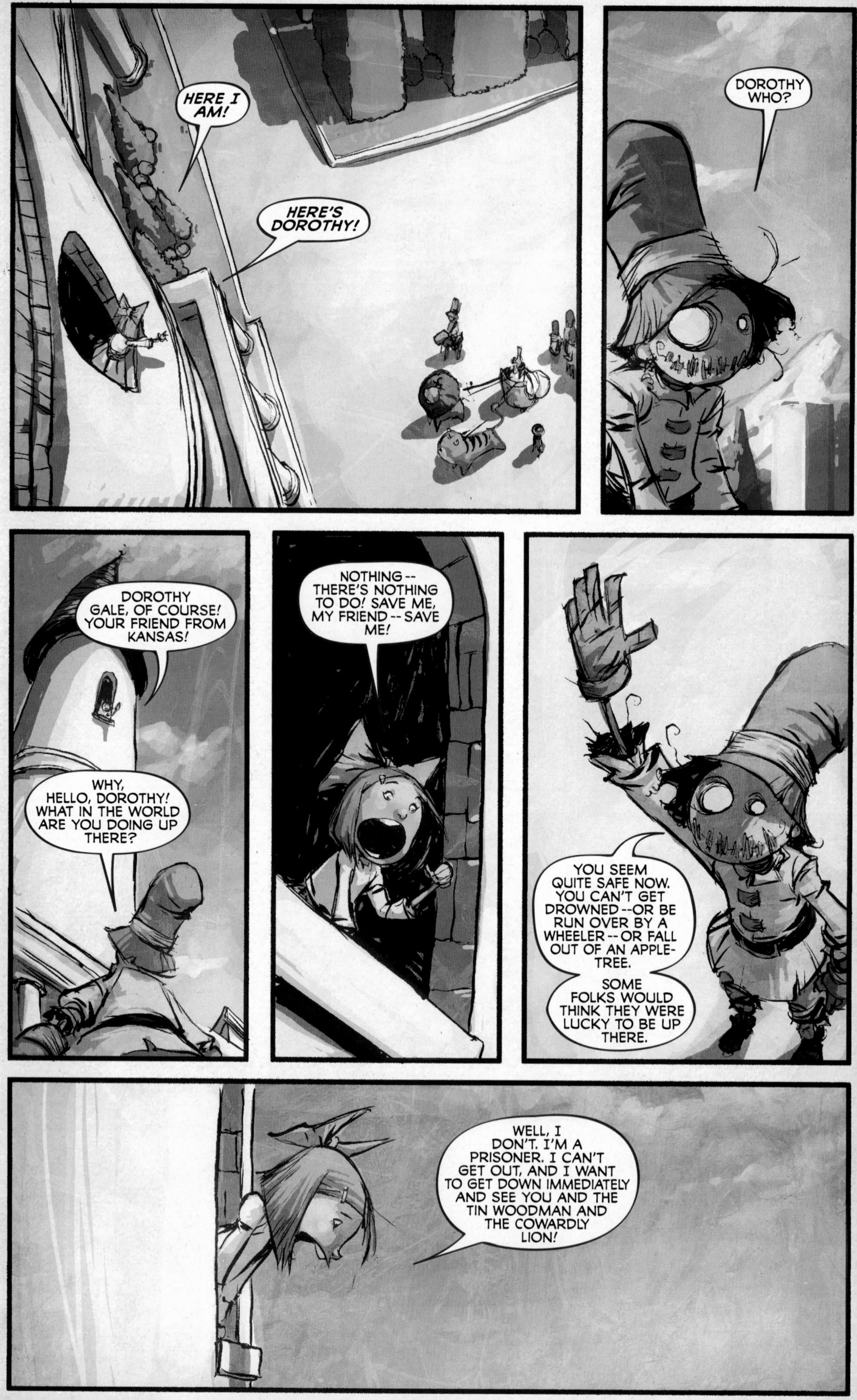
HERE I AM!
HERE'S DOROTHY!
DOROTHY WHO?
DOROTHY GALE, OF COURSE! YOUR FRIEND FROM KANSAS!
WHY, HELLO, DOROTHY! WHAT IN THE WORLD ARE YOU DOING UP THERE?
NOTHING -- THERE'S NOTHING TO DO! SAVE ME, MY FRIEND -- SAVE ME!
YOU SEEM QUITE SAFE NOW. YOU CAN'T GET DROWNED -- OR BE RUN OVER BY A WHEELER -- OR FALL OUT OF AN APPLE-TREE.
SOME FOLKS WOULD THINK THEY WERE LUCKY TO BE UP THERE.
WELL, I DON'T. I'M A PRISONER. I CAN'T GET OUT, AND I WANT TO GET DOWN IMMEDIATELY AND SEE YOU AND THE TIN WOODMAN AND THE COWARDLY LION!

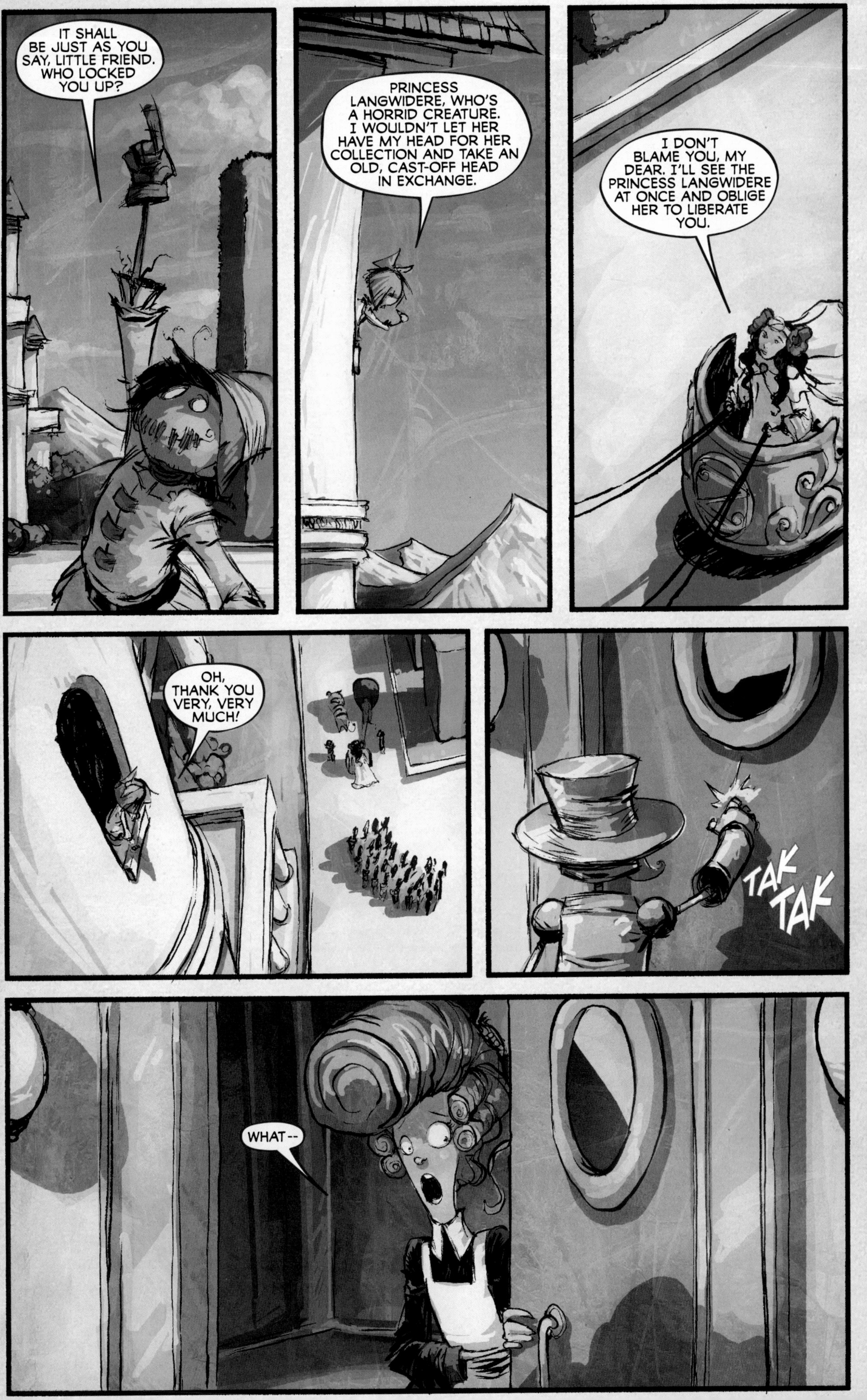
IT SHALL BE JUST AS YOU SAY, LITTLE FRIEND. WHO LOCKED YOU UP?
PRINCESS LANGWIDERE, WHO'S A HORRID CREATURE. I WOULDN'T LET HER HAVE MY HEAD FOR HER COLLECTION AND TAKE AN OLD, CAST-OFF HEAD IN EXCHANGE.
I DON'T BLAME YOU, MY DEAR. I'LL SEE THE PRINCESS LANGWIDERE AT ONCE AND OBLIGE HER TO LIBERATE YOU.
OH, THANK YOU VERY, VERY MUCH!
TAK TAK
WHAT--

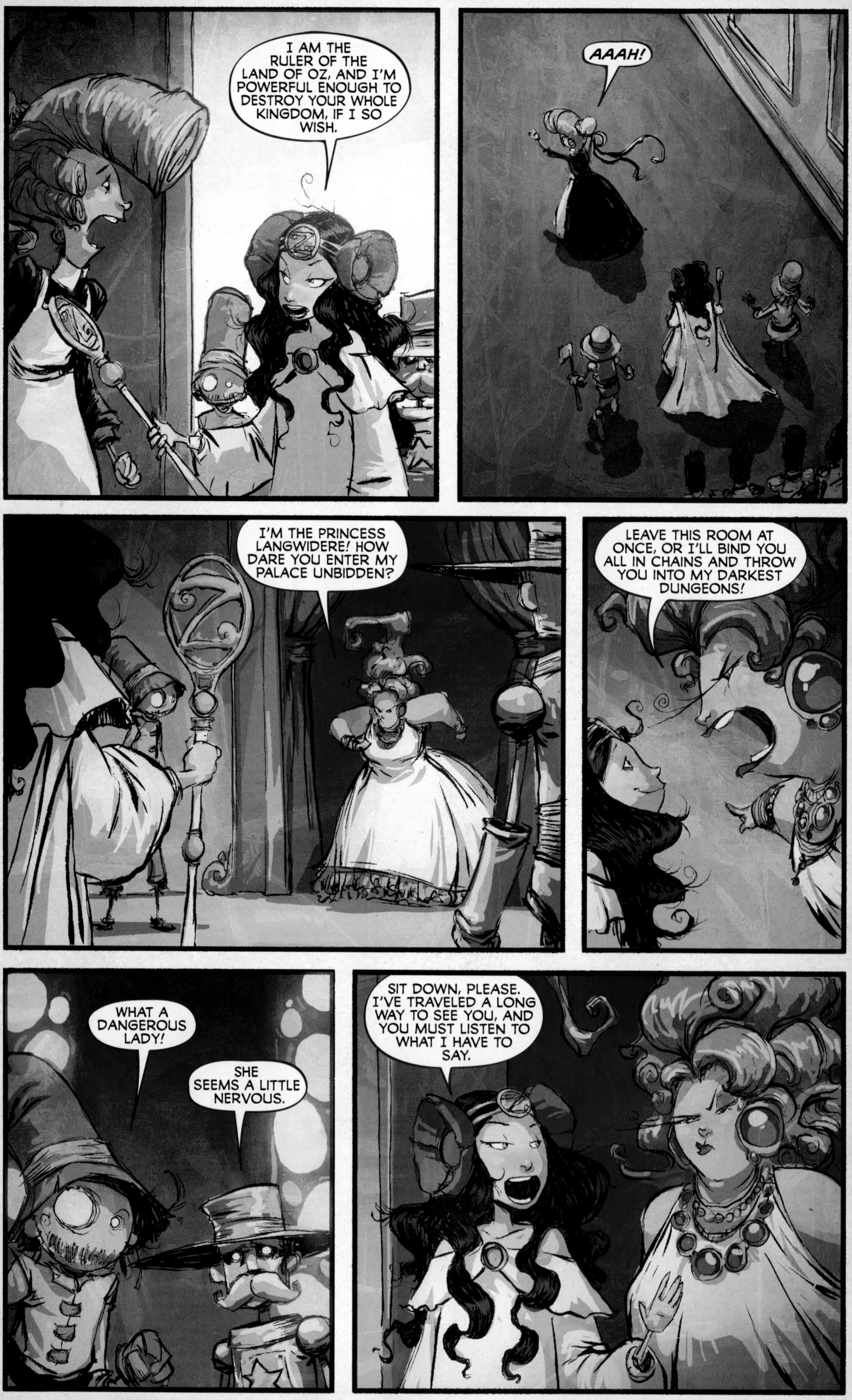
I AM THE RULER OF THE LAND OF OZ, AND I'M POWERFUL ENOUGH TO DESTROY YOUR WHOLE KINGDOM, IF I SO WISH.
AAAH!
I'M THE PRINCESS LANGWIDERE! HOW DARE YOU ENTER MY PALACE UNBIDDEN?
LEAVE THIS ROOM AT ONCE, OR I'LL BIND YOU ALL IN CHAINS AND THROW YOU INTO MY DARKEST DUNGEONS!
WHAT A DANGEROUS LADY!
SHE SEEMS A LITTLE NERVOUS.
SIT DOWN, PLEASE. I'VE TRAVELED A LONG WAY TO SEE YOU, AND YOU MUST LISTEN TO WHAT I HAVE TO SAY.

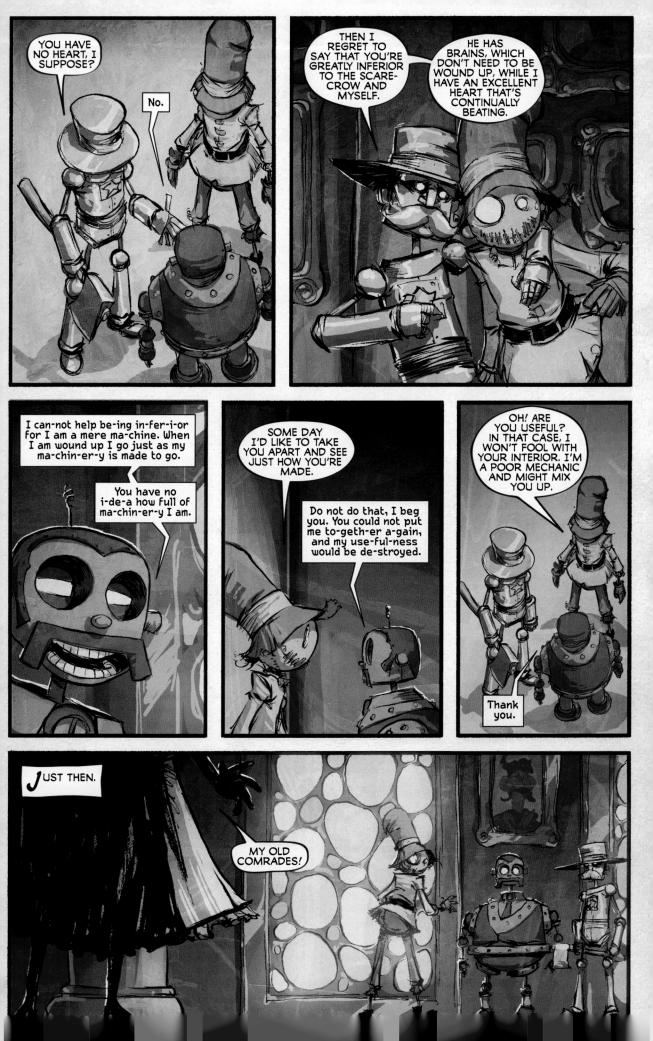

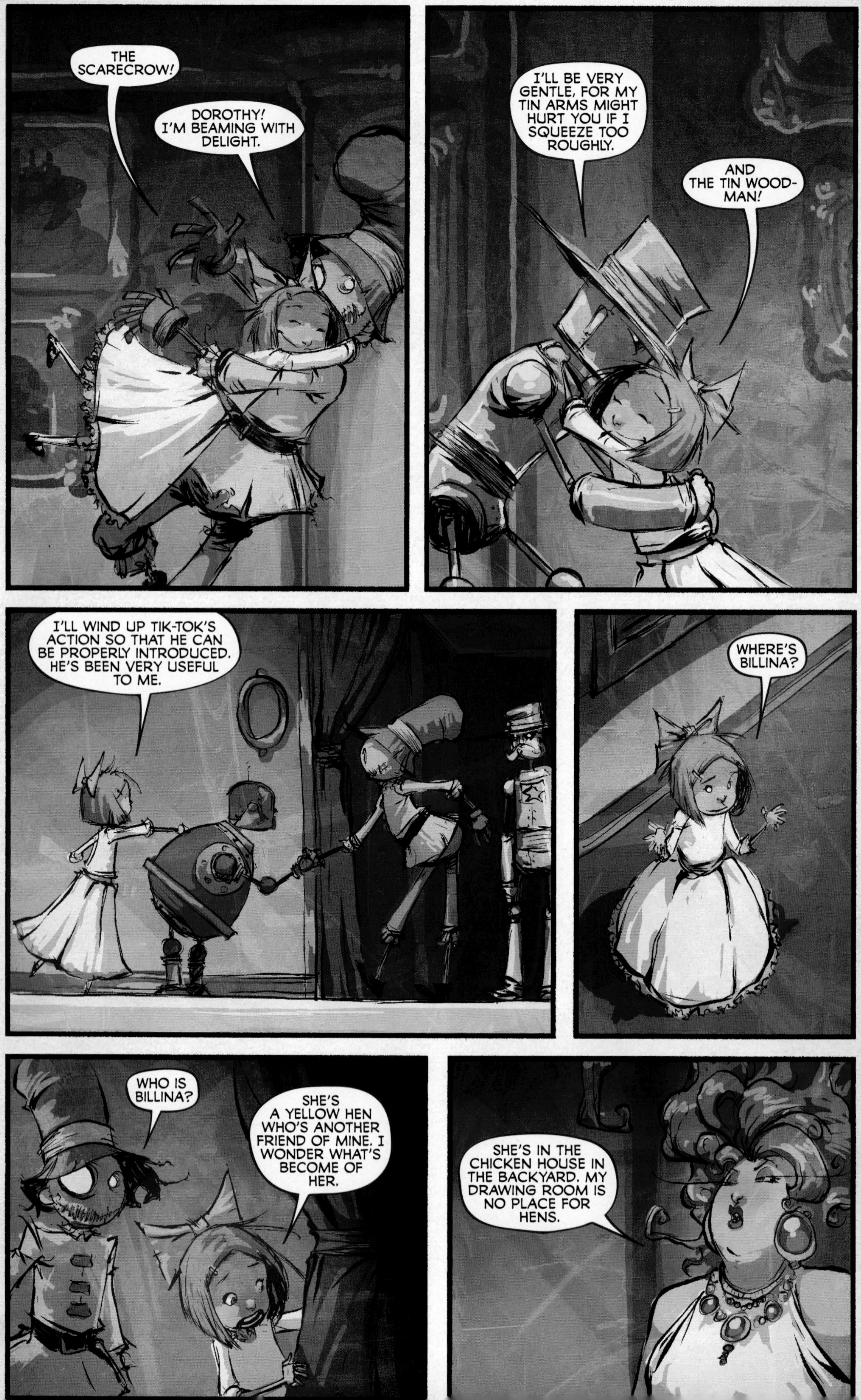
THE SCARECROW!
DOROTHY! I'M BEAMING WITH DELIGHT.
I'LL BE VERY GENTLE, FOR MY TIN ARMS MIGHT HURT YOU IF I SQUEEZE TOO ROUGHLY.
AND THE TIN WOOD-MAN!
I'LL WIND UP TIK-TOK'S ACTION SO THAT HE CAN BE PROPERLY INTRODUCED. HE'S BEEN VERY USEFUL TO ME.
WHERE'S BILLINA?
WHO IS BILLINA?
SHE'S A YELLOW HEN WHO'S ANOTHER FRIEND OF MINE. I WONDER WHAT'S BECOME OF HER.
SHE'S IN THE CHICKEN HOUSE IN THE BACKYARD. MY DRAWING ROOM IS NO PLACE FOR HENS.

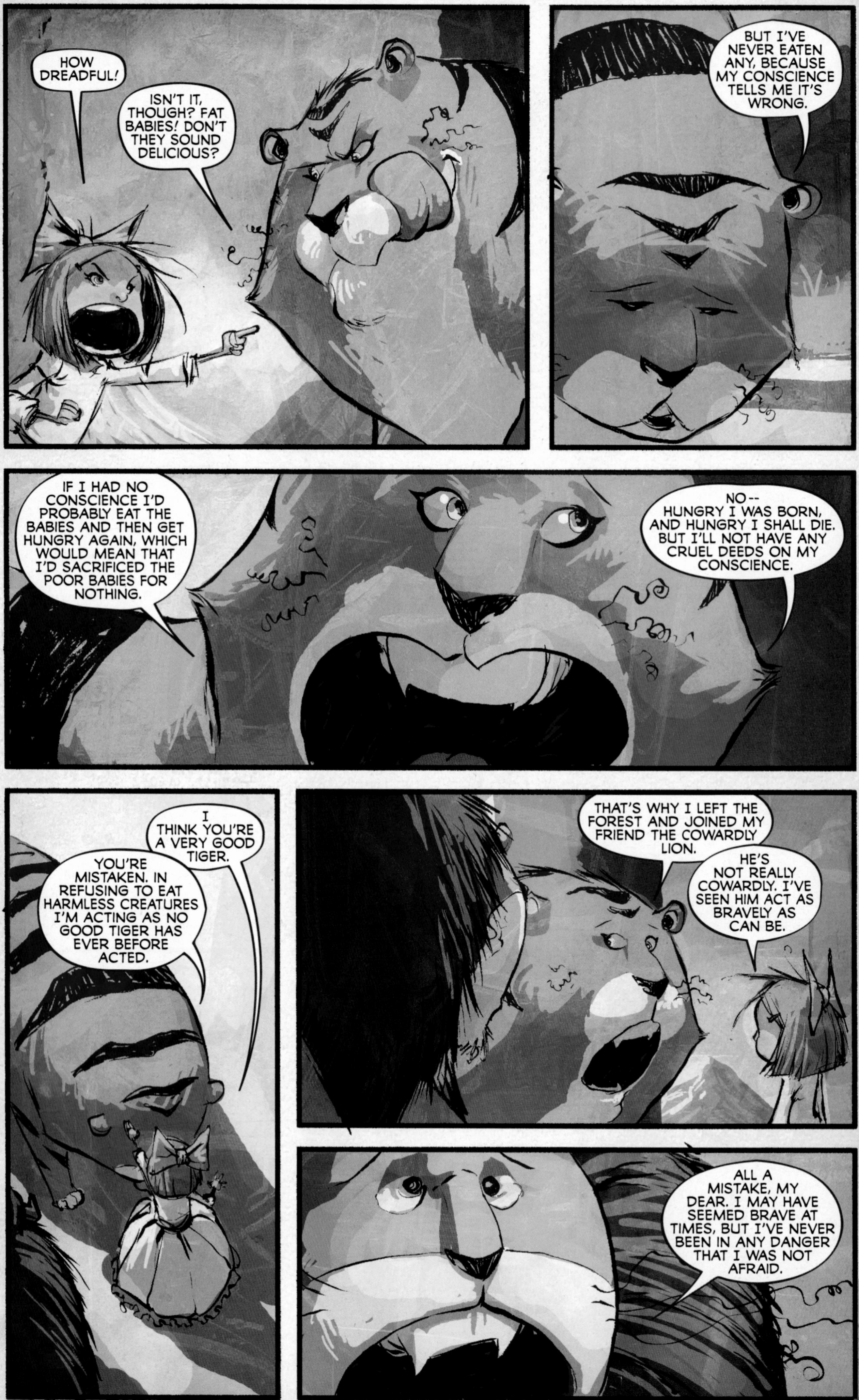
HOW DREADFUL!
ISN'T IT, THOUGH? FAT BABIES! DON'T THEY SOUND DELICIOUS?
BUT I'VE NEVER EATEN ANY, BECAUSE MY CONSCIENCE TELLS ME IT'S WRONG.
IF I HAD NO CONSCIENCE I'D PROBABLY EAT THE BABIES AND THEN GET HUNGRY AGAIN, WHICH WOULD MEAN THAT I'D SACRIFICED THE POOR BABIES FOR NOTHING.
NO-- HUNGRY I WAS BORN, AND HUNGRY I SHALL DIE. BUT I'LL NOT HAVE ANY CRUEL DEEDS ON MY CONSCIENCE.
I THINK YOU'RE A VERY GOOD TIGER.
YOU'RE MISTAKEN. IN REFUSING TO EAT HARMLESS CREATURES I'M ACTING AS NO GOOD TIGER HAS EVER BEFORE ACTED.
THAT'S WHY I LEFT THE FOREST AND JOINED MY FRIEND THE COWARDLY LION.
HE'S NOT REALLY COWARDLY. I'VE SEEN HIM ACT AS BRAVELY AS CAN BE.
ALL A MISTAKE, MY DEAR. I MAY HAVE SEEMED BRAVE AT TIMES, BUT I'VE NEVER BEEN IN ANY DANGER THAT I WAS NOT AFRAID.

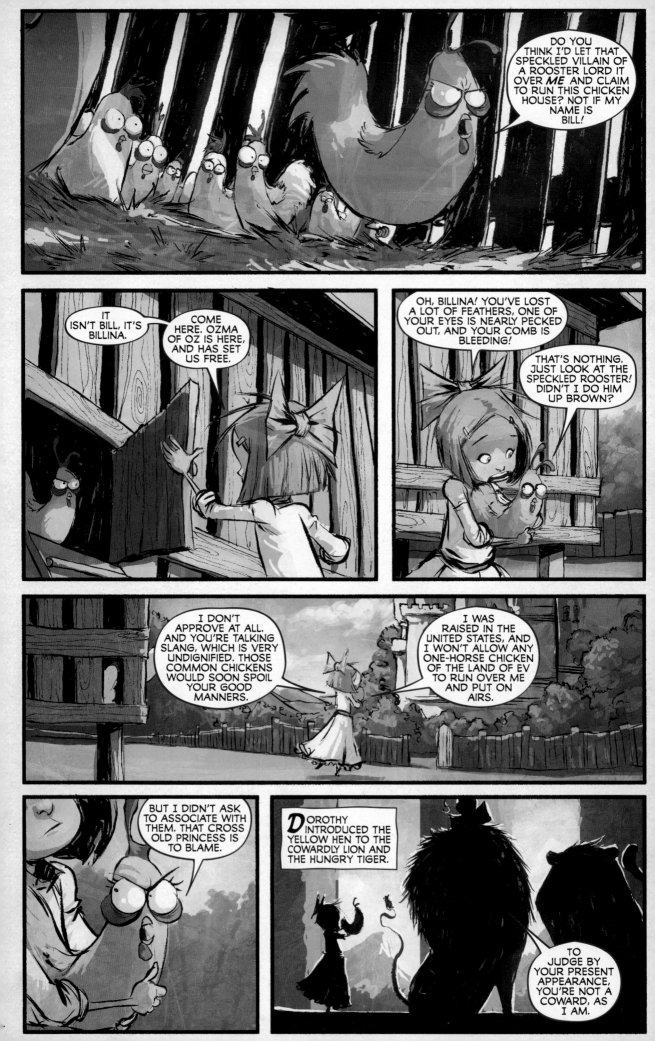

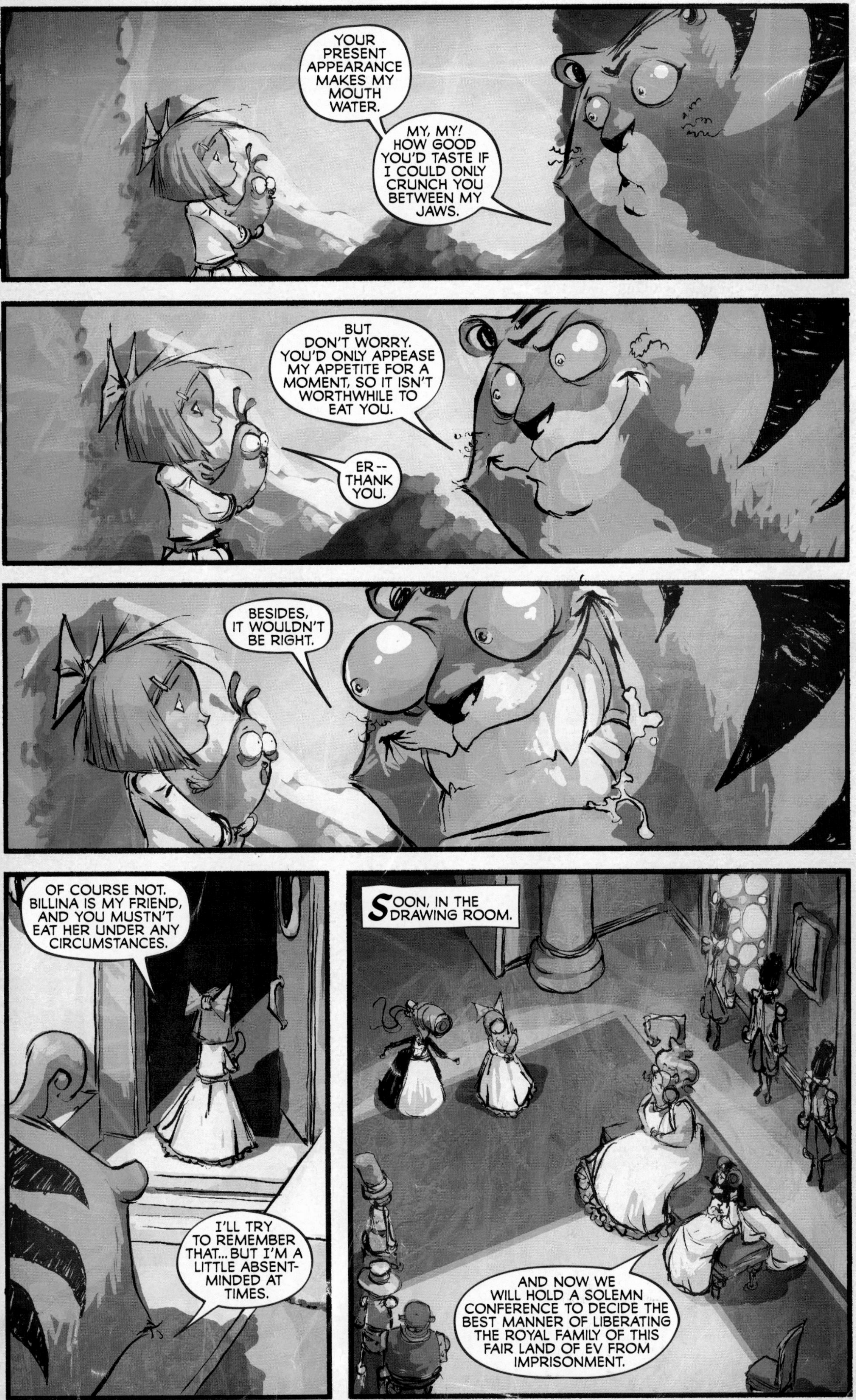
YOUR PRESENT APPEARANCE MAKES MY MOUTH WATER.
MY, MY! HOW GOOD YOU'D TASTE IF I COULD ONLY CRUNCH YOU BETWEEN MY JAWS.
BUT DON'T WORRY. YOU'D ONLY APPEASE MY APPETITE FOR A MOMENT, SO IT ISN'T WORTHWHILE TO EAT YOU.
ER-- THANK YOU.
BESIDES, IT WOULDN'T BE RIGHT.
OF COURSE NOT. BILLINA IS MY FRIEND, AND YOU MUSTN'T EAT HER UNDER ANY CIRCUMSTANCES.
I'LL TRY TO REMEMBER THAT... BUT I'M A LITTLE ABSENT-MINDED AT TIMES.
SOON, IN THE DRAWING ROOM.
AND NOW WE WILL HOLD A SOLEMN CONFERENCE TO DECIDE THE BEST MANNER OF LIBERATING THE ROYAL FAMILY OF THIS FAIR LAND OF EV FROM IMPRISONMENT.

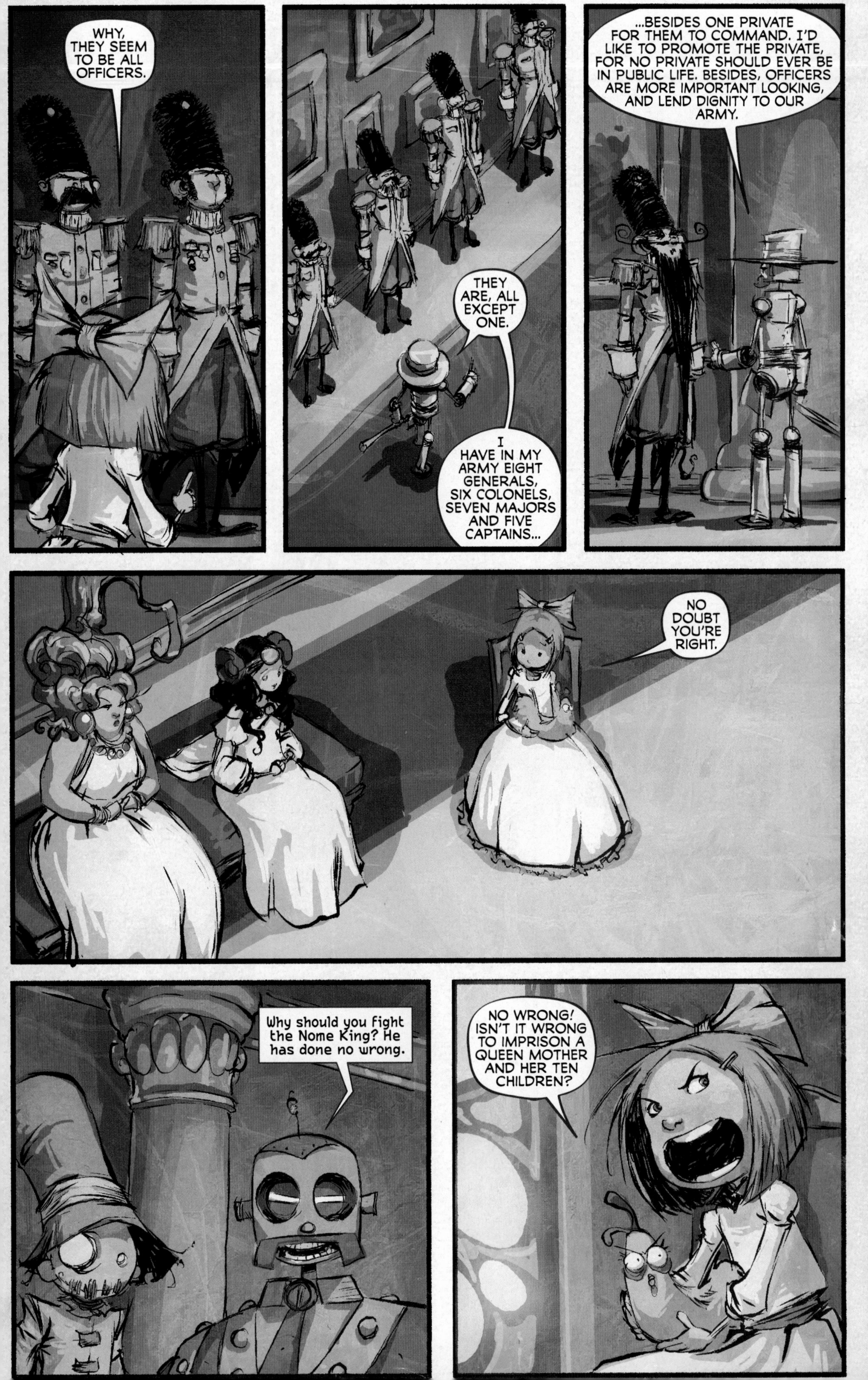
WHY, THEY SEEM TO BE ALL OFFICERS.
THEY ARE, ALL EXCEPT ONE.
I HAVE IN MY ARMY EIGHT GENERALS, SIX COLONELS, SEVEN MAJORS AND FIVE CAPTAINS...
...BESIDES ONE PRIVATE FOR THEM TO COMMAND. I'D LIKE TO PROMOTE THE PRIVATE, FOR NO PRIVATE SHOULD EVER BE IN PUBLIC LIFE. BESIDES, OFFICERS ARE MORE IMPORTANT LOOKING, AND LEND DIGNITY TO OUR ARMY.
NO DOUBT YOU'RE RIGHT.
Why should you fight the Nome King? He has done no wrong.
NO WRONG! ISN'T IT WRONG TO IMPRISON A QUEEN MOTHER AND HER TEN CHILDREN?

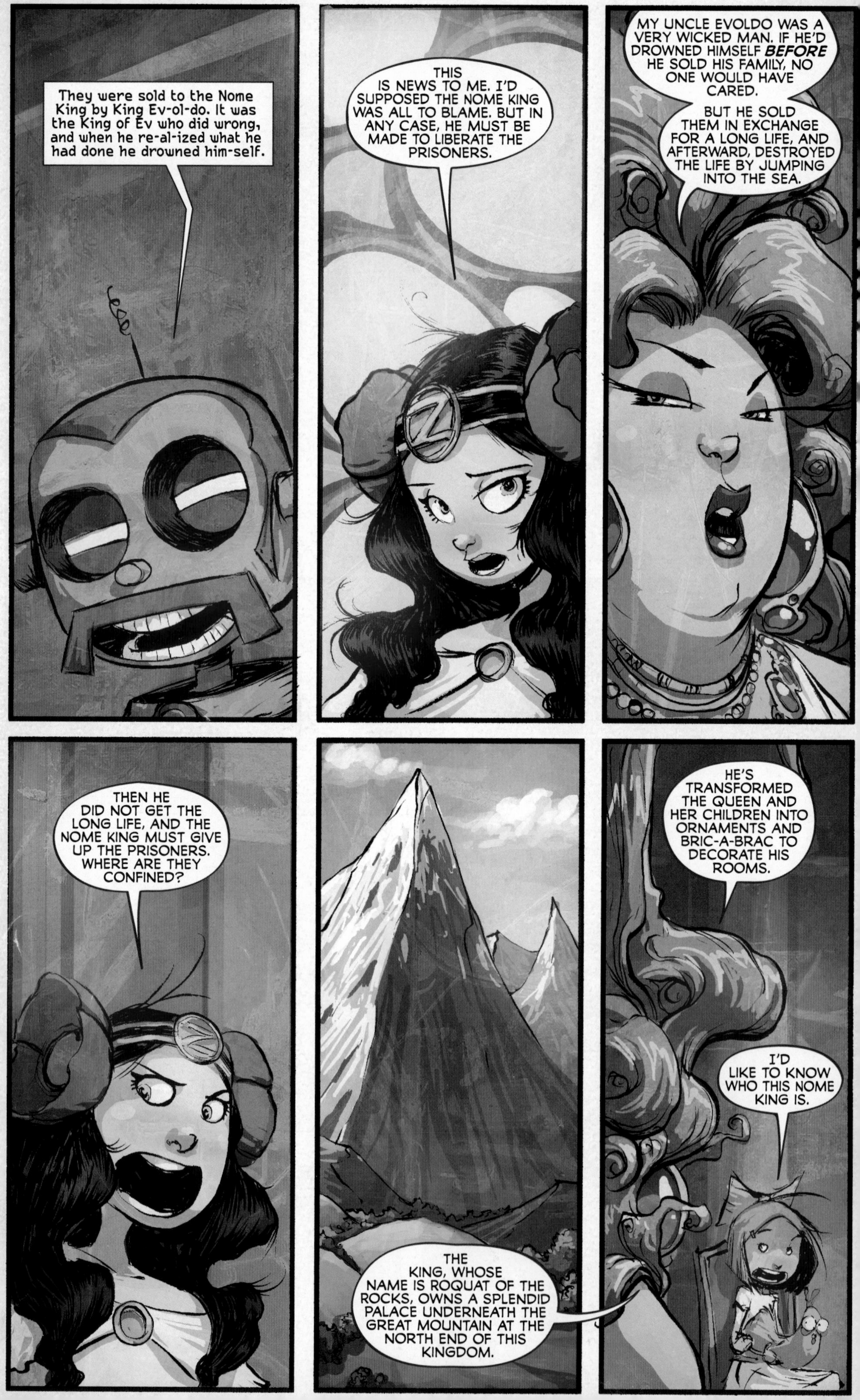
They were sold to the Nome King by King Ev-ol-do. It was the King of Ev who did wrong, and when he re-al-ized what he had done he drowned him-self.
THIS IS NEWS TO ME. I'D SUPPOSED THE NOME KING WAS ALL TO BLAME. BUT IN ANY CASE, HE MUST BE MADE TO LIBERATE THE PRISONERS.
MY UNCLE EVOLDO WAS A VERY WICKED MAN. IF HE'D DROWNED HIMSELF BEFORE HE SOLD HIS FAMILY, NO ONE WOULD HAVE CARED.
BUT HE SOLD THEM IN EXCHANGE FOR A LONG LIFE, AND AFTERWARD, DESTROYED THE LIFE BY JUMPING INTO THE SEA.
THEN HE DID NOT GET THE LONG LIFE, AND THE NOME KING MUST GIVE UP THE PRISONERS. WHERE ARE THEY CONFINED?
THE KING, WHOSE NAME IS ROQUAT OF THE ROCKS, OWNS A SPLENDID PALACE UNDERNEATH THE GREAT MOUNTAIN AT THE NORTH END OF THIS KINGDOM.
HE'S TRANSFORMED THE QUEEN AND HER CHILDREN INTO ORNAMENTS AND BRIC-A-BRAC TO DECORATE HIS ROOMS.
I'D LIKE TO KNOW WHO THIS NOME KING IS.

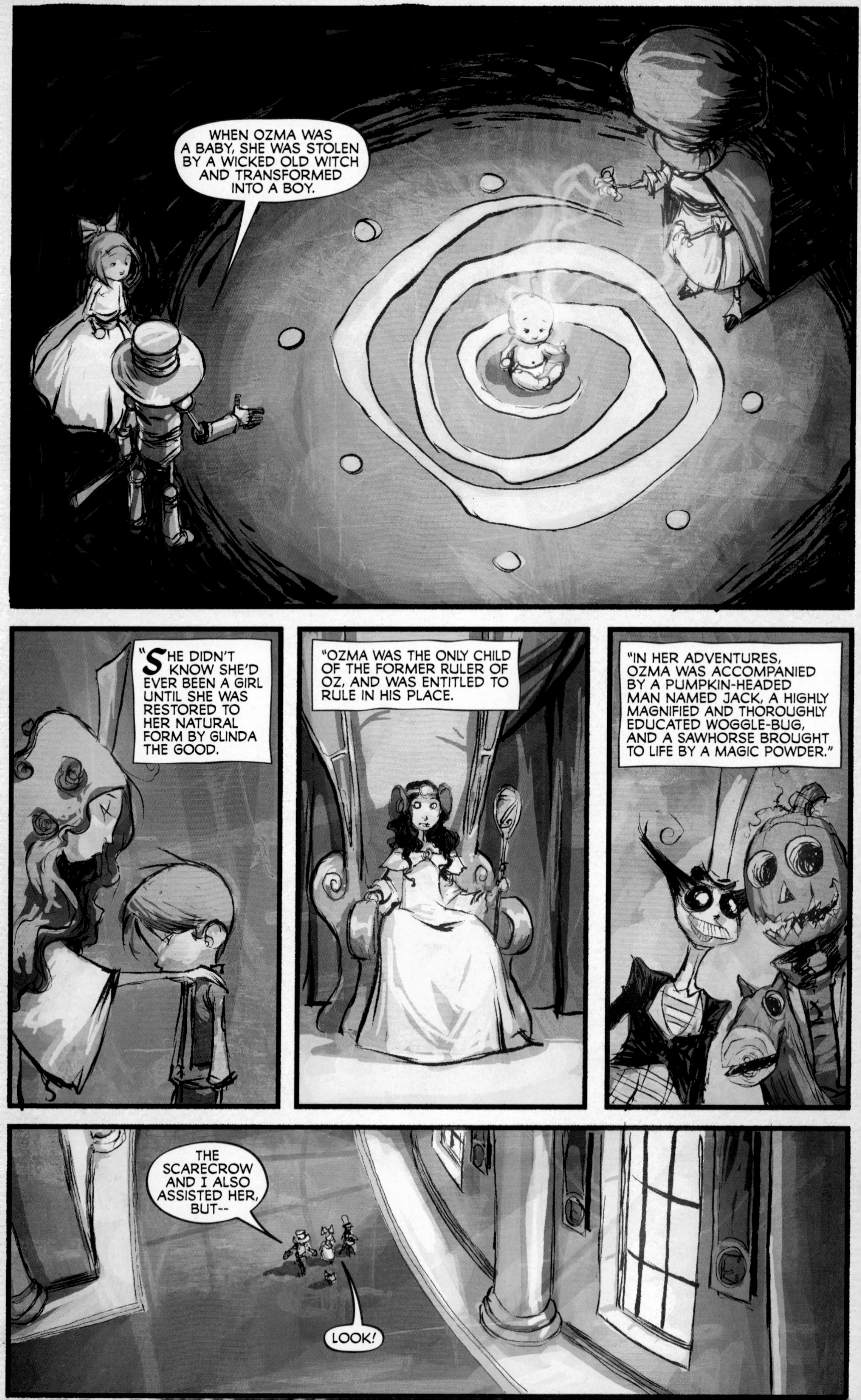
WHEN OZMA WAS A BABY, SHE WAS STOLEN BY A WICKED OLD WITCH AND TRANSFORMED INTO A BOY.
"SHE DIDN'T KNOW SHE'D EVER BEEN A GIRL UNTIL SHE WAS RESTORED TO HER NATURAL FORM BY GLINDA THE GOOD.
"OZMA WAS THE ONLY CHILD OF THE FORMER RULER OF OZ, AND WAS ENTITLED TO RULE IN HIS PLACE.
"IN HER ADVENTURES, OZMA WAS ACCOMPANIED BY A PUMPKIN-HEADED MAN NAMED JACK, A HIGHLY MAGNIFIED AND THOROUGHLY EDUCATED WOGGLE-BUG, AND A SAWHORSE BROUGHT TO LIFE BY A MAGIC POWDER."
THE SCARECROW AND I ALSO ASSISTED HER, BUT--
LOOK!

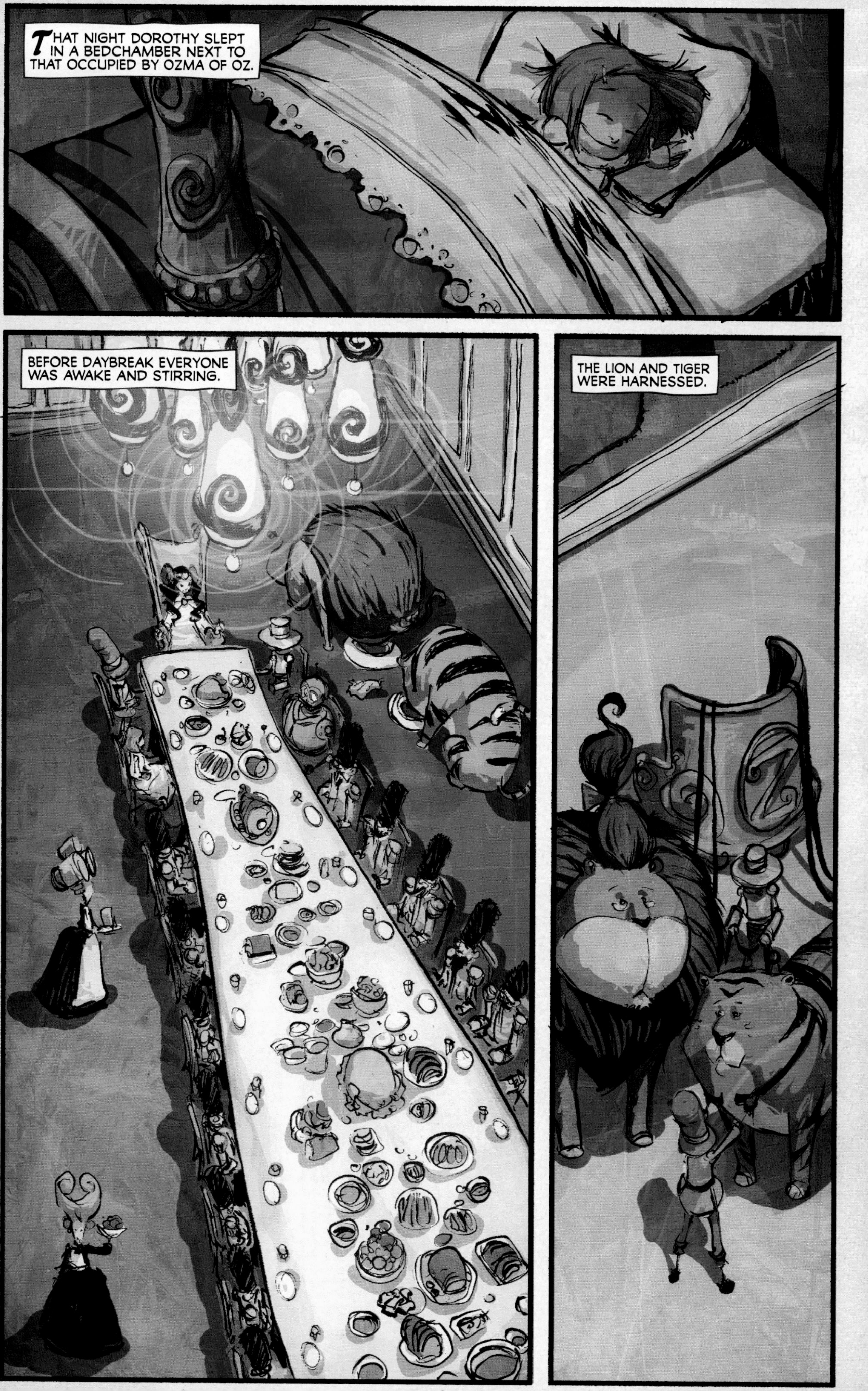
THAT NIGHT DOROTHY SLEPT IN A BEDCHAMBER NEXT TO THAT OCCUPIED BY OZMA OF OZ.
BEFORE DAYBREAK EVERYONE WAS AWAKE AND STIRRING.
THE LION AND TIGER WERE HARNESSED.

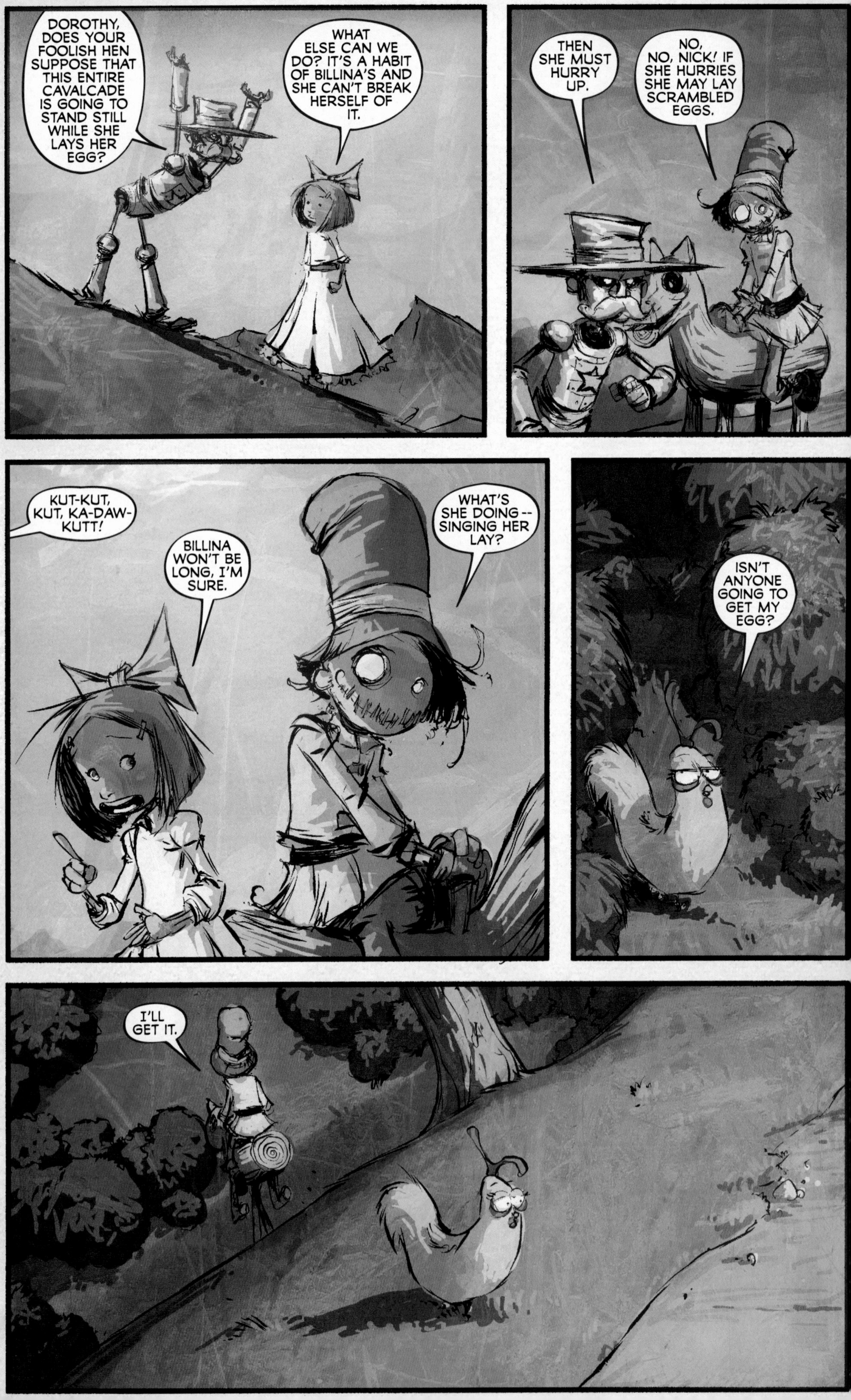
DOROTHY, DOES YOUR FOOLISH HEN SUPPOSE THAT THIS ENTIRE CAVALCADE IS GOING TO STAND STILL WHILE SHE LAYS HER EGG?
WHAT ELSE CAN WE DO? IT'S A HABIT OF BILLINA'S AND SHE CAN'T BREAK HERSELF OF IT.
THEN SHE MUST HURRY UP.
NO, NO, NICK! IF SHE HURRIES SHE MAY LAY SCRAMBLED EGGS.
KUT-KUT, KUT, KA-DAW-KUTT!
BILLINA WON'T BE LONG, I'M SURE.
WHAT'S SHE DOING -- SINGING HER LAY?
ISN'T ANYONE GOING TO GET MY EGG?
I'LL GET IT.

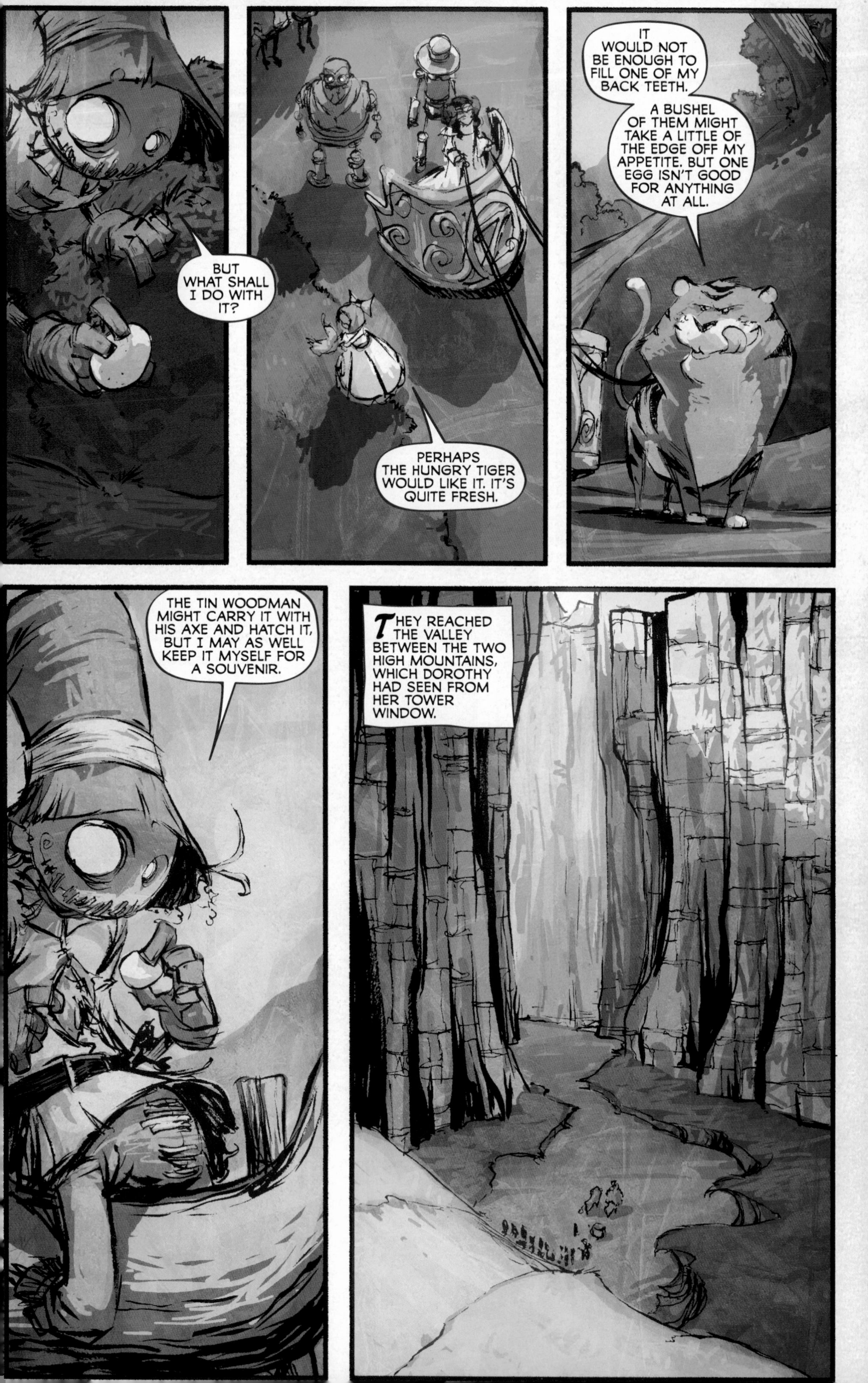
BUT WHAT SHALL I DO WITH IT?
PERHAPS THE HUNGRY TIGER WOULD LIKE IT. IT'S QUITE FRESH.
IT WOULD NOT BE ENOUGH TO FILL ONE OF MY BACK TEETH.
A BUSHEL OF THEM MIGHT TAKE A LITTLE OF THE EDGE OFF MY APPETITE. BUT ONE EGG ISN'T GOOD FOR ANYTHING AT ALL.
THE TIN WOODMAN MIGHT CARRY IT WITH HIS AXE AND HATCH IT, BUT I MAY AS WELL KEEP IT MYSELF FOR A SOUVENIR.
THEY REACHED THE VALLEY BETWEEN THE TWO HIGH MOUNTAINS, WHICH DOROTHY HAD SEEN FROM HER TOWER WINDOW.

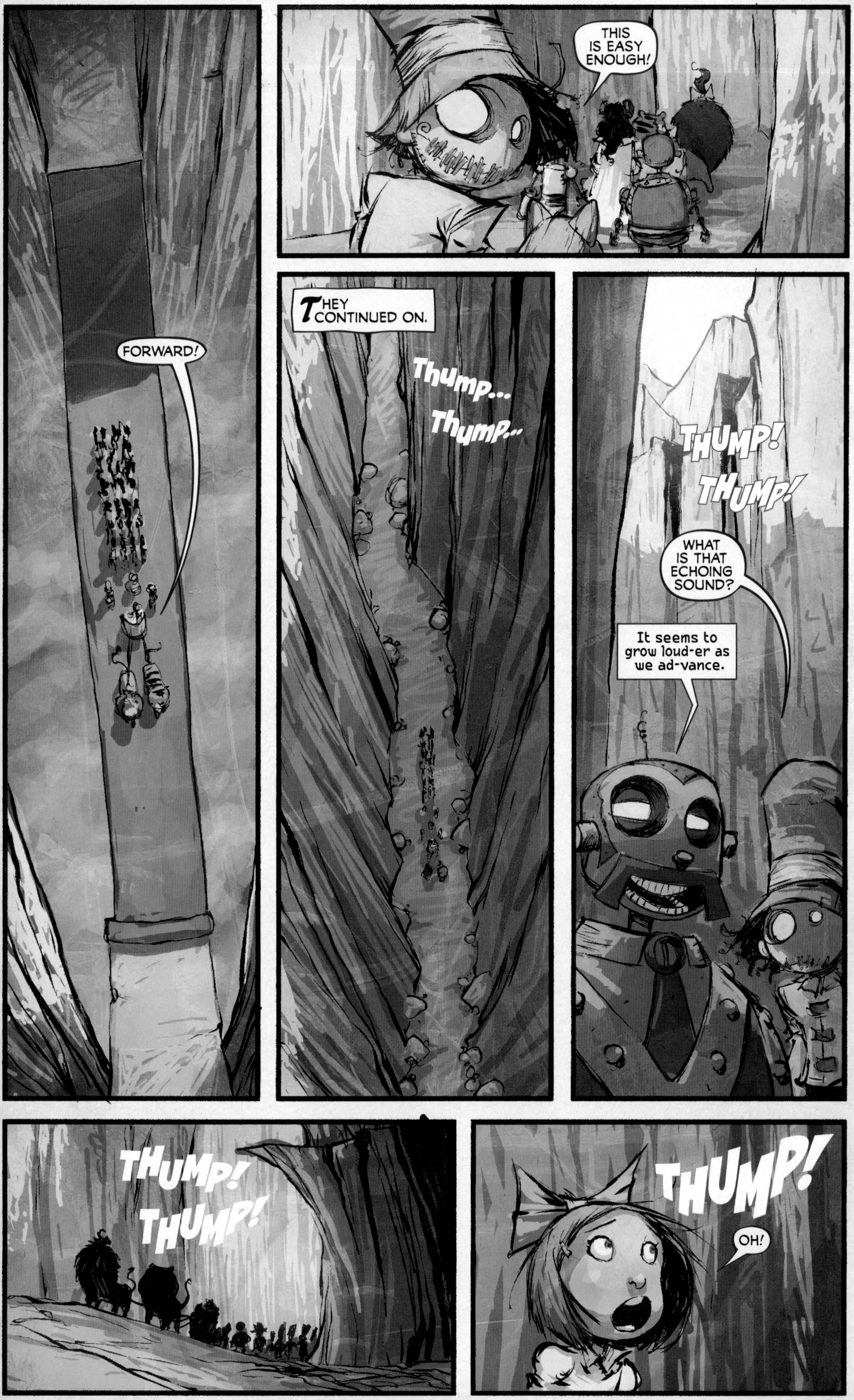
FORWARD!
THIS IS EASY ENOUGH!
THEY CONTINUED ON.
Thump...
Thump...
THUMP!
THUMP!
WHAT IS THAT ECHOING SOUND?
It seems to grow loud-er as we ad-vance.
THUMP!
THUMP!
THUMP!
OH!

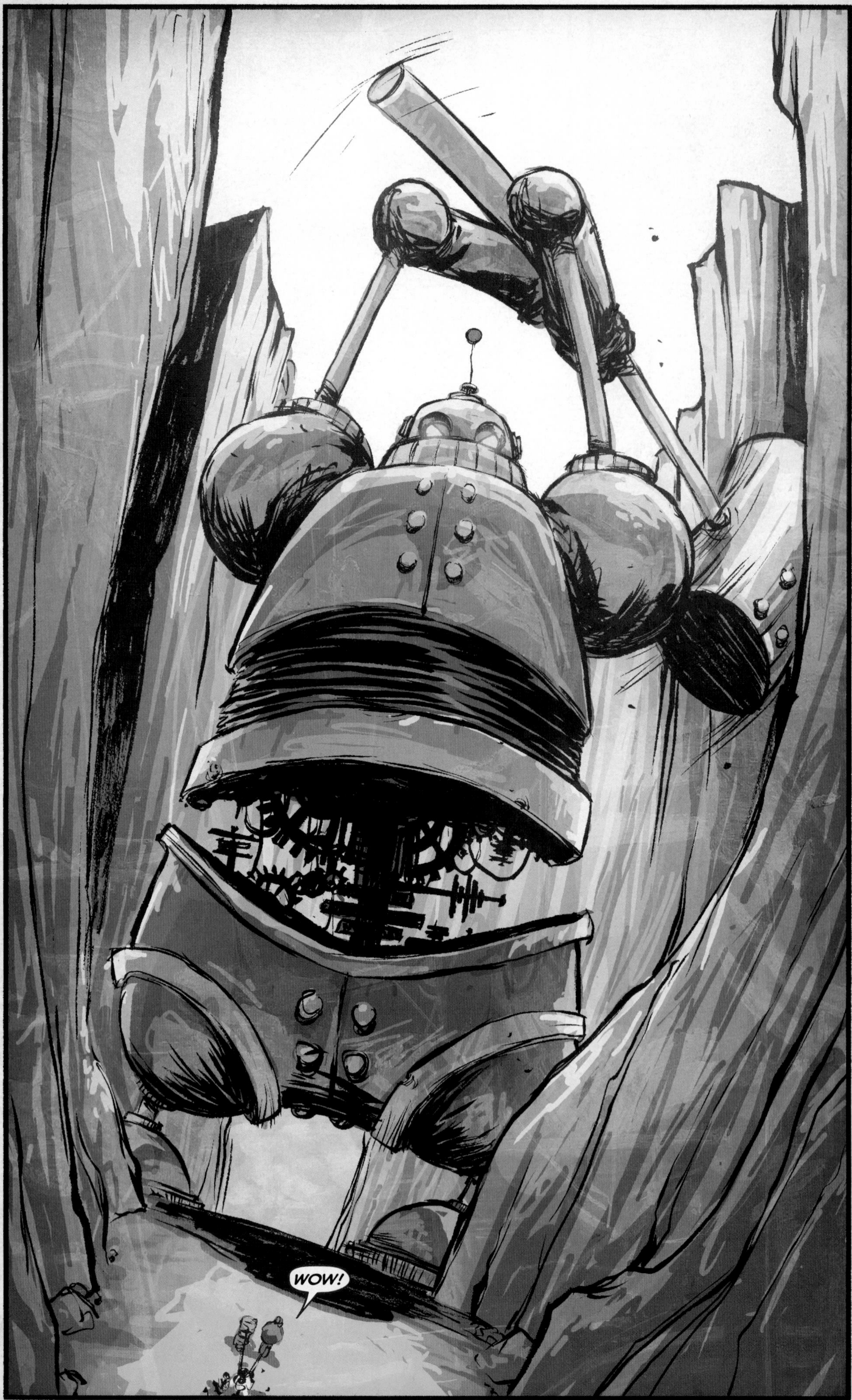
WOW!

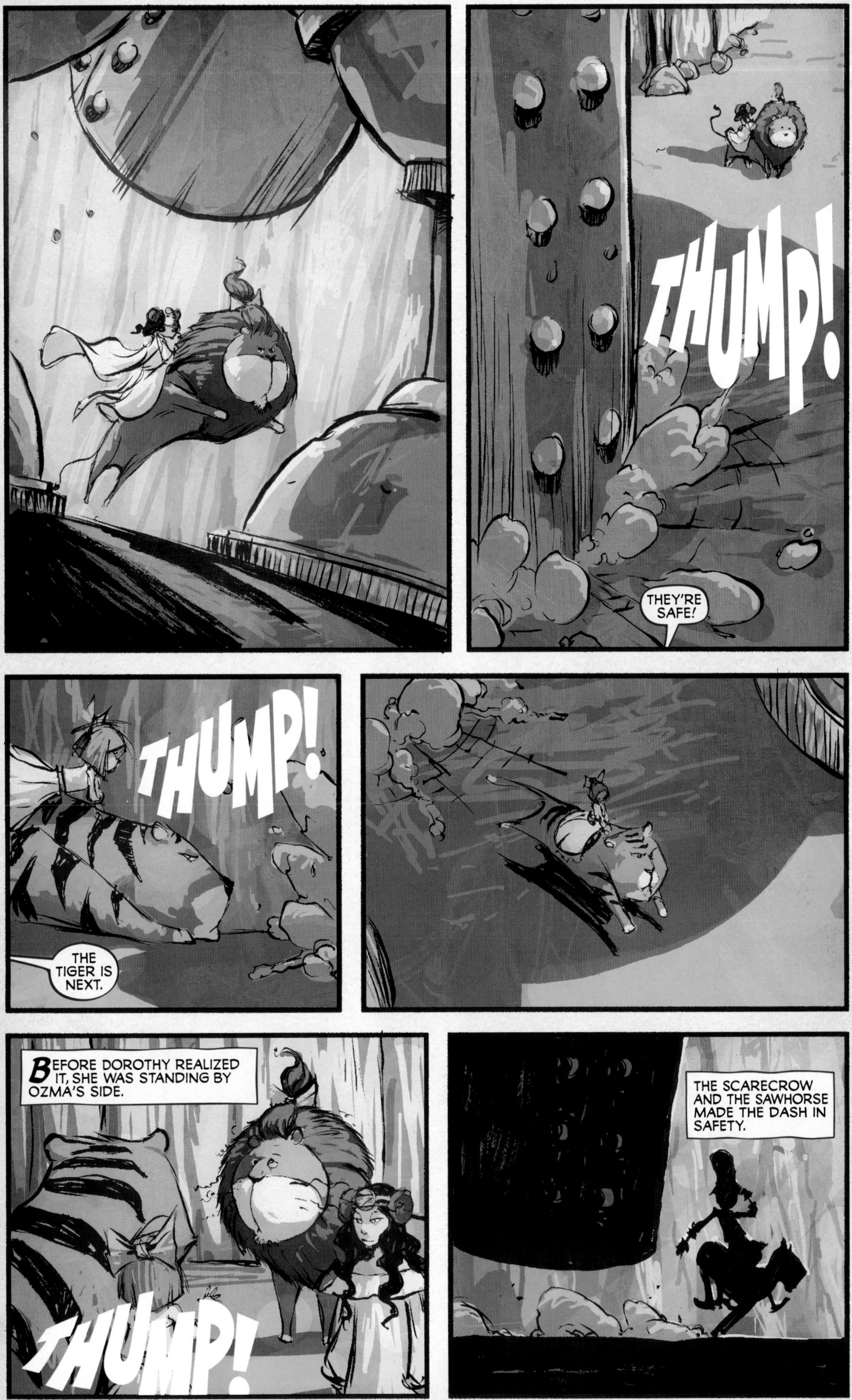
THUMP!
THEY'RE SAFE!
THUMP!
THE TIGER IS NEXT.
BEFORE DOROTHY REALIZED IT, SHE WAS STANDING BY OZMA'S SIDE.
THUMP!
THE SCARECROW AND THE SAWHORSE MADE THE DASH IN SAFETY.

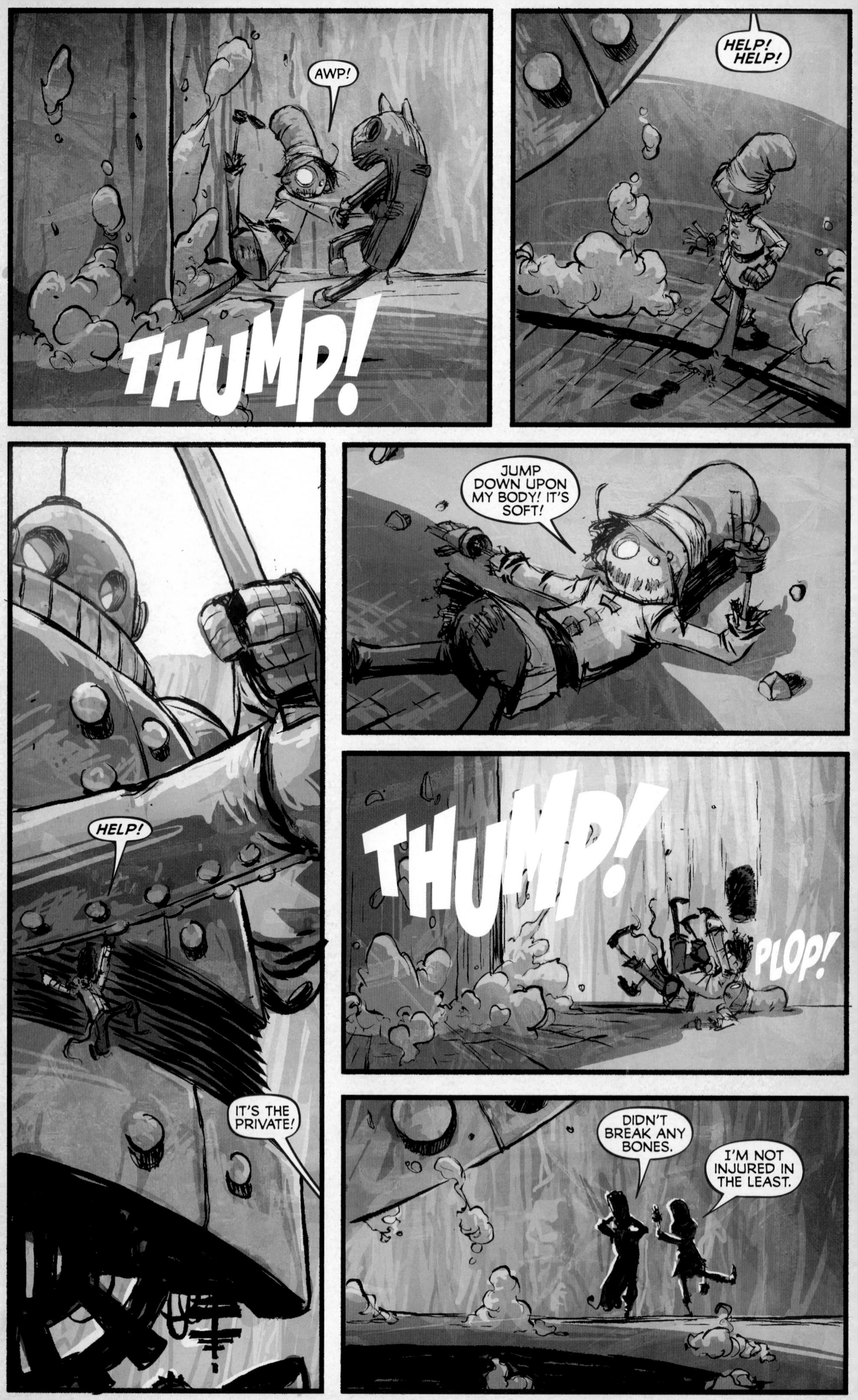
AWP!
THUMP!
HELP! HELP!
HELP!
IT'S THE PRIVATE!
JUMP DOWN UPON MY BODY! IT'S SOFT!
THUMP!
PLOP!
DIDN'T BREAK ANY BONES.
I'M NOT INJURED IN THE LEAST.

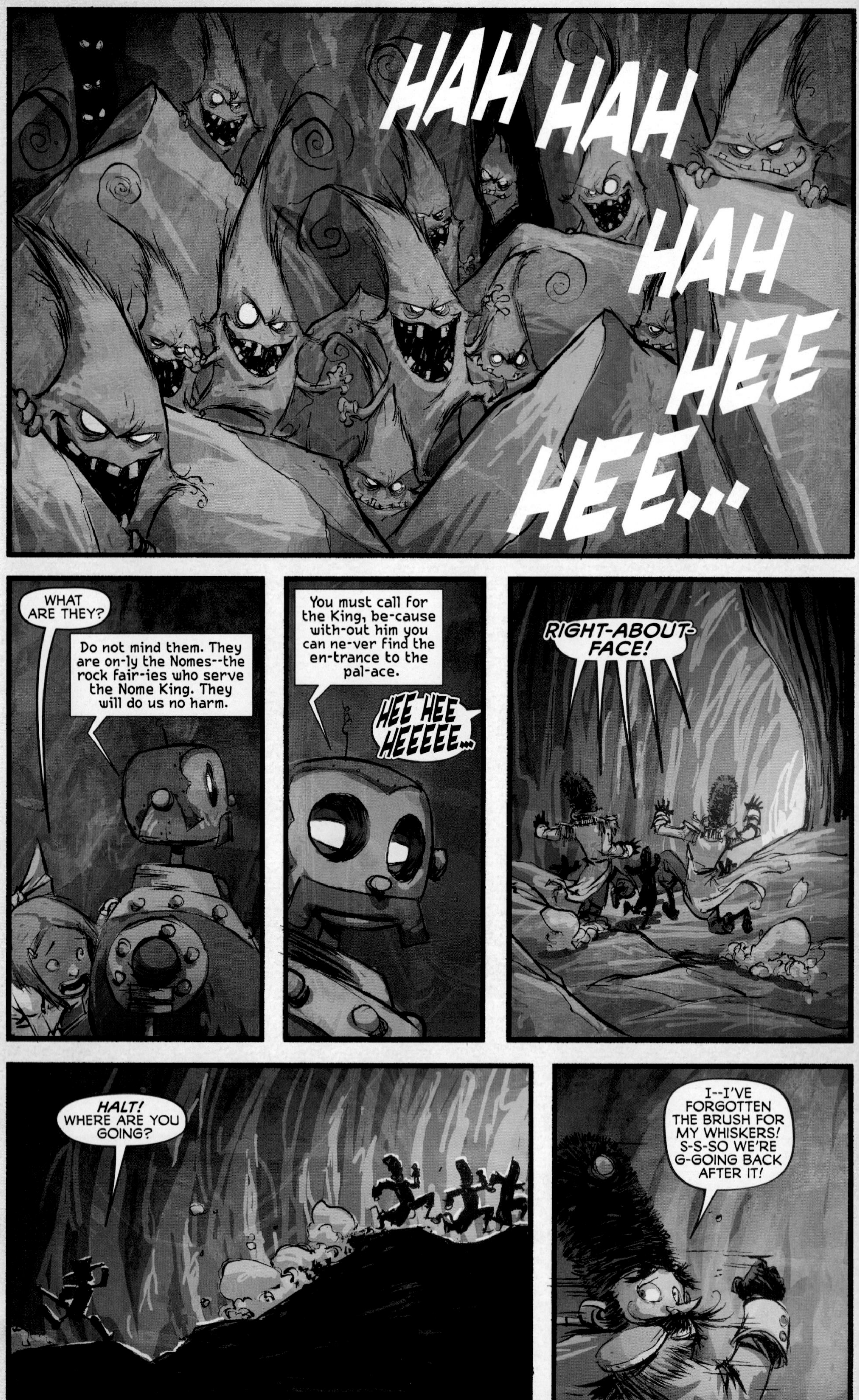
HAH HAH HAH HEE HEE...
WHAT ARE THEY?
Do not mind them. They are on-ly the Nomes--the rock fair-ies who serve the Nome King. They will do us no harm.
You must call for the King, be-cause with-out him you can ne-ver find the en-trance to the pal-ace.
HEE HEE HEEEEE...
RIGHT-ABOUT-FACE!
HALT! WHERE ARE YOU GOING?
I--I'VE FORGOTTEN THE BRUSH FOR MY WHISKERS! S-S-SO WE'RE G-GOING BACK AFTER IT!

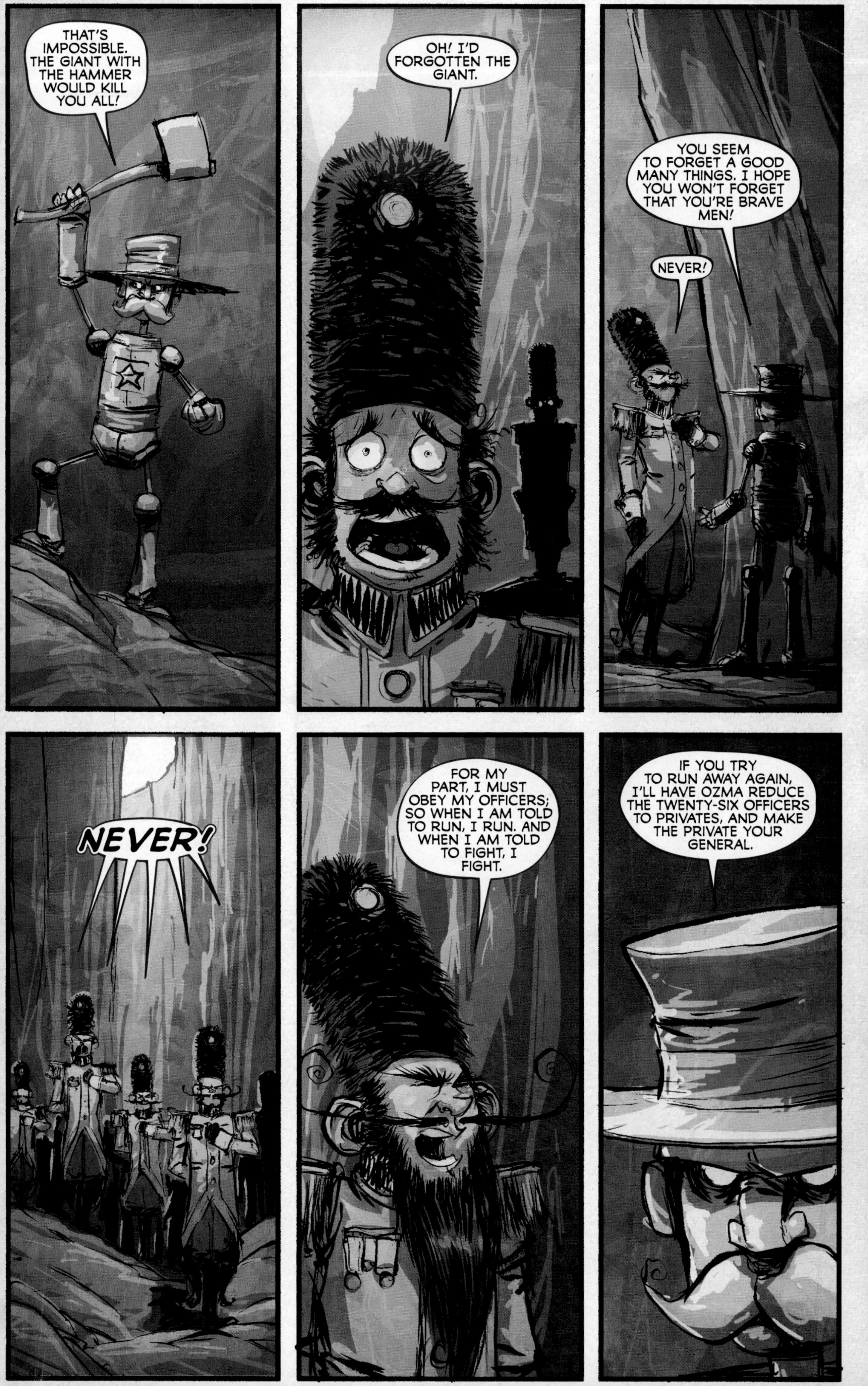
THAT'S IMPOSSIBLE. THE GIANT WITH THE HAMMER WOULD KILL YOU ALL!
OH! I'D FORGOTTEN THE GIANT.
YOU SEEM TO FORGET A GOOD MANY THINGS. I HOPE YOU WON'T FORGET THAT YOU'RE BRAVE MEN!
NEVER!
NEVER!
FOR MY PART, I MUST OBEY MY OFFICERS; SO WHEN I AM TOLD TO RUN, I RUN. AND WHEN I AM TOLD TO FIGHT, I FIGHT.
IF YOU TRY TO RUN AWAY AGAIN, I'LL HAVE OZMA REDUCE THE TWENTY-SIX OFFICERS TO PRIVATES, AND MAKE THE PRIVATE YOUR GENERAL.

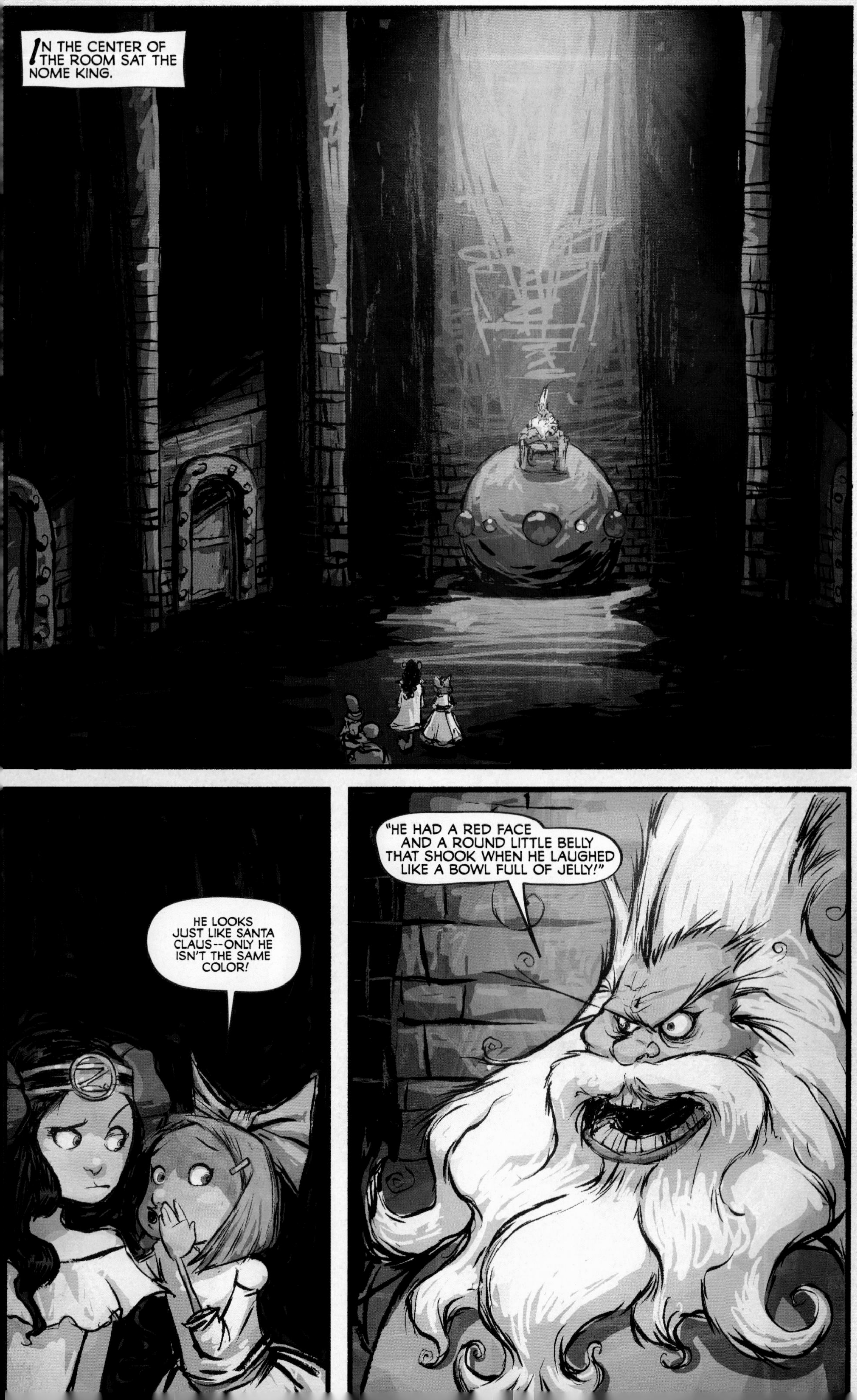
IN THE CENTER OF THE ROOM SAT THE NOME KING.
HE LOOKS JUST LIKE SANTA CLAUS--ONLY HE ISN'T THE SAME COLOR!
"HE HAD A RED FACE AND A ROUND LITTLE BELLY THAT SHOOK WHEN HE LAUGHED LIKE A BOWL FULL OF JELLY!"

COME WITH ME FOR A MOMENT, MY DEAR OZMA.

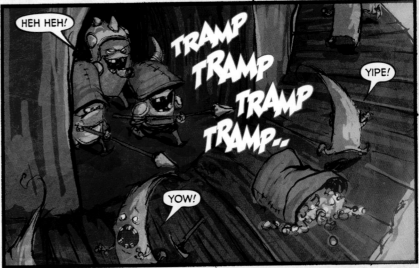

HEH HEH!

TRAMP TRAMP TRAMP TRAMP--

YIPE!

YOW!

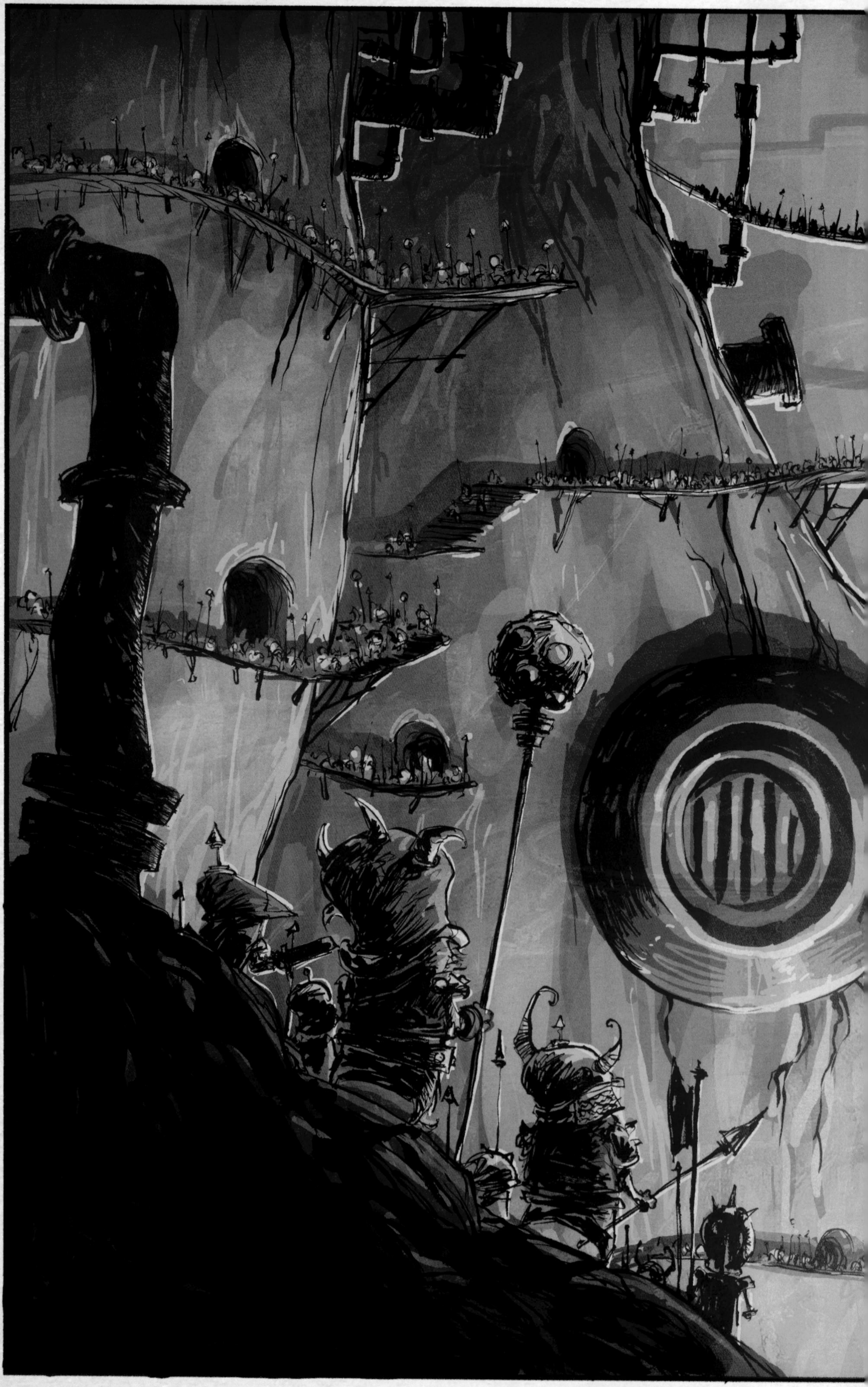

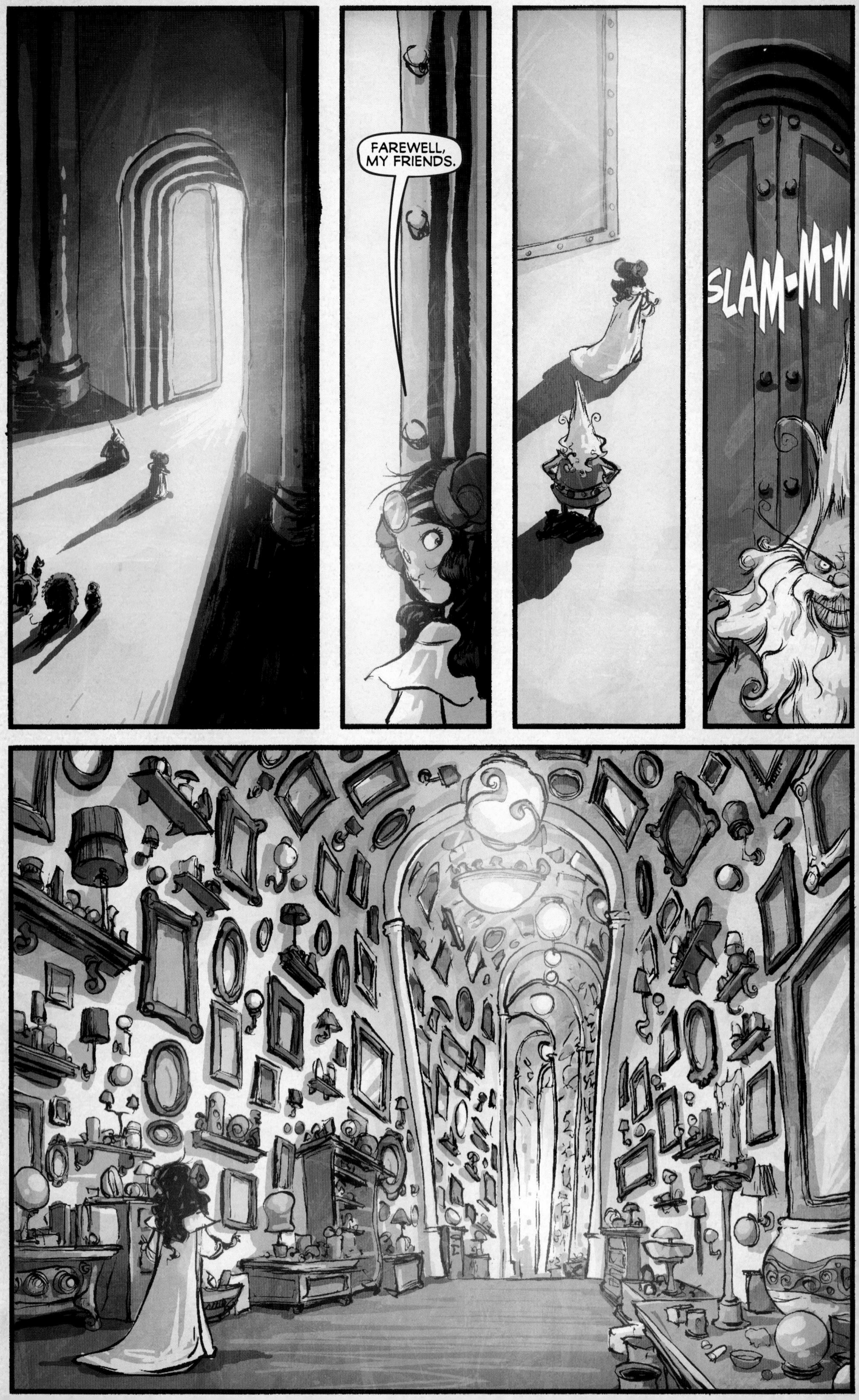
FAREWELL, MY FRIENDS.
SLAM-M-M

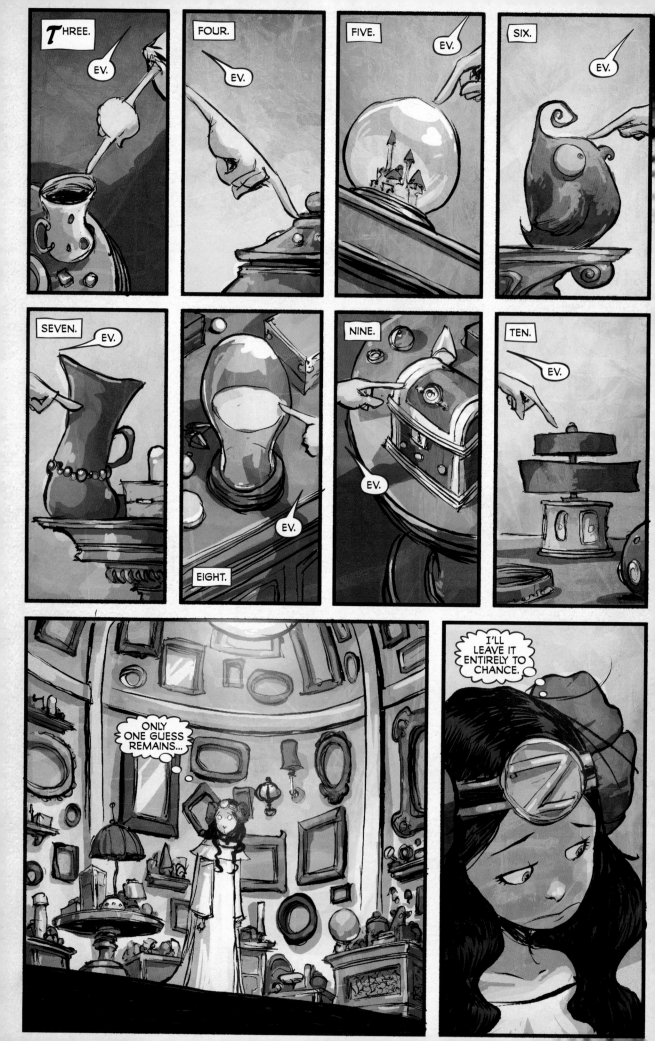

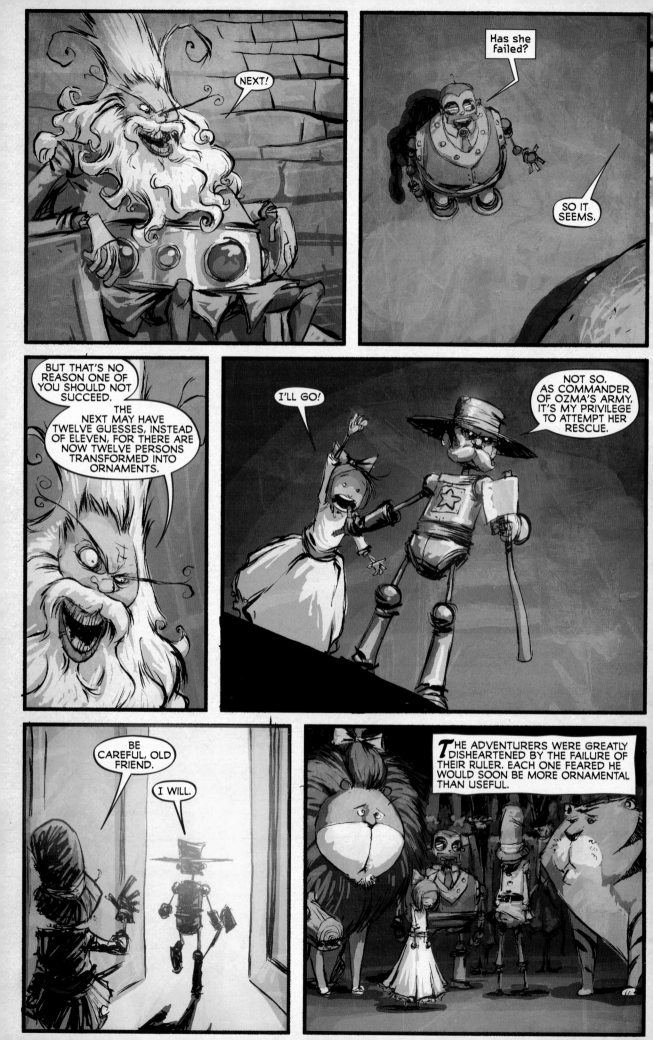

NEXT!

Has she failed?

SO IT SEEMS.

BUT THAT'S NO REASON ONE OF YOU SHOULD NOT SUCCEED.

THE NEXT MAY HAVE TWELVE GUESSES, INSTEAD OF ELEVEN, FOR THERE ARE NOW TWELVE PERSONS TRANSFORMED INTO ORNAMENTS.

I'LL GO!

NOT SO. AS COMMANDER OF OZMA'S ARMY, IT'S MY PRIVILEGE TO ATTEMPT HER RESCUE.

BE CAREFUL, OLD FRIEND.

I WILL.

*T*HE ADVENTURERS WERE GREATLY DISHEARTENED BY THE FAILURE OF THEIR RULER. EACH ONE FEARED HE WOULD SOON BE MORE ORNAMENTAL THAN USEFUL.

YOU'VE NO BUSINESS TO SIT UP SO LATE. YOU'LL BE CROSS AS A GRIFFIN TOMORROW.

AS SOON AS THAT STUPID PRIVATE IS TRANSFORMED, KALIKO, WE'LL ALL GO TO BED AND LEAVE THE JOB TO BE FINISHED IN THE MORNING.

IS IT SO VERY LATE?

WHY, IT'S AFTER MIDNIGHT--THAT STRIKES ME AS BEING LATE ENOUGH.

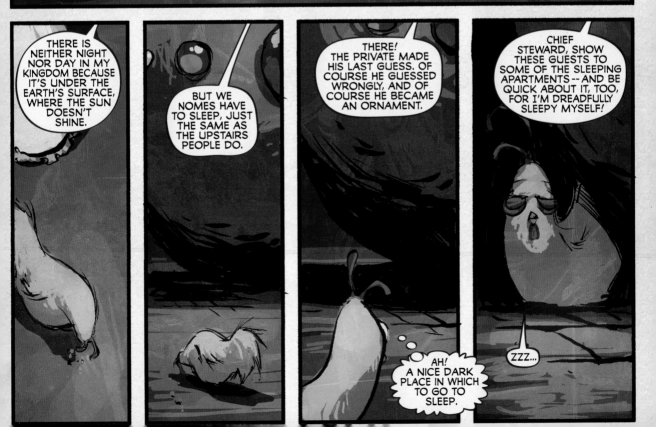

THERE IS NEITHER NIGHT NOR DAY IN MY KINGDOM BECAUSE IT'S UNDER THE EARTH'S SURFACE, WHERE THE SUN DOESN'T SHINE.

BUT WE NOMES HAVE TO SLEEP, JUST THE SAME AS THE UPSTAIRS PEOPLE DO.

THERE! THE PRIVATE MADE HIS LAST GUESS. OF COURSE HE GUESSED WRONGLY, AND OF COURSE HE BECAME AN ORNAMENT.

AH! A NICE DARK PLACE IN WHICH TO GO TO SLEEP.

CHIEF STEWARD, SHOW THESE GUESTS TO SOME OF THE SLEEPING APARTMENTS -- AND BE QUICK ABOUT IT, TOO, FOR I'M DREADFULLY SLEEPY MYSELF!

ZZZ...

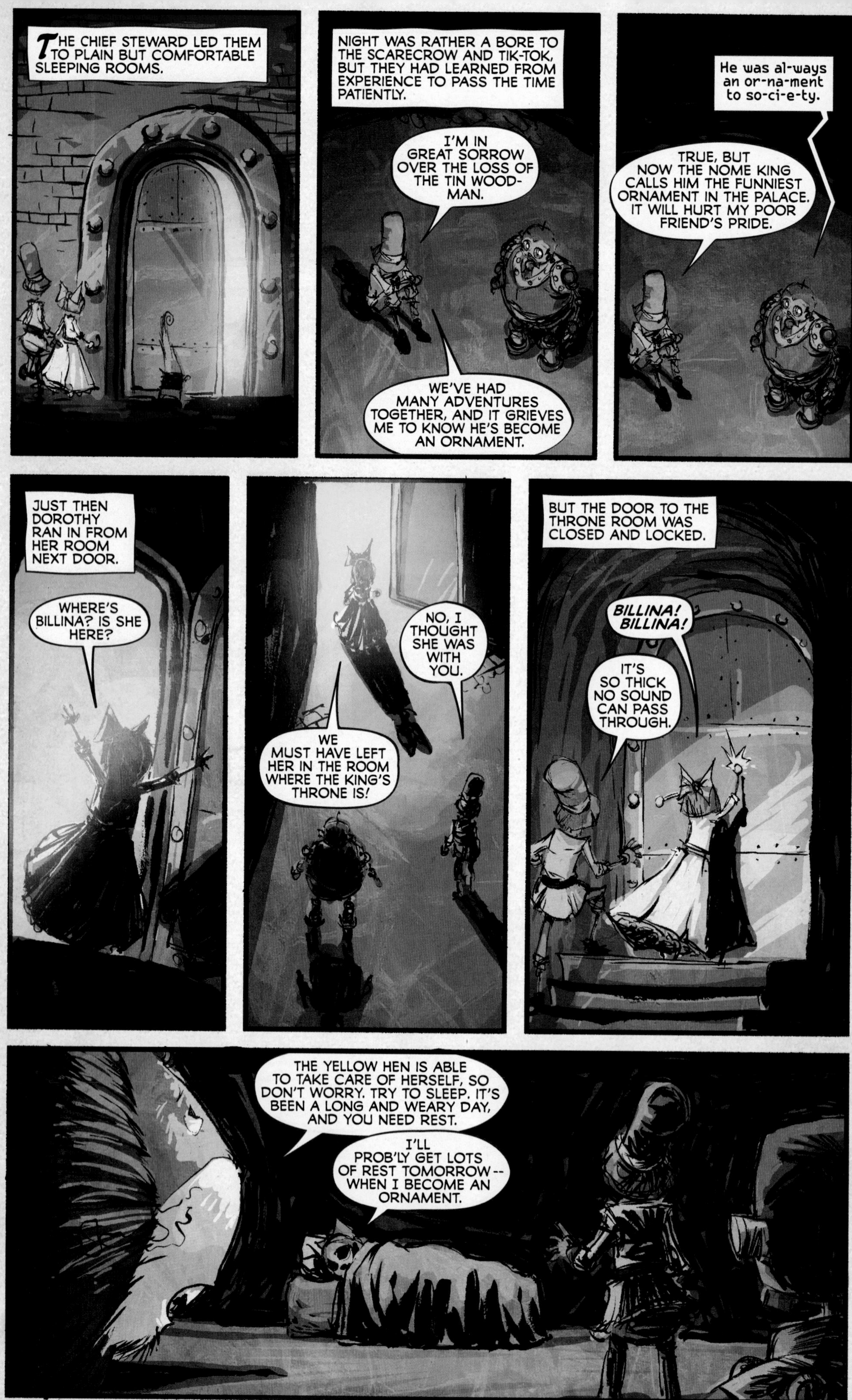
THE CHIEF STEWARD LED THEM TO PLAIN BUT COMFORTABLE SLEEPING ROOMS.
NIGHT WAS RATHER A BORE TO THE SCARECROW AND TIK-TOK, BUT THEY HAD LEARNED FROM EXPERIENCE TO PASS THE TIME PATIENTLY.
I'M IN GREAT SORROW OVER THE LOSS OF THE TIN WOOD-MAN.
WE'VE HAD MANY ADVENTURES TOGETHER, AND IT GRIEVES ME TO KNOW HE'S BECOME AN ORNAMENT.
He was al-ways an or-na-ment to so-ci-e-ty.
TRUE, BUT NOW THE NOME KING CALLS HIM THE FUNNIEST ORNAMENT IN THE PALACE. IT WILL HURT MY POOR FRIEND'S PRIDE.
JUST THEN DOROTHY RAN IN FROM HER ROOM NEXT DOOR.
WHERE'S BILLINA? IS SHE HERE?
NO, I THOUGHT SHE WAS WITH YOU.
WE MUST HAVE LEFT HER IN THE ROOM WHERE THE KING'S THRONE IS!
BUT THE DOOR TO THE THRONE ROOM WAS CLOSED AND LOCKED.
BILLINA! BILLINA!
IT'S SO THICK NO SOUND CAN PASS THROUGH.
THE YELLOW HEN IS ABLE TO TAKE CARE OF HERSELF, SO DON'T WORRY. TRY TO SLEEP. IT'S BEEN A LONG AND WEARY DAY, AND YOU NEED REST.
I'LL PROB'LY GET LOTS OF REST TOMORROW-- WHEN I BECOME AN ORNAMENT.

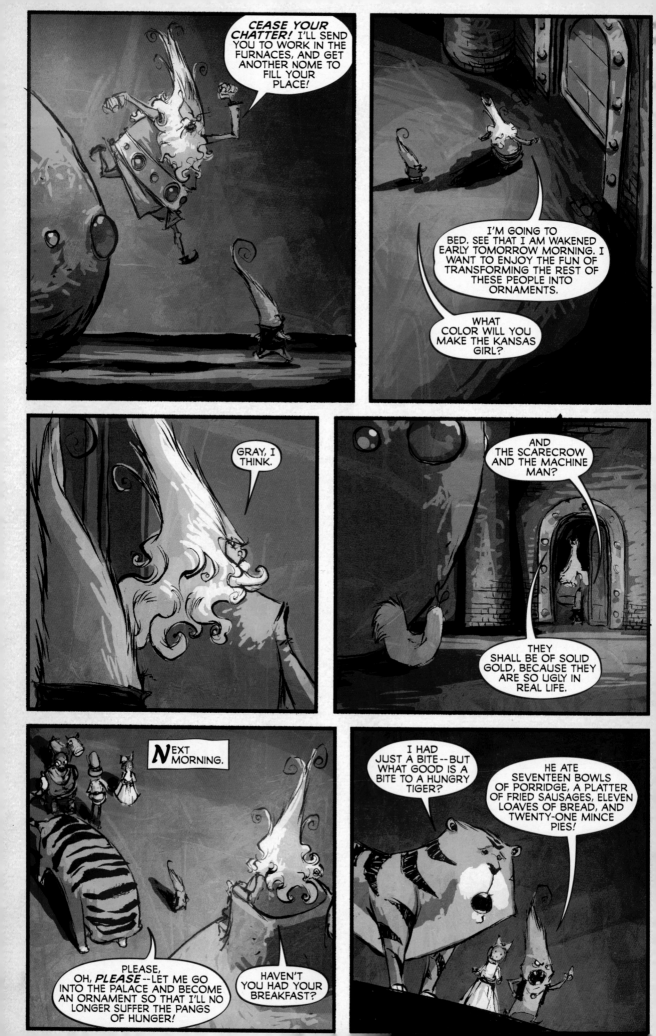

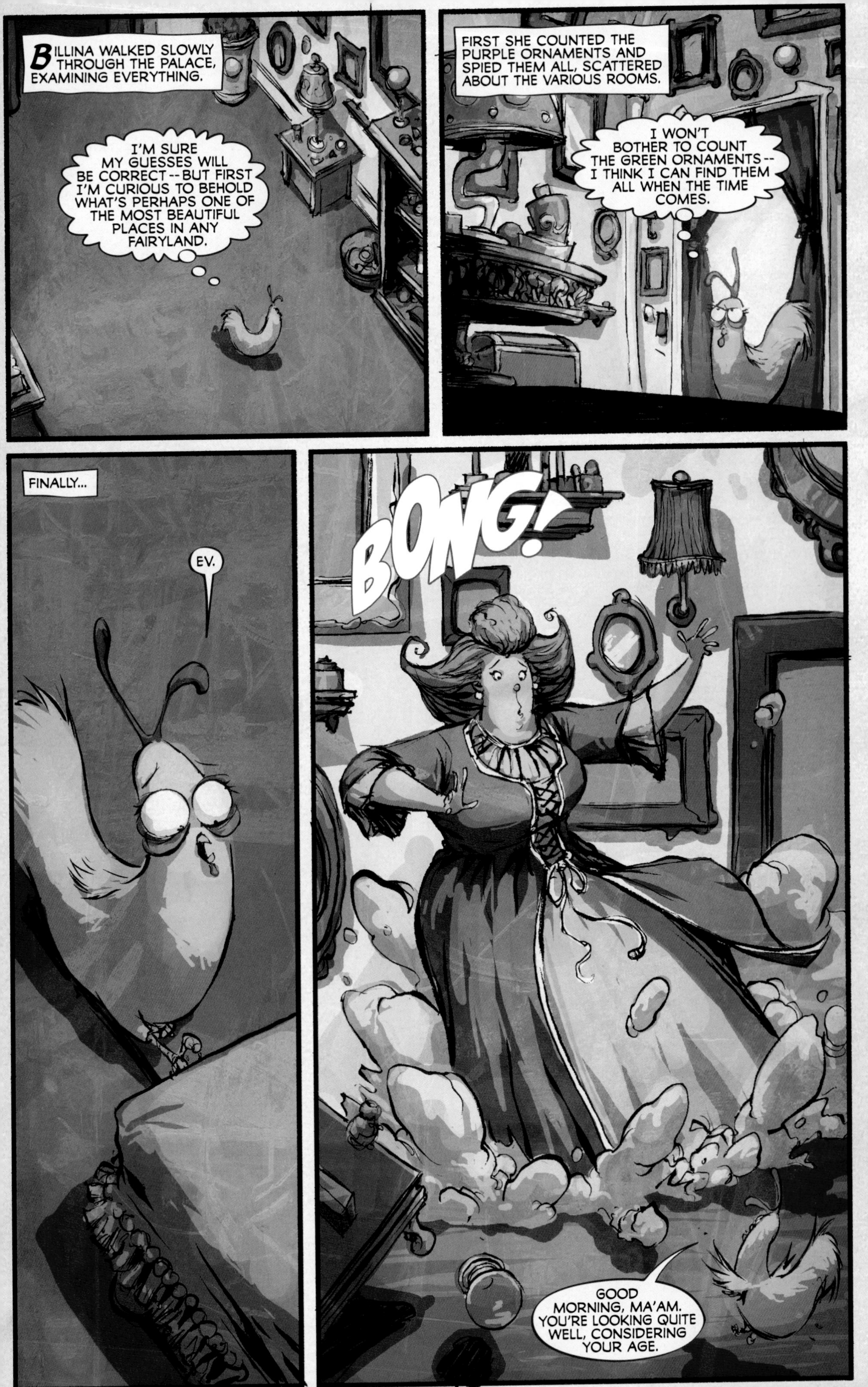
BILLINA WALKED SLOWLY THROUGH THE PALACE, EXAMINING EVERYTHING.
I'M SURE MY GUESSES WILL BE CORRECT -- BUT FIRST I'M CURIOUS TO BEHOLD WHAT'S PERHAPS ONE OF THE MOST BEAUTIFUL PLACES IN ANY FAIRYLAND.
FIRST SHE COUNTED THE PURPLE ORNAMENTS AND SPIED THEM ALL, SCATTERED ABOUT THE VARIOUS ROOMS.
I WON'T BOTHER TO COUNT THE GREEN ORNAMENTS -- I THINK I CAN FIND THEM ALL WHEN THE TIME COMES.
FINALLY...
EV.
BONG!
GOOD MORNING, MA'AM. YOU'RE LOOKING QUITE WELL, CONSIDERING YOUR AGE.

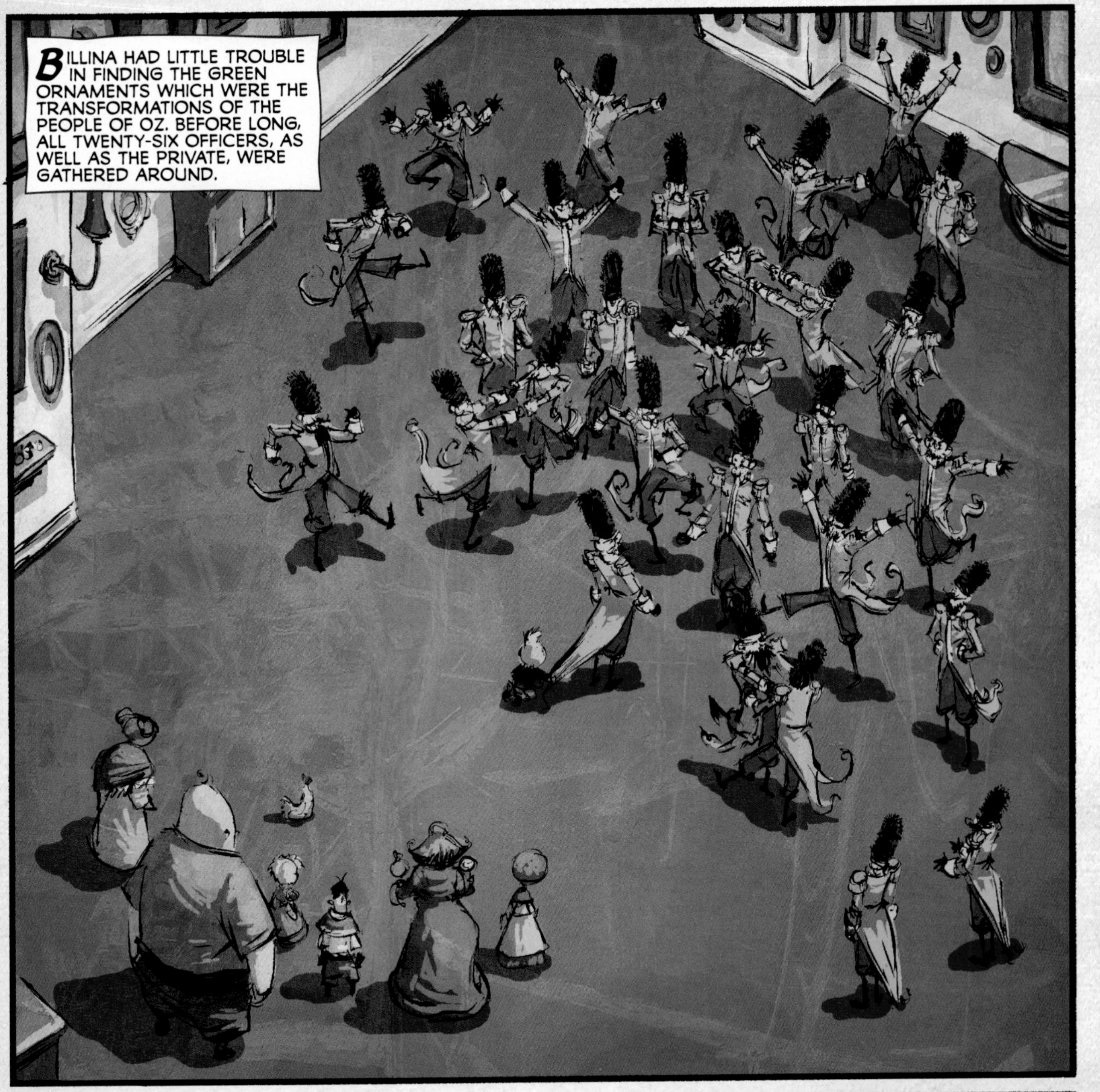
BILLINA HAD LITTLE TROUBLE IN FINDING THE GREEN ORNAMENTS WHICH WERE THE TRANSFORMATIONS OF THE PEOPLE OF OZ. BEFORE LONG, ALL TWENTY-SIX OFFICERS, AS WELL AS THE PRIVATE, WERE GATHERED AROUND.

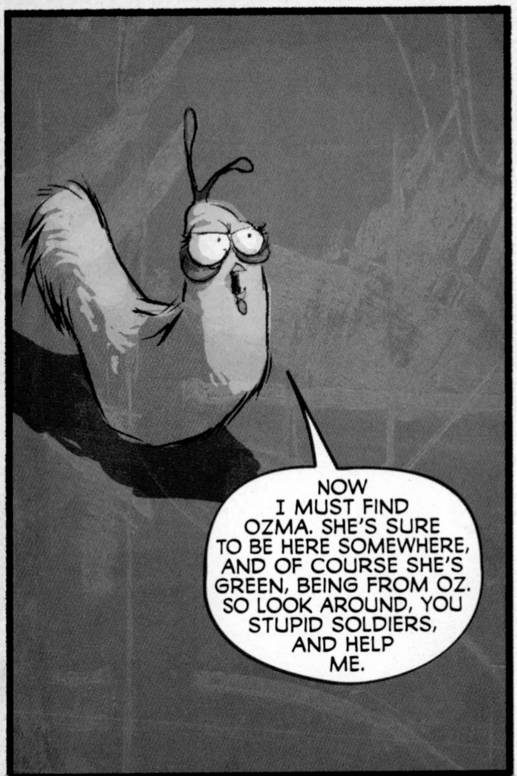
NOW I MUST FIND OZMA. SHE'S SURE TO BE HERE SOMEWHERE, AND OF COURSE SHE'S GREEN, BEING FROM OZ. SO LOOK AROUND, YOU STUPID SOLDIERS, AND HELP ME.

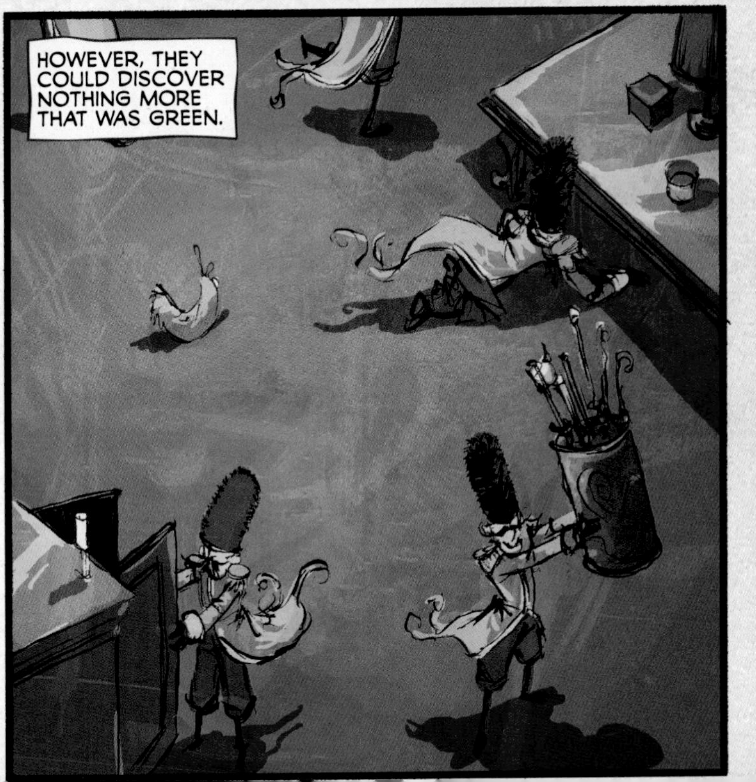
HOWEVER, THEY COULD DISCOVER NOTHING MORE THAT WAS GREEN.

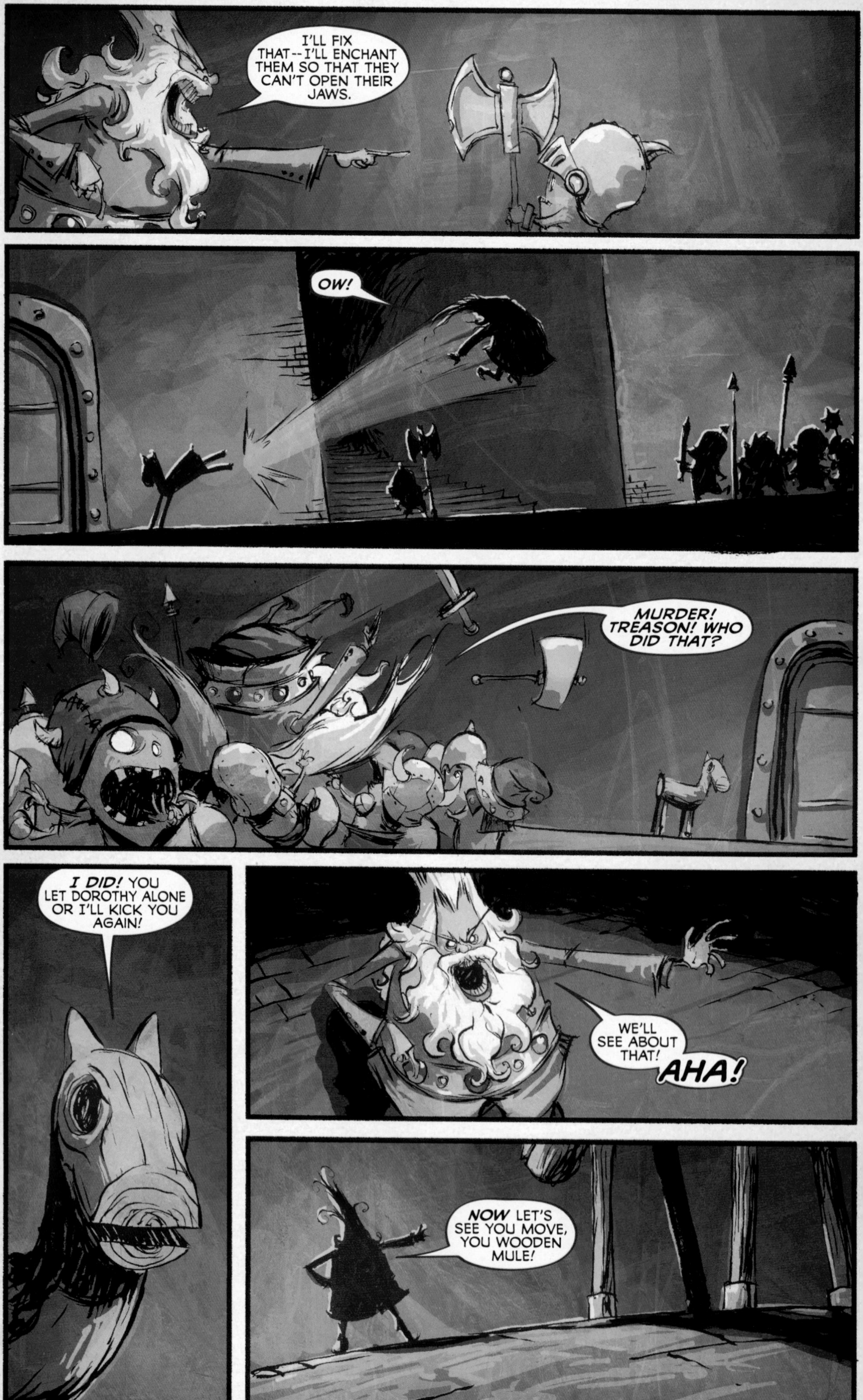
I'LL FIX THAT--I'LL ENCHANT THEM SO THAT THEY CAN'T OPEN THEIR JAWS.
OW!
MURDER! TREASON! WHO DID THAT?
I DID! YOU LET DOROTHY ALONE OR I'LL KICK YOU AGAIN!
WE'LL SEE ABOUT THAT! AHA!
NOW LET'S SEE YOU MOVE, YOU WOODEN MULE!

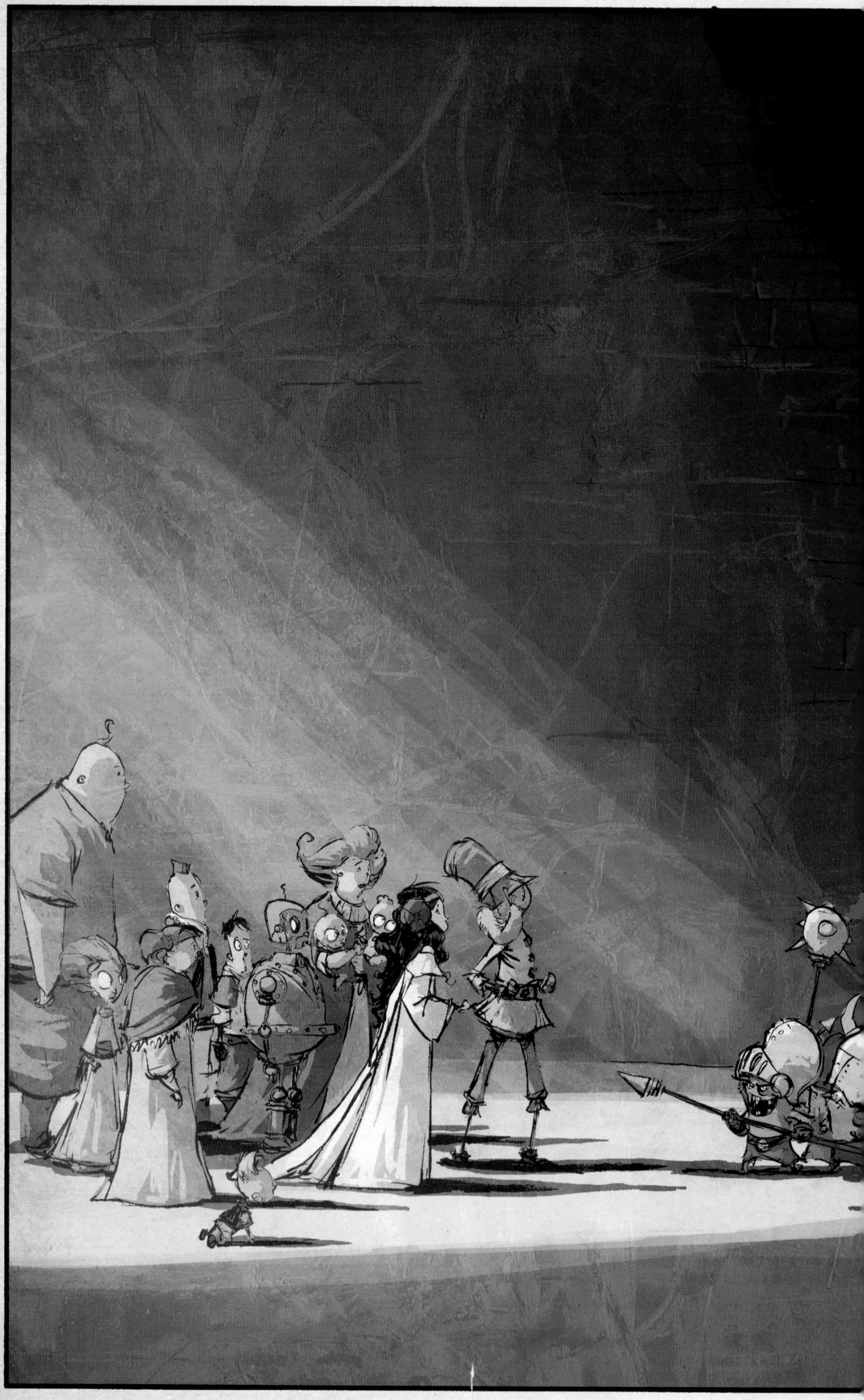

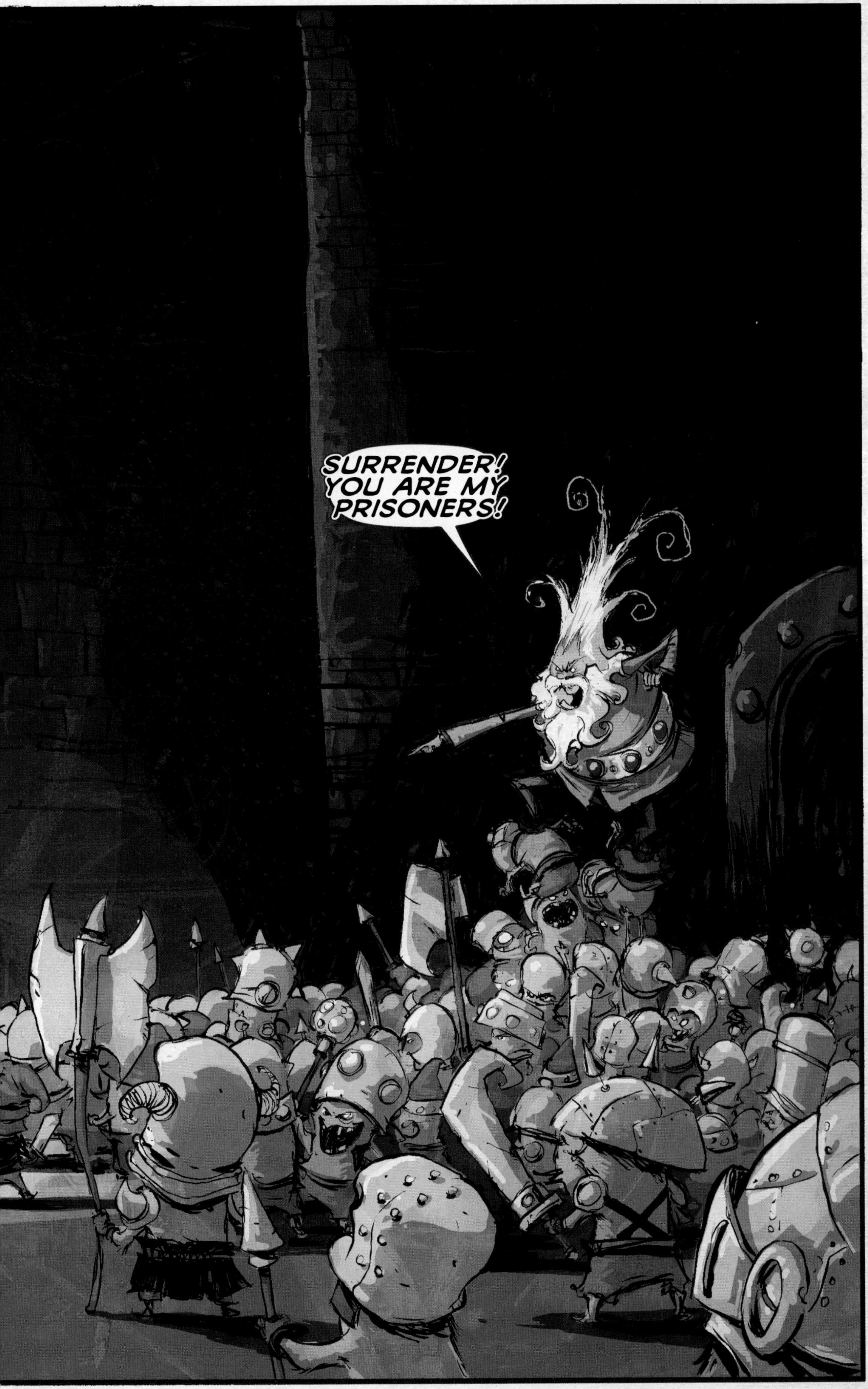
SURRENDER! YOU ARE MY PRISONERS!

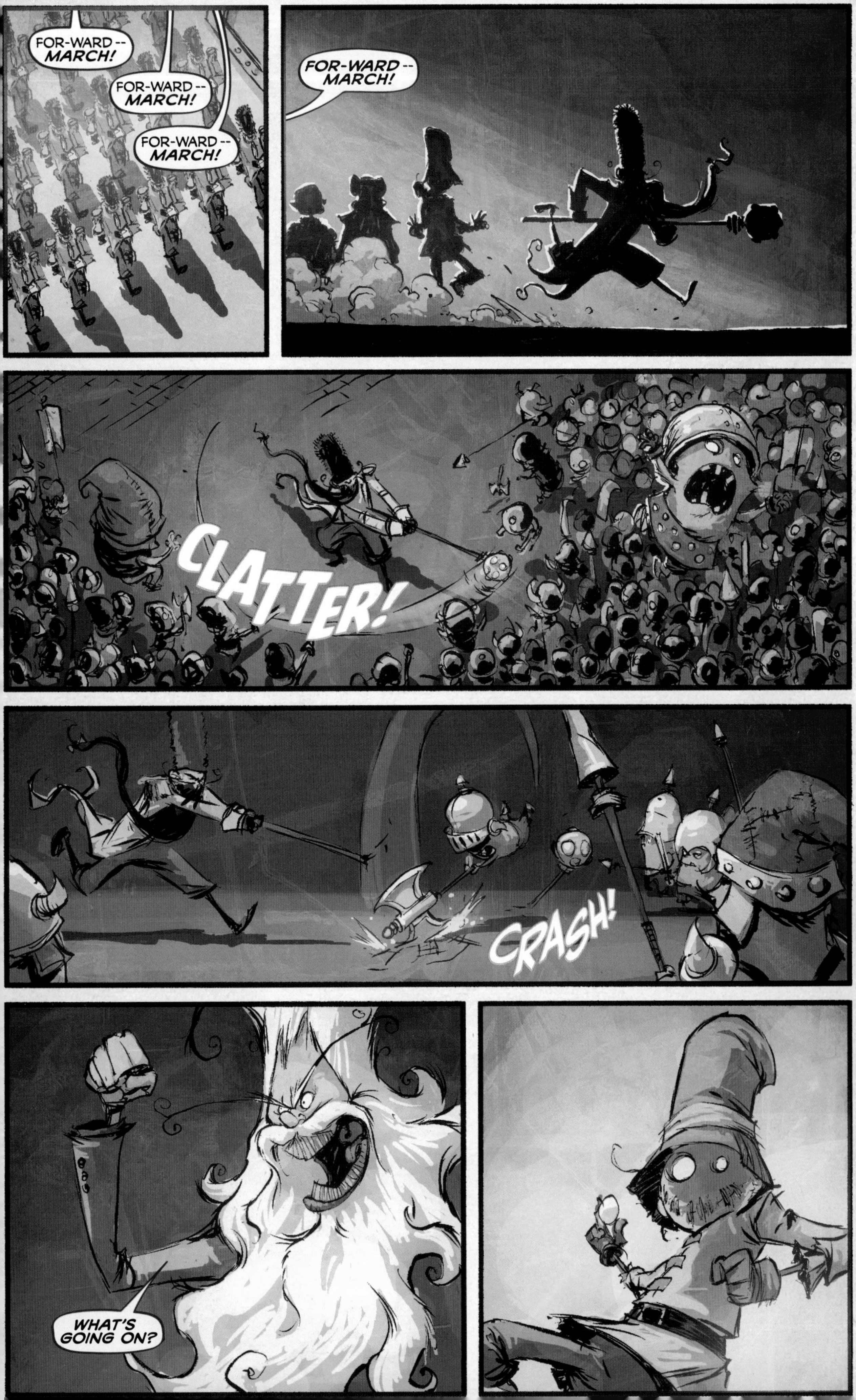
FOR-WARD -- MARCH!
FOR-WARD -- MARCH!
FOR-WARD -- MARCH!
FOR-WARD -- MARCH!
CLATTER!
CRASH!
WHAT'S GOING ON?

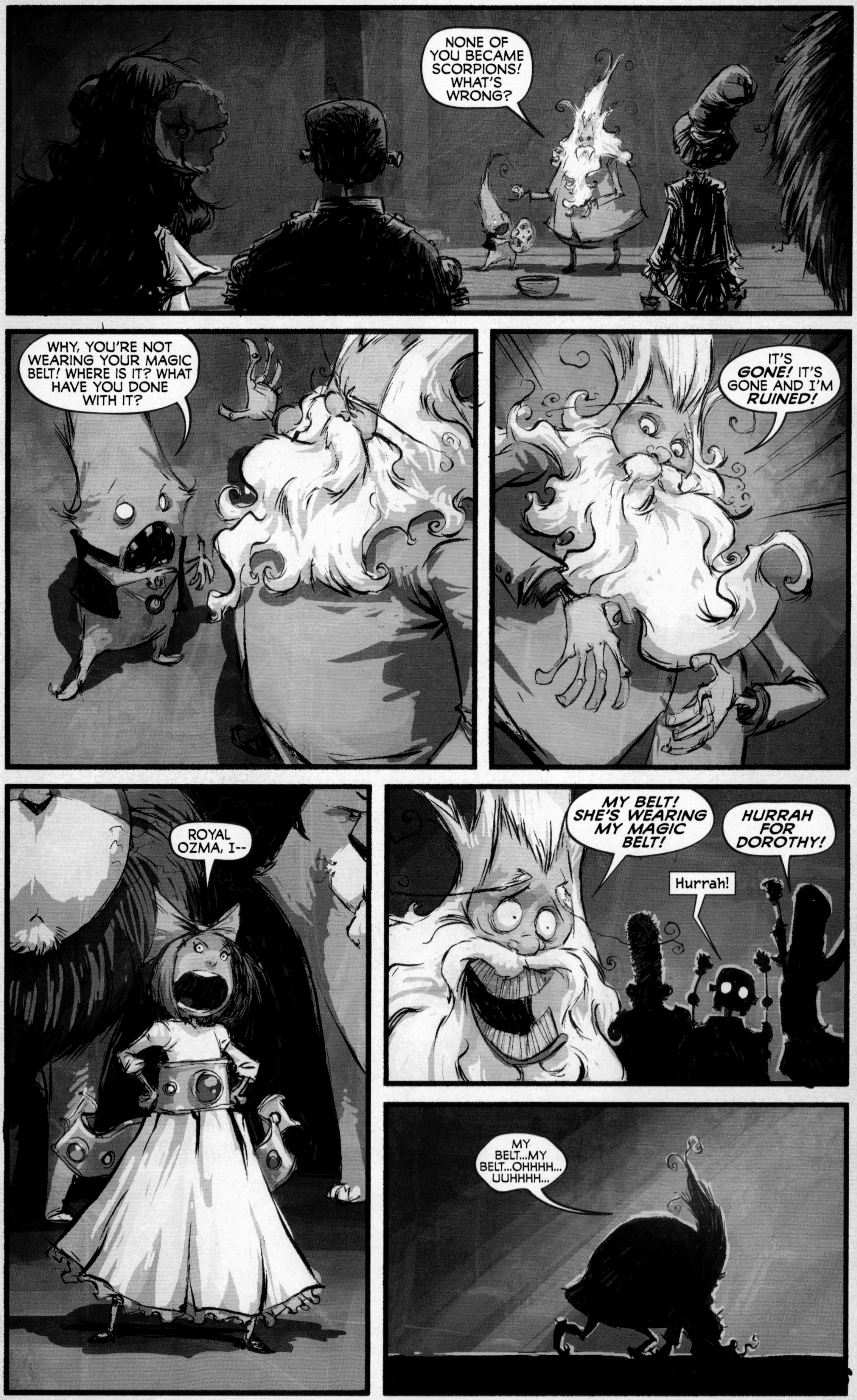
NONE OF YOU BECAME SCORPIONS! WHAT'S WRONG?
WHY, YOU'RE NOT WEARING YOUR MAGIC BELT! WHERE IS IT? WHAT HAVE YOU DONE WITH IT?
IT'S GONE! IT'S GONE AND I'M RUINED!
ROYAL OZMA, I--
MY BELT! SHE'S WEARING MY MAGIC BELT!
HURRAH FOR DOROTHY!
Hurrah!
MY BELT...MY BELT...OHHHH... UUHHHH...

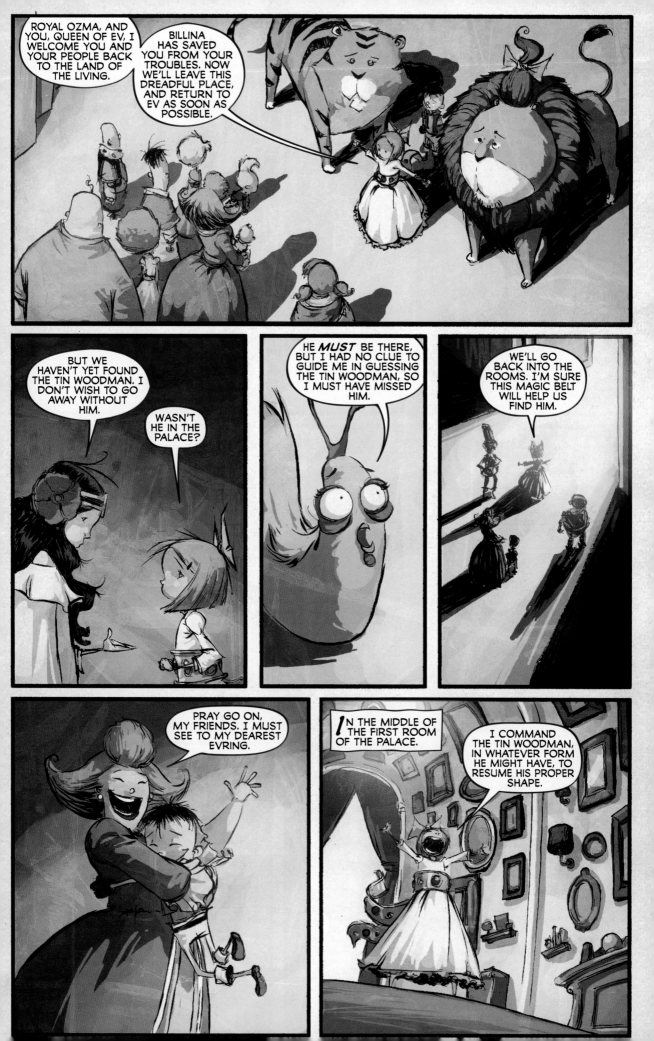

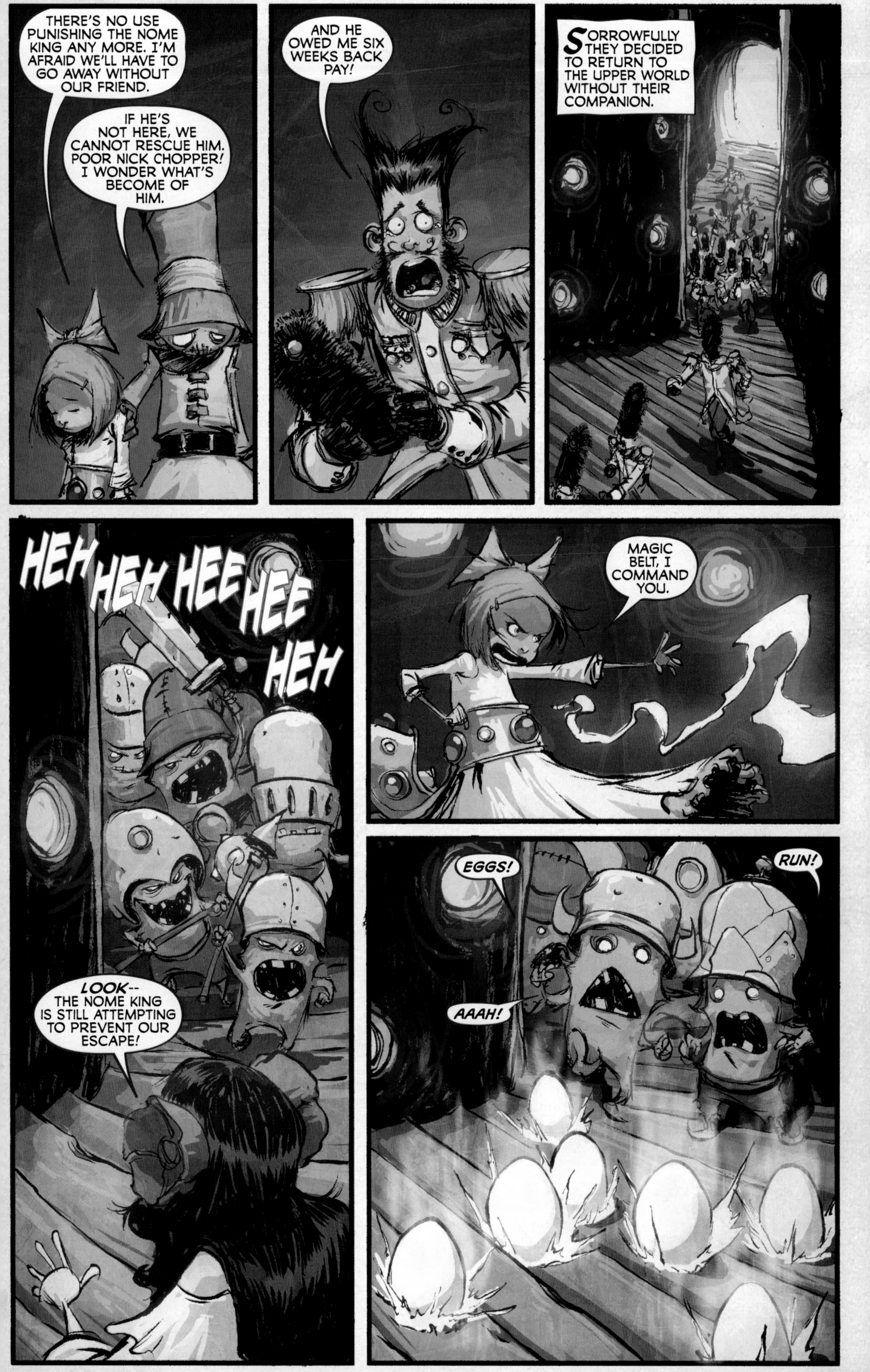
THERE'S NO USE PUNISHING THE NOME KING ANY MORE. I'M AFRAID WE'LL HAVE TO GO AWAY WITHOUT OUR FRIEND.
IF HE'S NOT HERE, WE CANNOT RESCUE HIM. POOR NICK CHOPPER! I WONDER WHAT'S BECOME OF HIM.
AND HE OWED ME SIX WEEKS BACK PAY!
SORROWFULLY THEY DECIDED TO RETURN TO THE UPPER WORLD WITHOUT THEIR COMPANION.
HEH HEH HEH HEE HEE HEH
LOOK-- THE NOME KING IS STILL ATTEMPTING TO PREVENT OUR ESCAPE!
MAGIC BELT, I COMMAND YOU.
EGGS!
RUN!
AAAH!

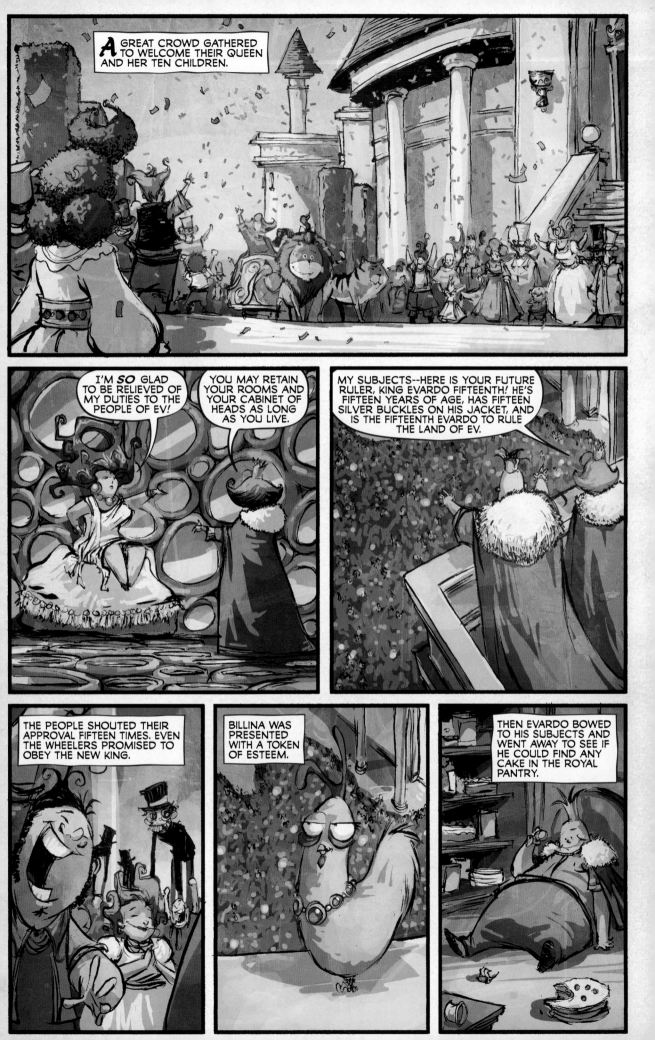

A GREAT CROWD GATHERED TO WELCOME THEIR QUEEN AND HER TEN CHILDREN.

I'M **SO** GLAD TO BE RELIEVED OF MY DUTIES TO THE PEOPLE OF EV!

YOU MAY RETAIN YOUR ROOMS AND YOUR CABINET OF HEADS AS LONG AS YOU LIVE.

MY SUBJECTS--HERE IS YOUR FUTURE RULER, KING EVARDO FIFTEENTH! HE'S FIFTEEN YEARS OF AGE, HAS FIFTEEN SILVER BUCKLES ON HIS JACKET, AND IS THE FIFTEENTH EVARDO TO RULE THE LAND OF EV.

THE PEOPLE SHOUTED THEIR APPROVAL FIFTEEN TIMES. EVEN THE WHEELERS PROMISED TO OBEY THE NEW KING.

BILLINA WAS PRESENTED WITH A TOKEN OF ESTEEM.

THEN EVARDO BOWED TO HIS SUBJECTS AND WENT AWAY TO SEE IF HE COULD FIND ANY CAKE IN THE ROYAL PANTRY.

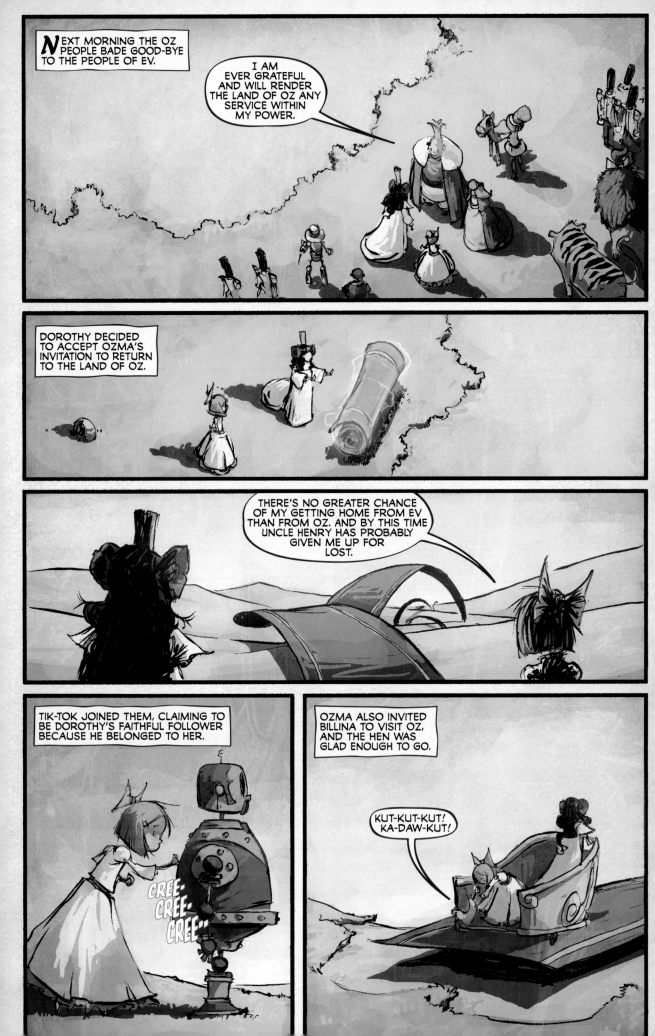

NEXT MORNING THE OZ PEOPLE BADE GOOD-BYE TO THE PEOPLE OF EV.

I AM EVER GRATEFUL AND WILL RENDER THE LAND OF OZ ANY SERVICE WITHIN MY POWER.

DOROTHY DECIDED TO ACCEPT OZMA'S INVITATION TO RETURN TO THE LAND OF OZ.

THERE'S NO GREATER CHANCE OF MY GETTING HOME FROM EV THAN FROM OZ. AND BY THIS TIME UNCLE HENRY HAS PROBABLY GIVEN ME UP FOR LOST.

TIK-TOK JOINED THEM, CLAIMING TO BE DOROTHY'S FAITHFUL FOLLOWER BECAUSE HE BELONGED TO HER.

CREE-CREE-CREE"

OZMA ALSO INVITED BILLINA TO VISIT OZ, AND THE HEN WAS GLAD ENOUGH TO GO.

KUT-KUT-KUT! KA-DAW-KUT!

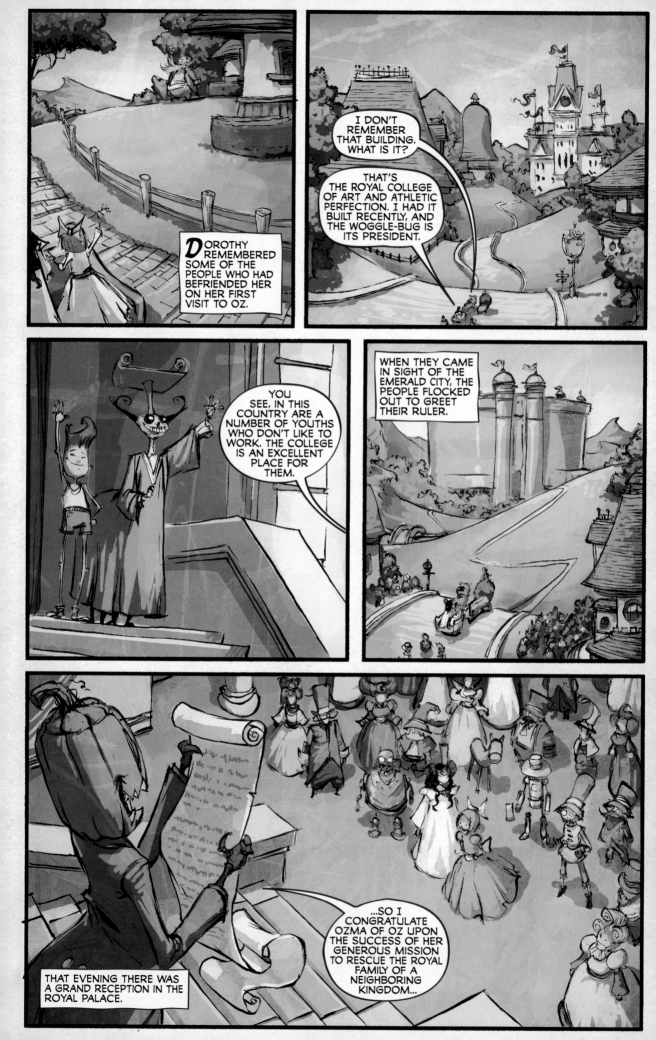

I DON'T REMEMBER THAT BUILDING. WHAT IS IT?

THAT'S THE ROYAL COLLEGE OF ART AND ATHLETIC PERFECTION. I HAD IT BUILT RECENTLY, AND THE WOGGLE-BUG IS ITS PRESIDENT.

*D*OROTHY REMEMBERED SOME OF THE PEOPLE WHO HAD BEFRIENDED HER ON HER FIRST VISIT TO OZ.

YOU SEE, IN THIS COUNTRY ARE A NUMBER OF YOUTHS WHO DON'T LIKE TO WORK. THE COLLEGE IS AN EXCELLENT PLACE FOR THEM.

WHEN THEY CAME IN SIGHT OF THE EMERALD CITY, THE PEOPLE FLOCKED OUT TO GREET THEIR RULER.

THAT EVENING THERE WAS A GRAND RECEPTION IN THE ROYAL PALACE.

...SO I CONGRATULATE OZMA OF OZ UPON THE SUCCESS OF HER GENEROUS MISSION TO RESCUE THE ROYAL FAMILY OF A NEIGHBORING KINGDOM...

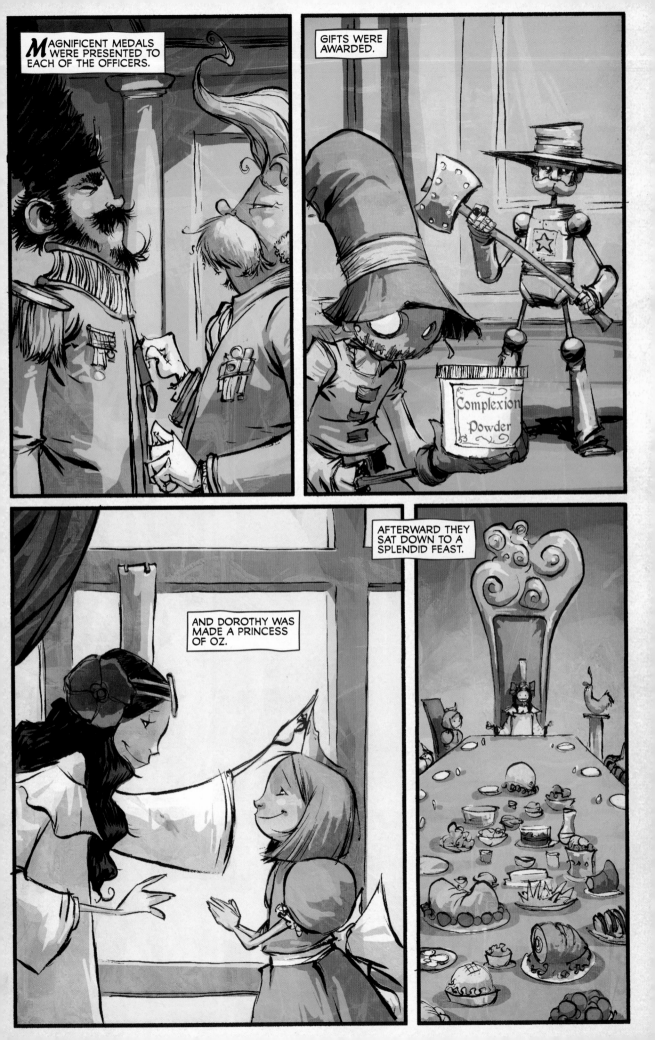

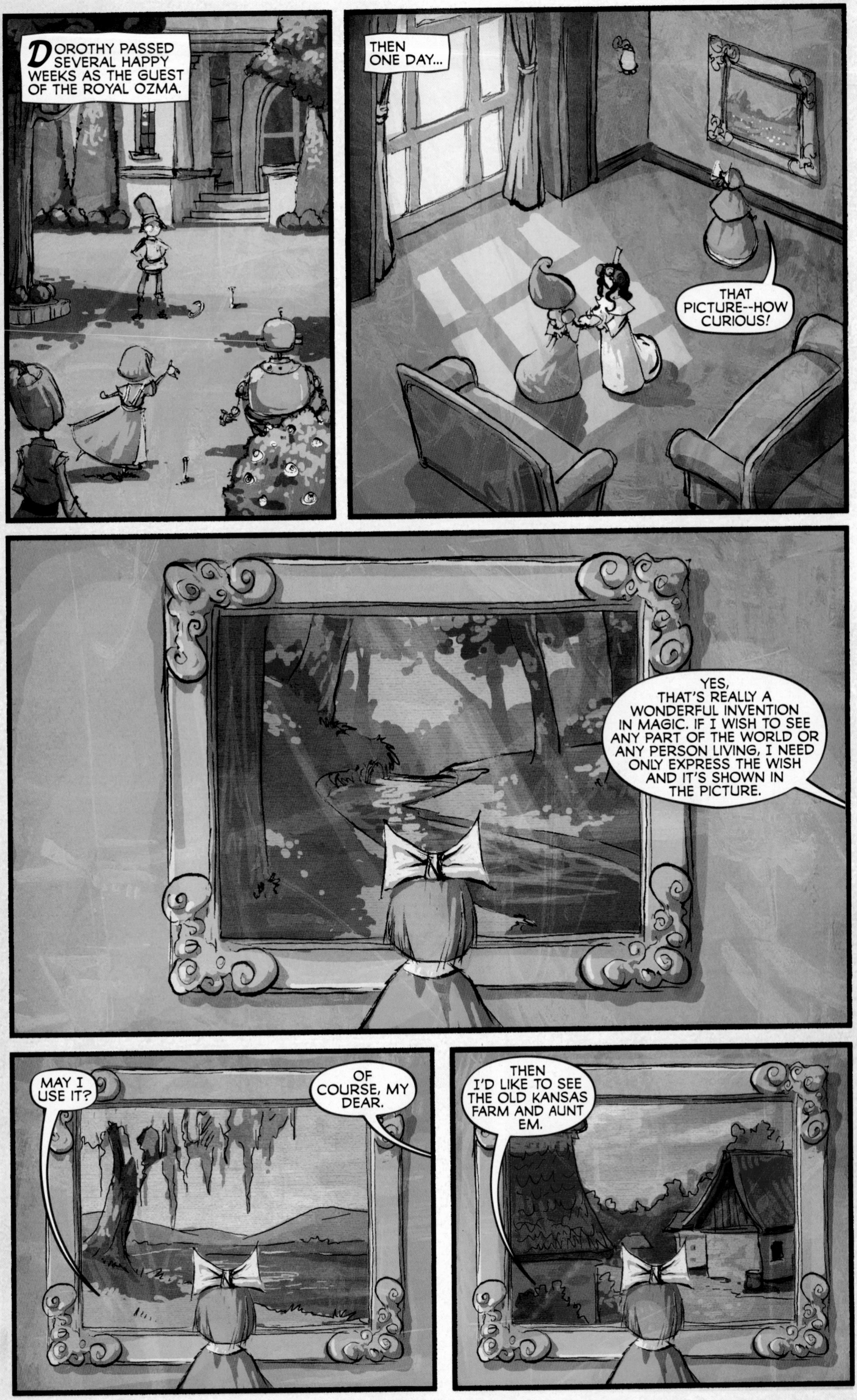
DOROTHY PASSED SEVERAL HAPPY WEEKS AS THE GUEST OF THE ROYAL OZMA.
THEN ONE DAY...
THAT PICTURE--HOW CURIOUS!
YES, THAT'S REALLY A WONDERFUL INVENTION IN MAGIC. IF I WISH TO SEE ANY PART OF THE WORLD OR ANY PERSON LIVING, I NEED ONLY EXPRESS THE WISH AND IT'S SHOWN IN THE PICTURE.
MAY I USE IT?
OF COURSE, MY DEAR.
THEN I'D LIKE TO SEE THE OLD KANSAS FARM AND AUNT EM.

THE STORY CONTINUES IN...

ONE

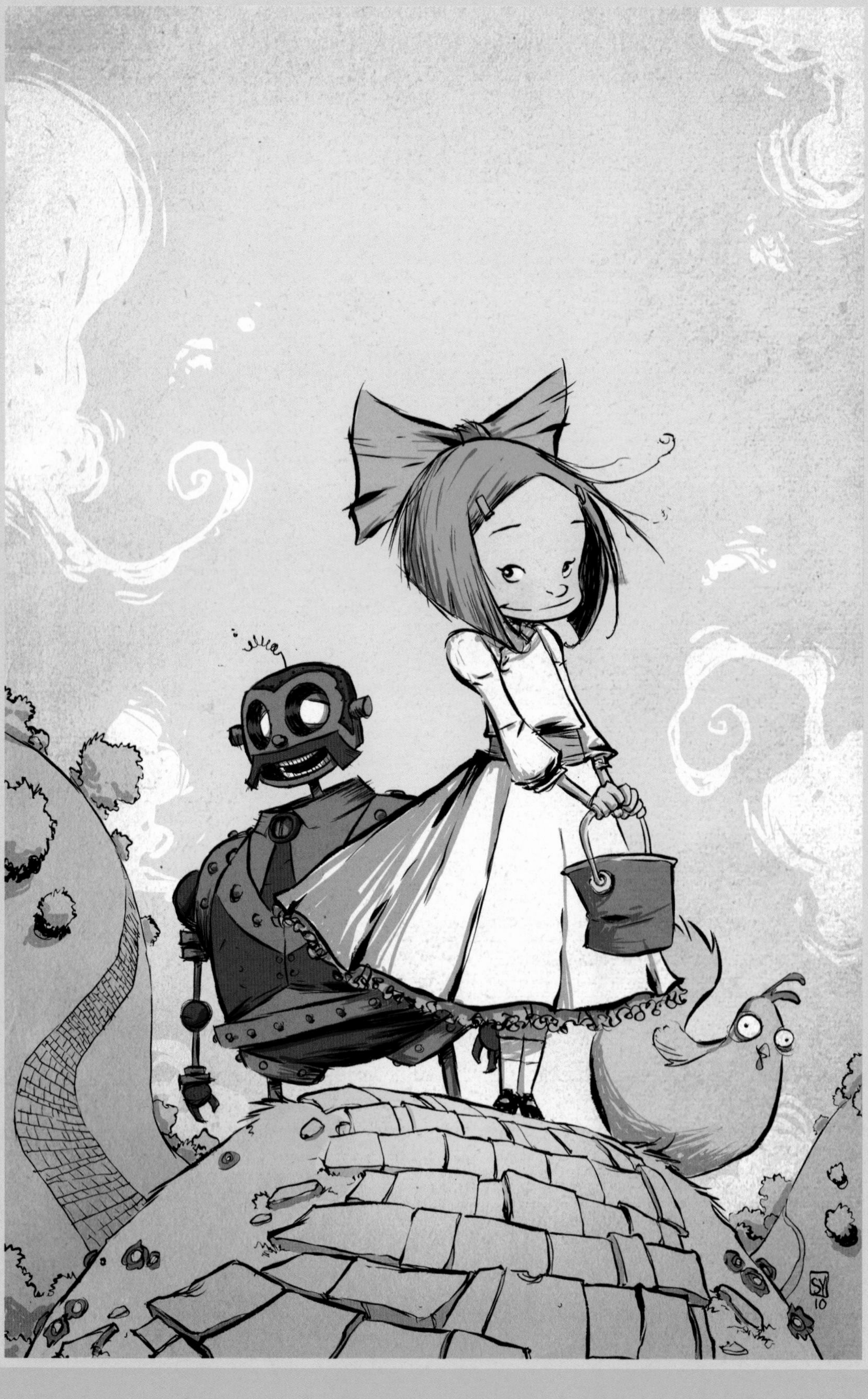
SY
10

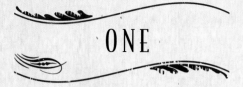

ONE

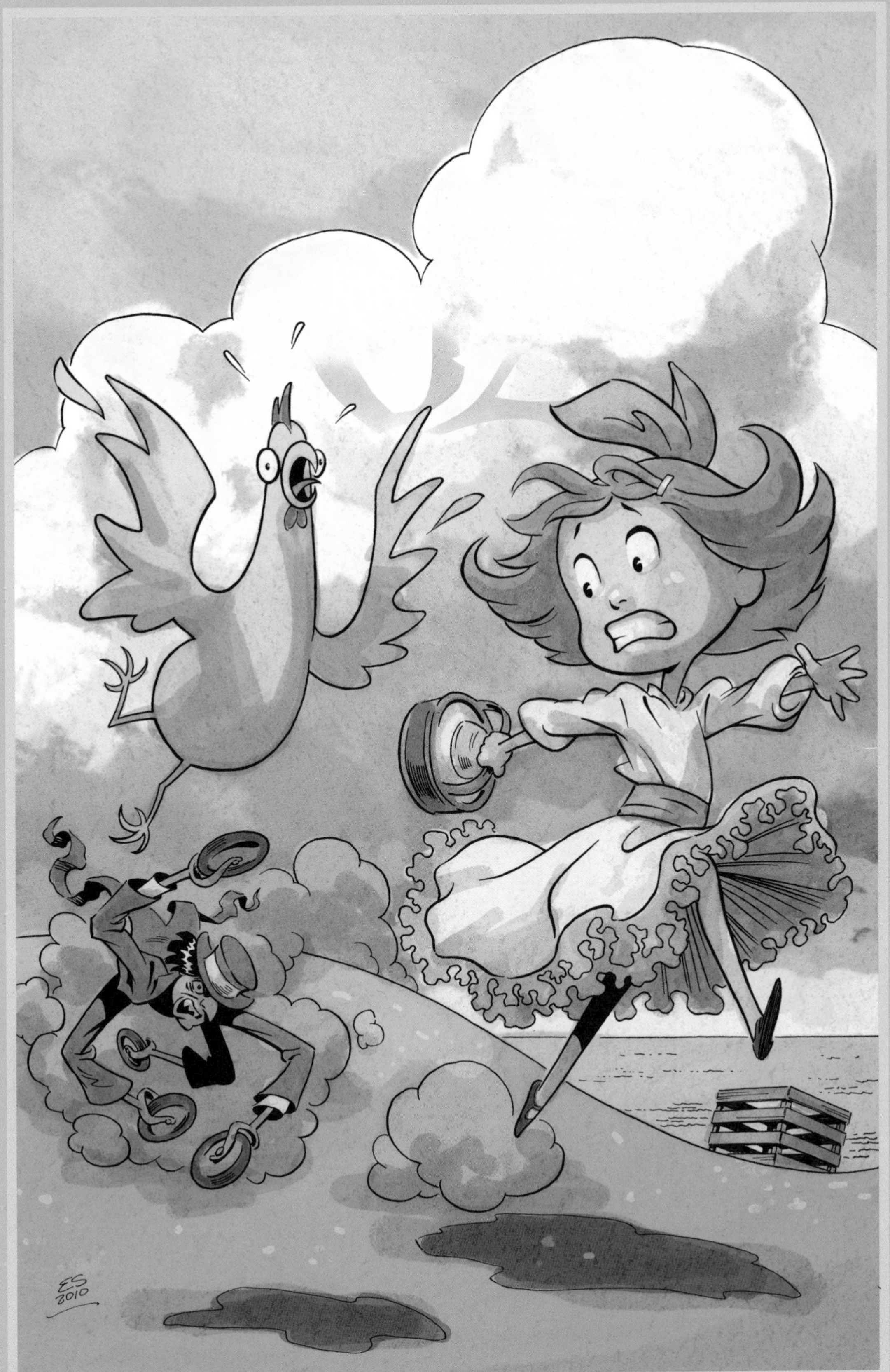
ES
2010

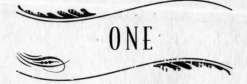

Variant Cover by Eric Shanower

ONE

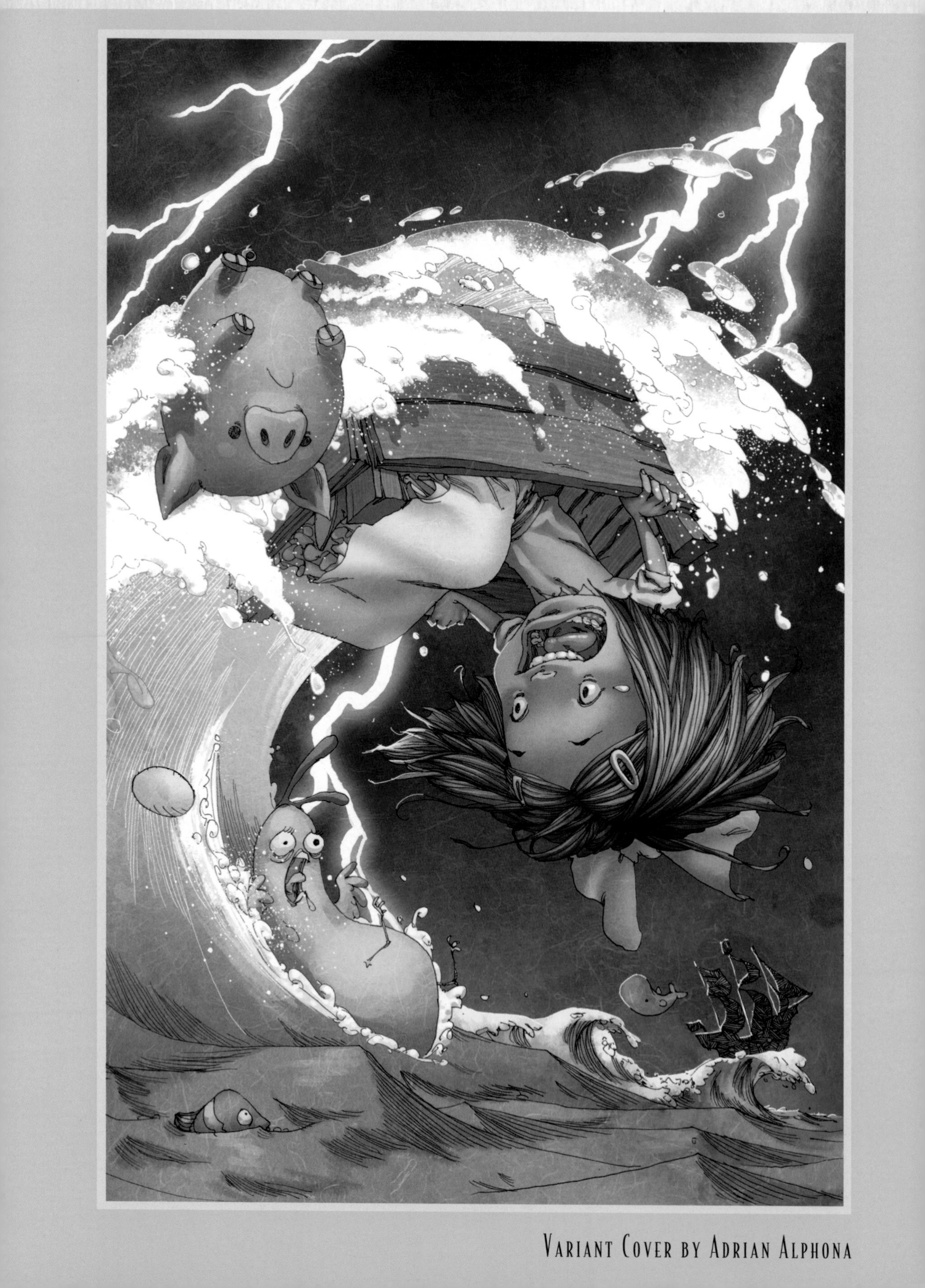

Variant Cover by Adrian Alphona

TWO

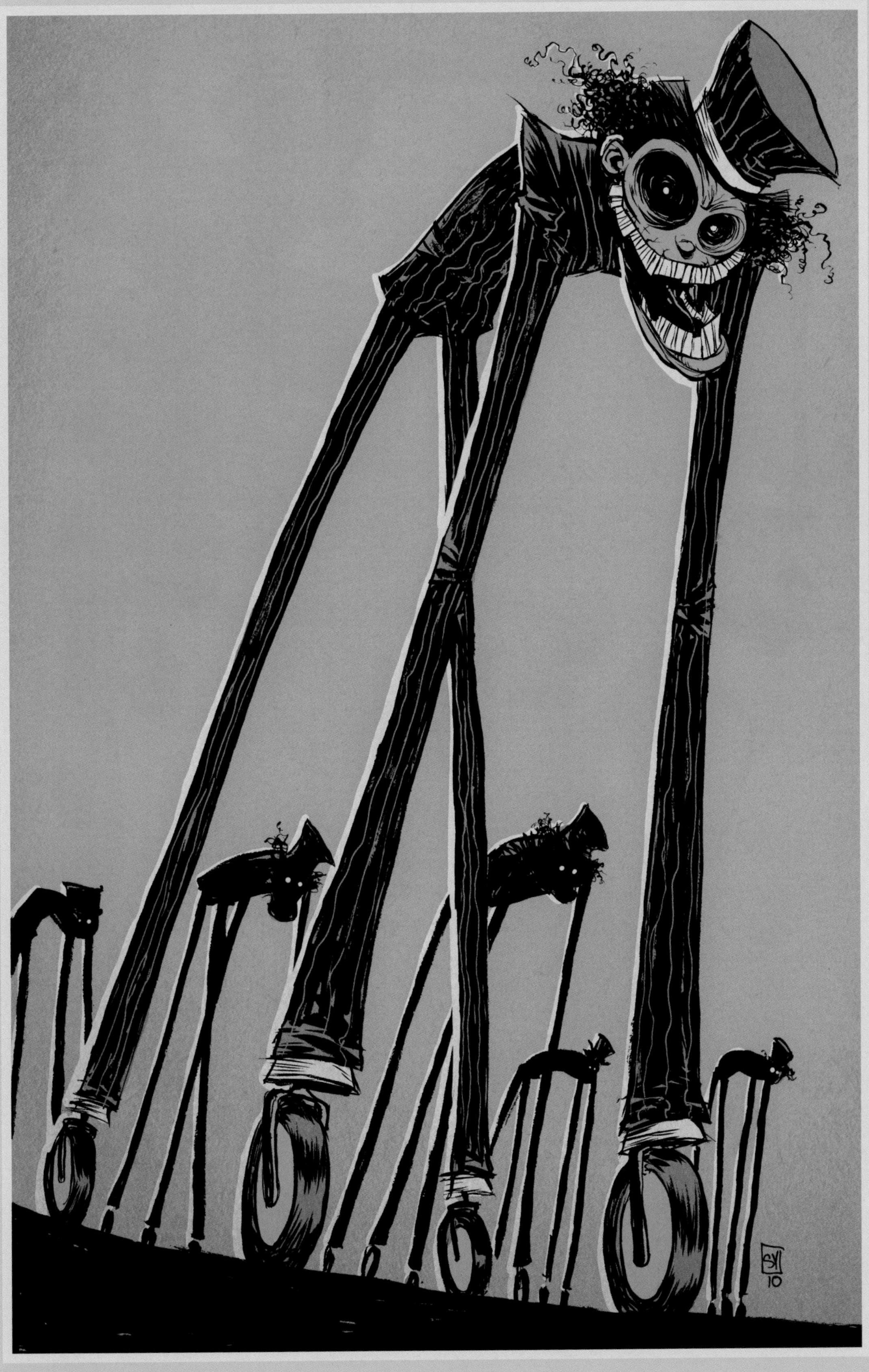

THREE

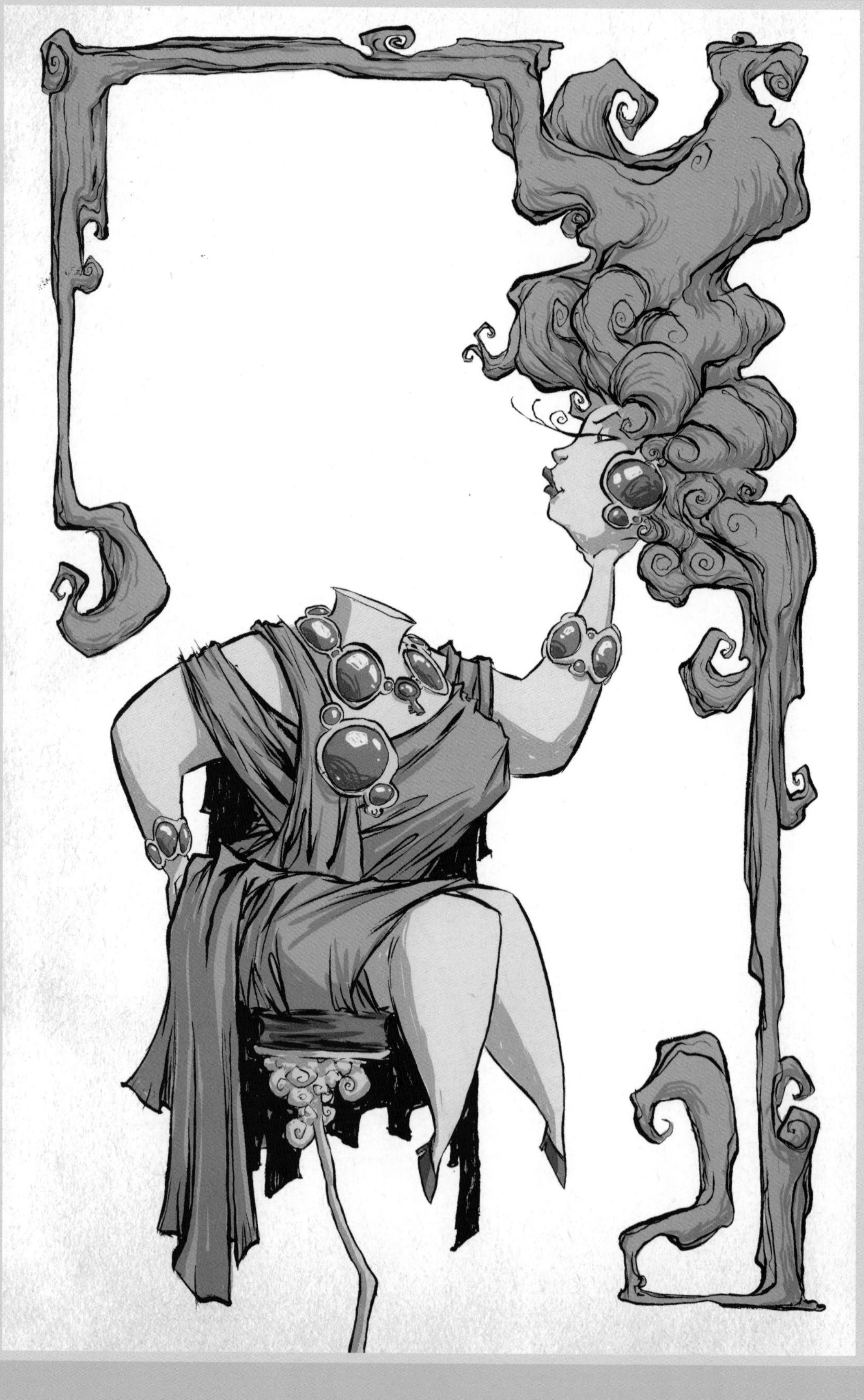

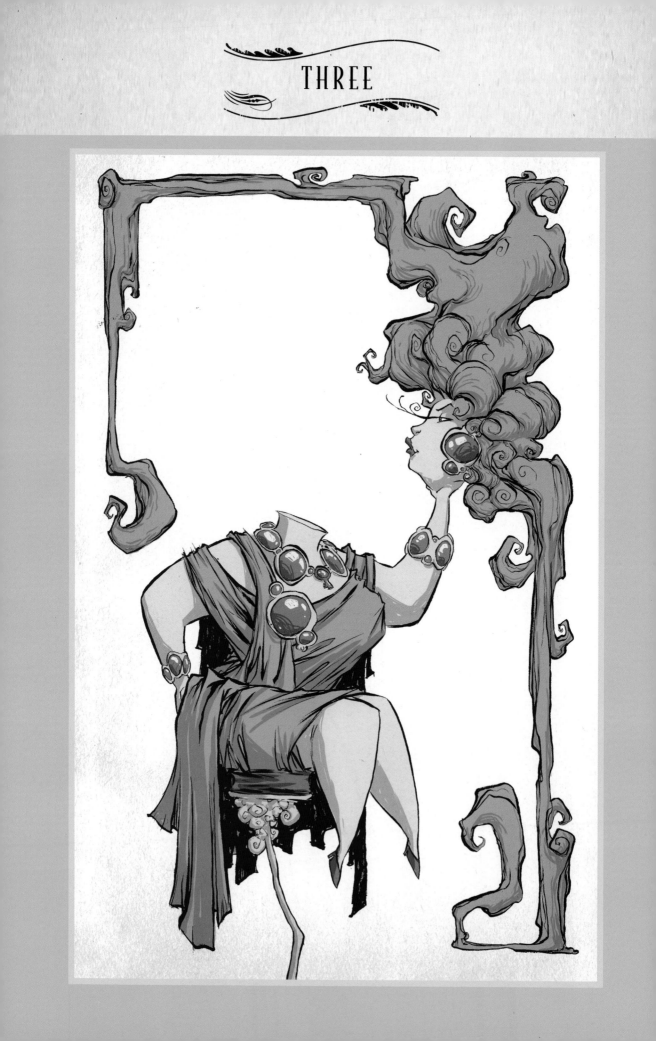

FOUR

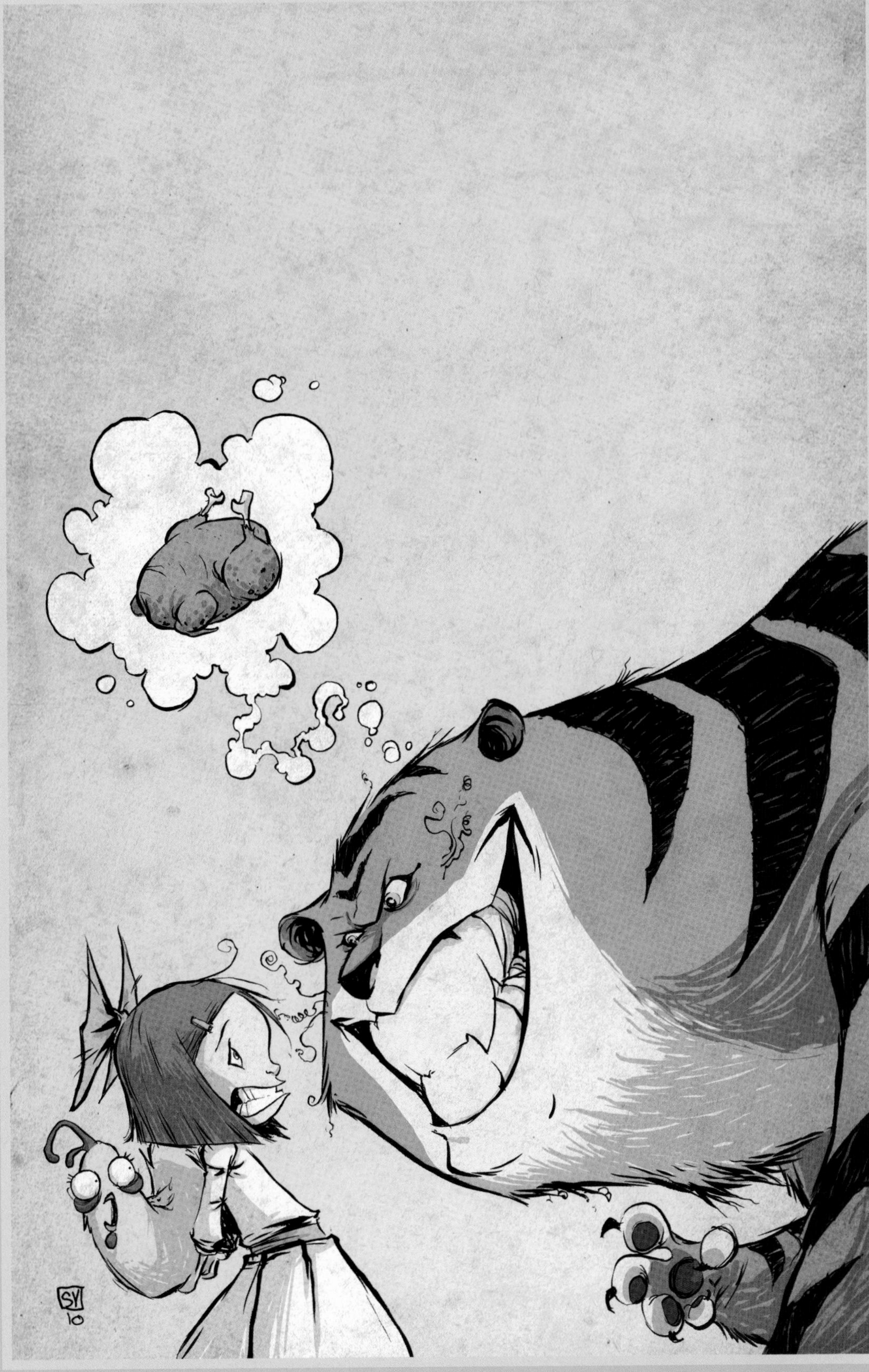

FIVE

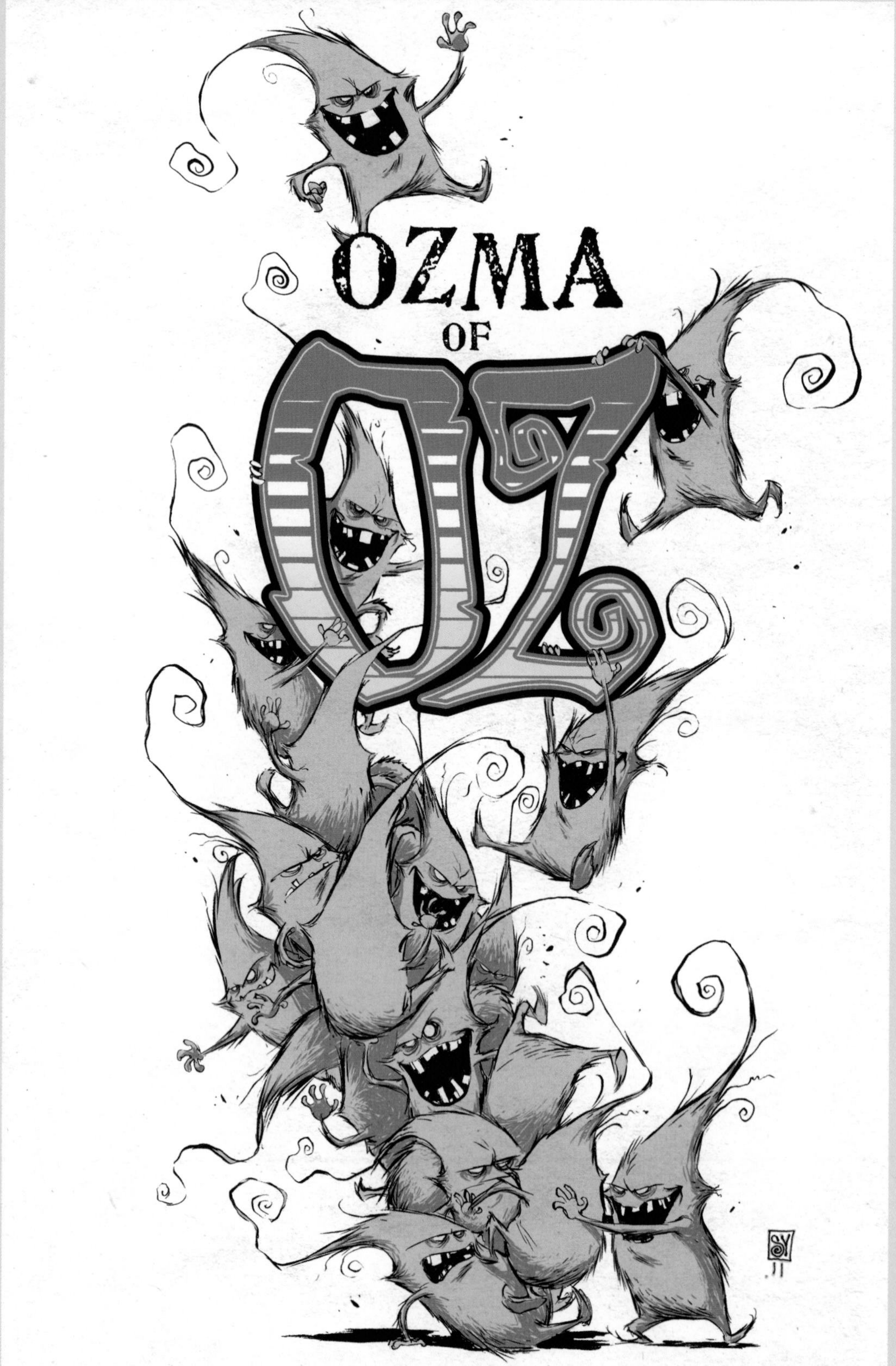
OZMA
OF
OZ

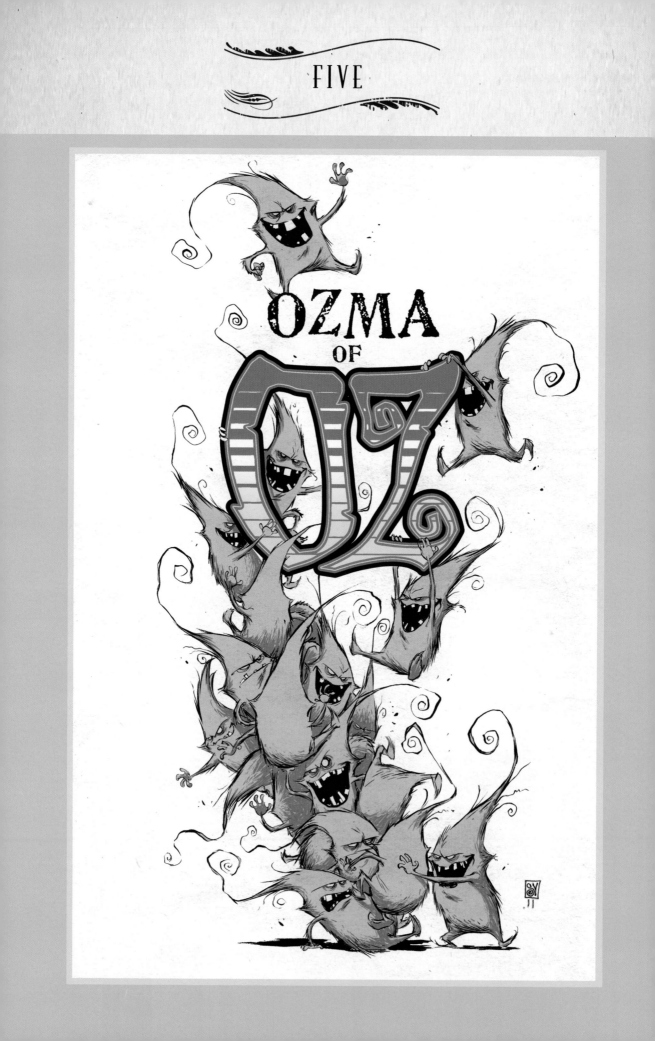

SIX

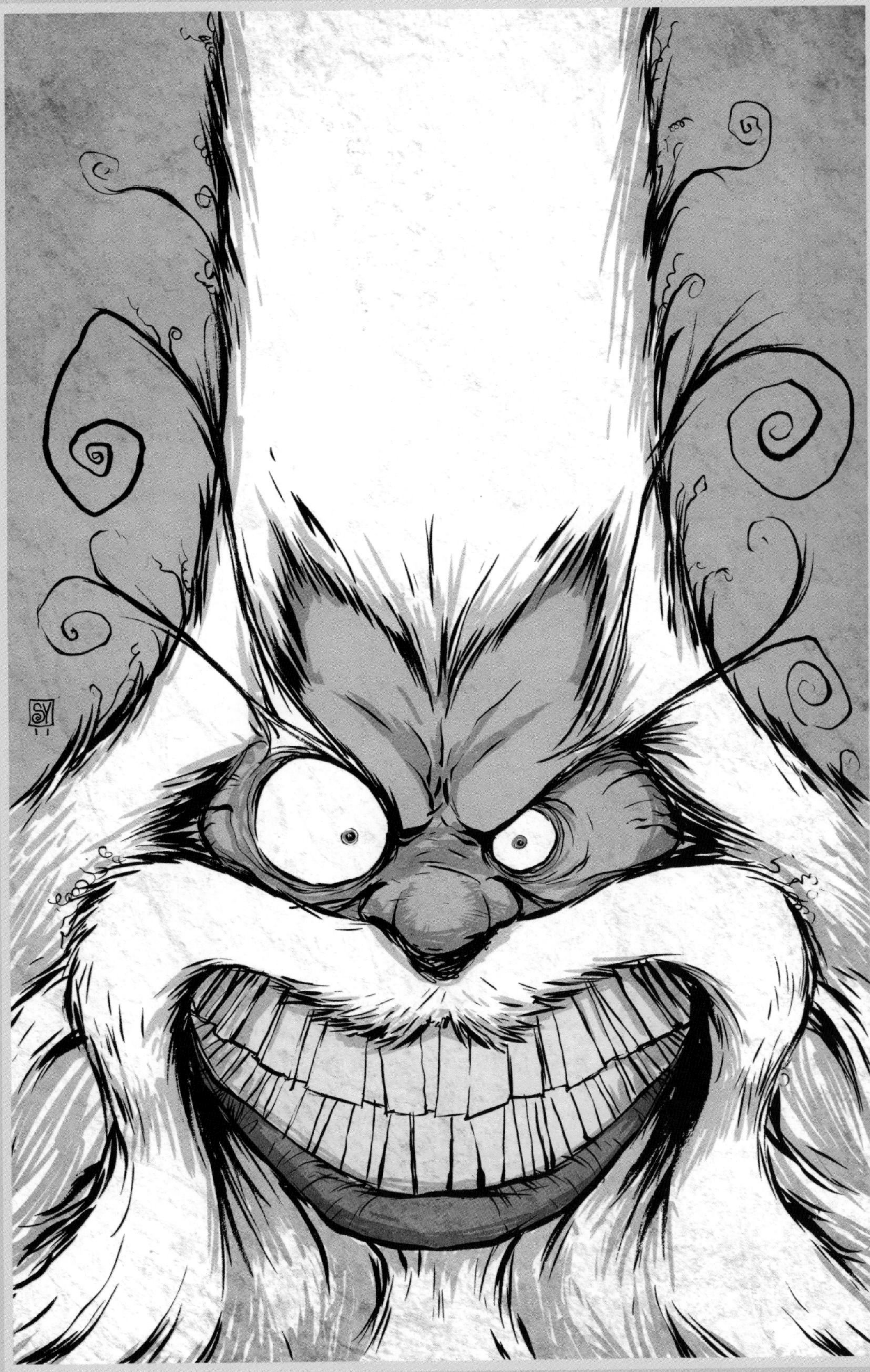

SEVEN

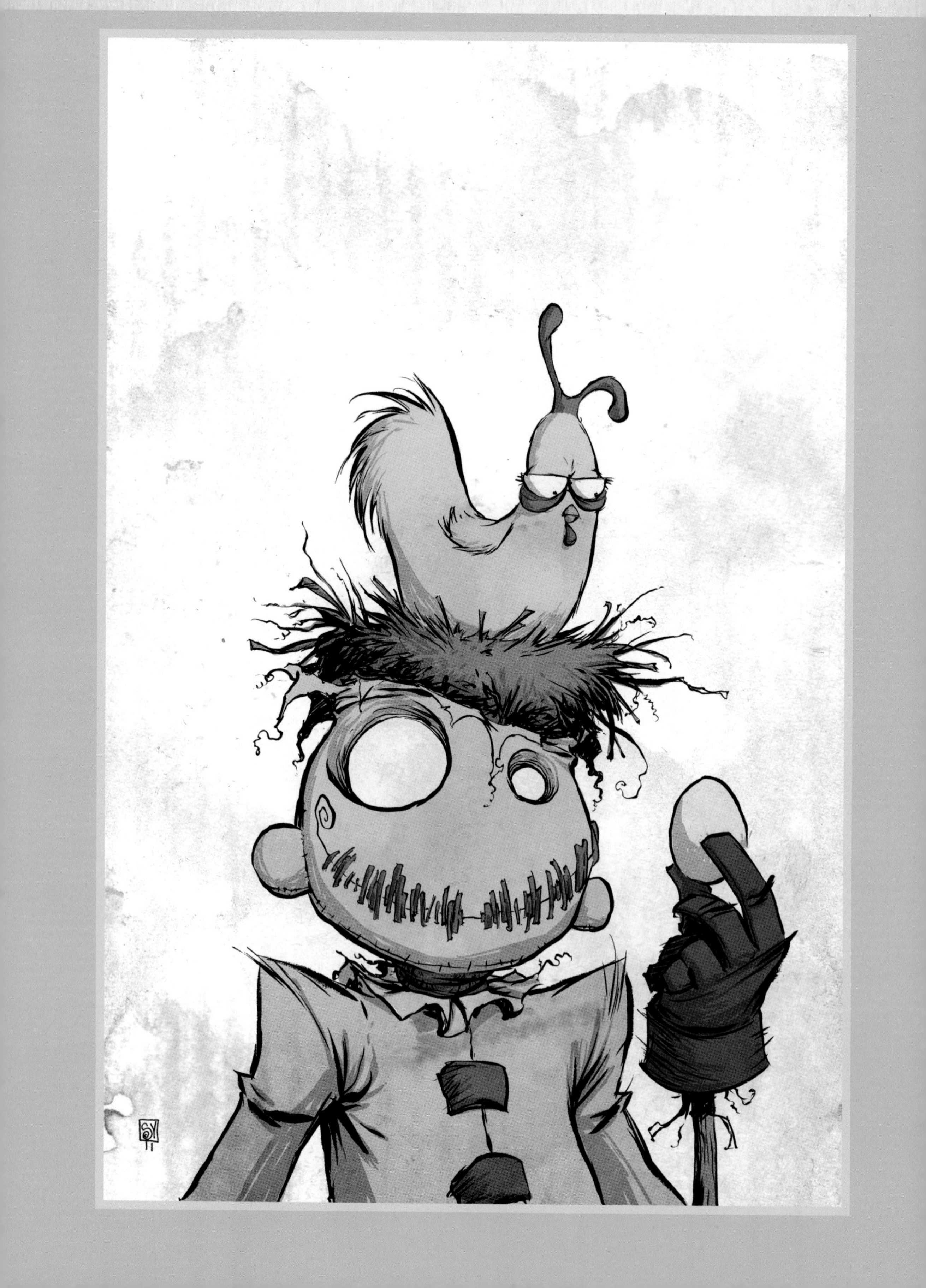

EIGHT

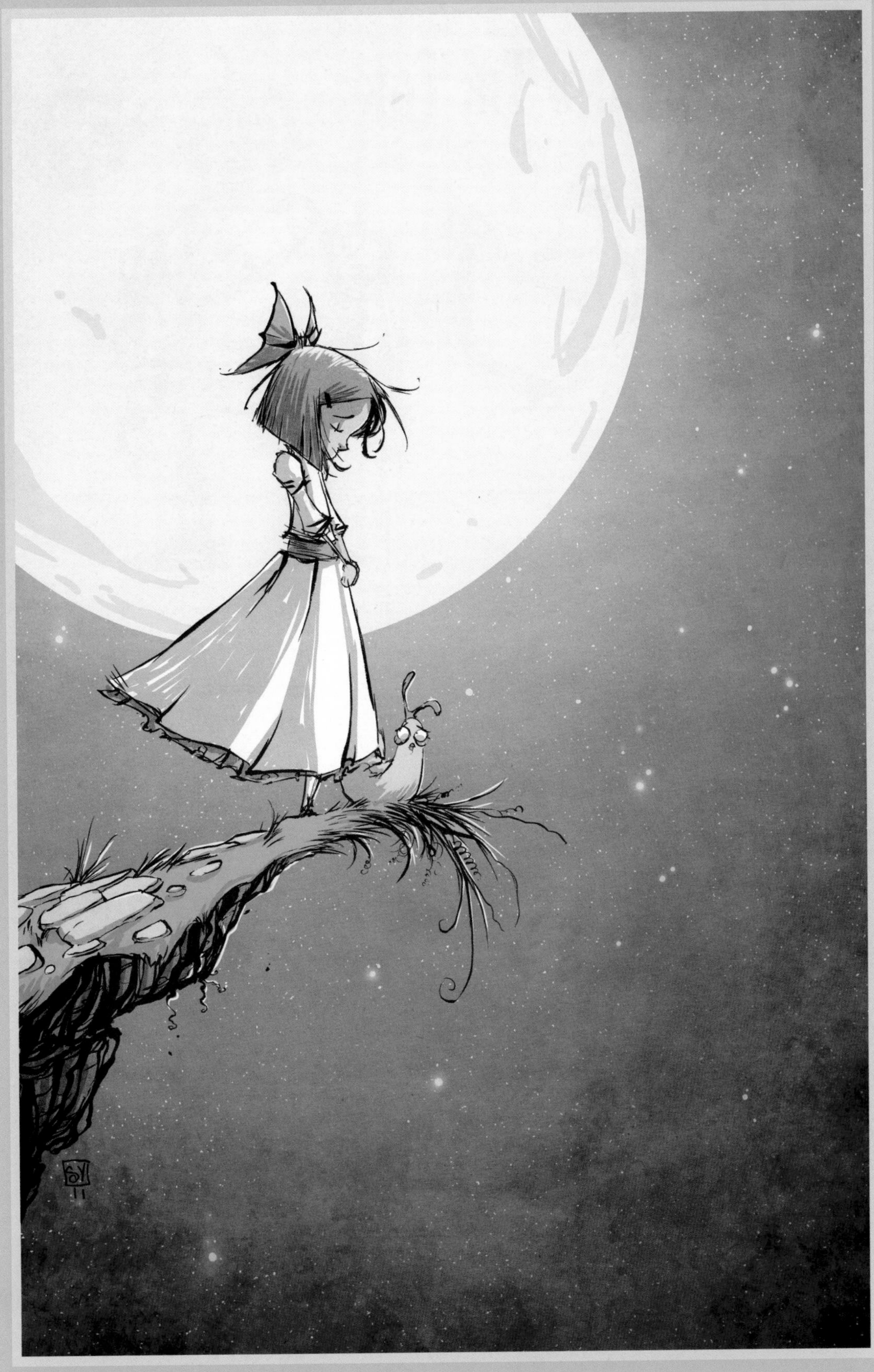

BILLINA AND TIK TOK

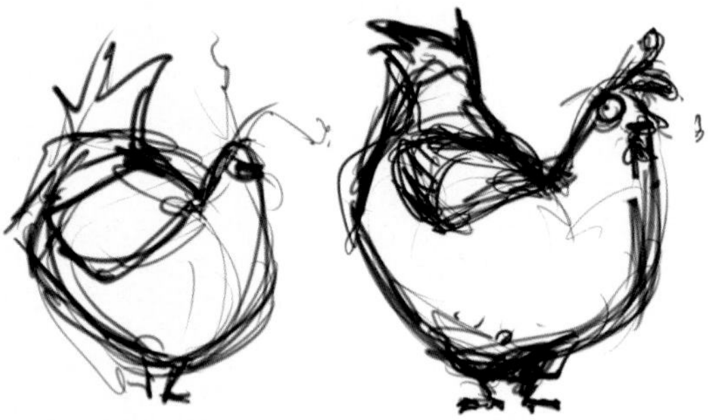

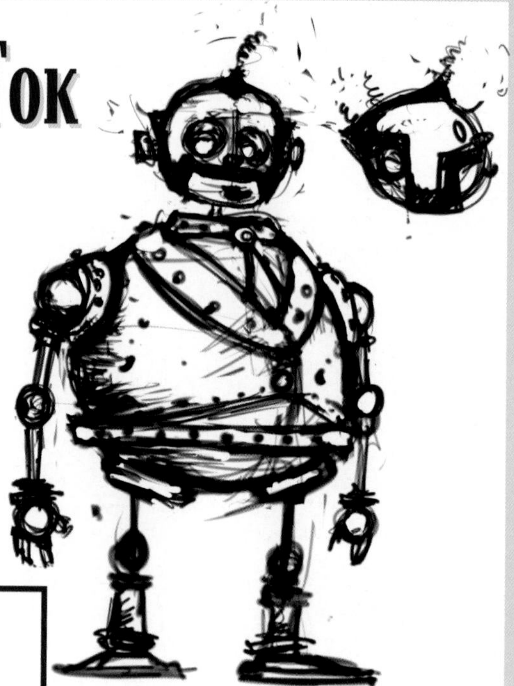

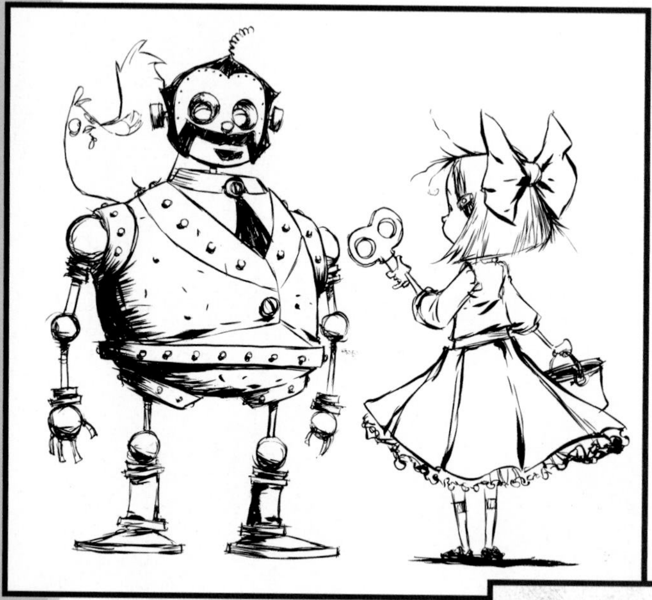

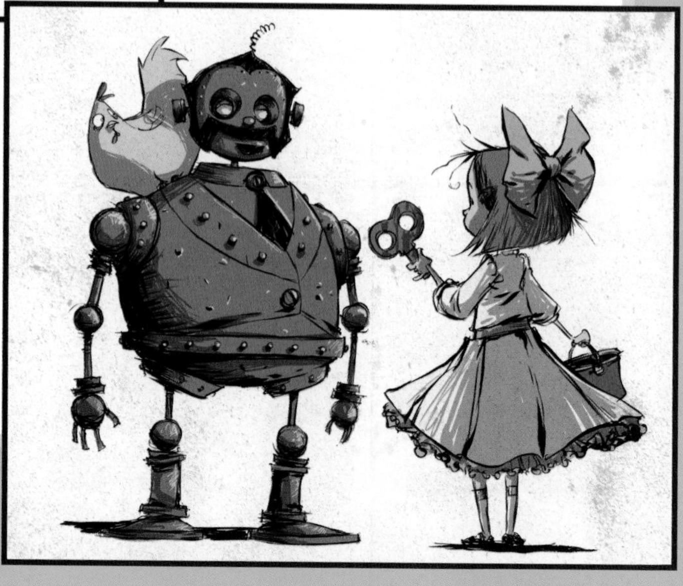

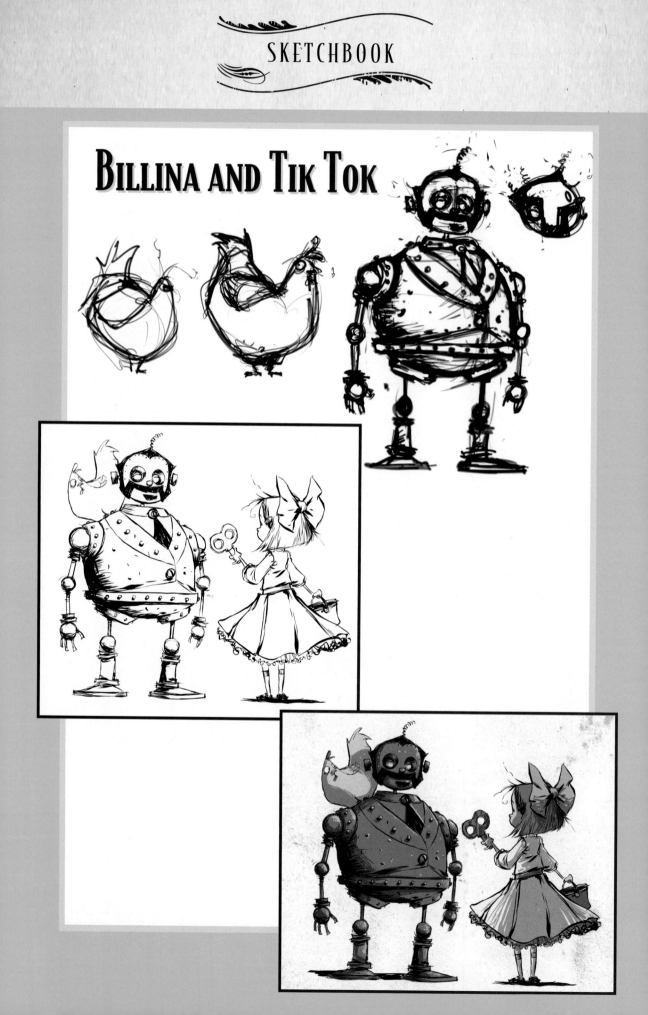

ISSUE ONE COVER PROCESS

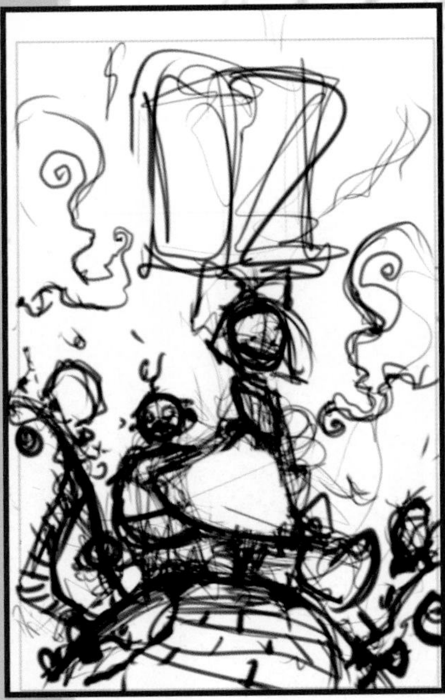

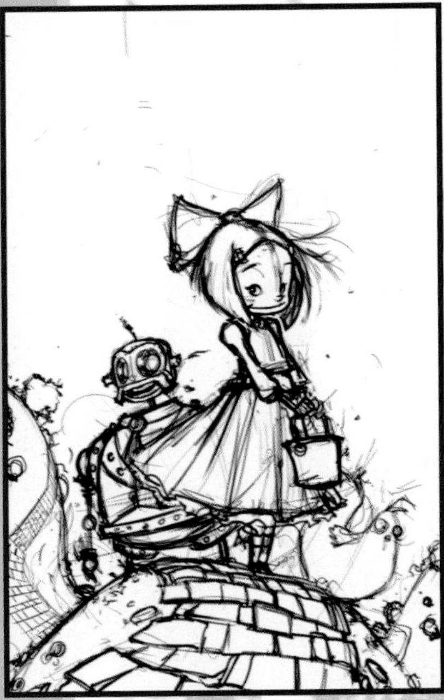

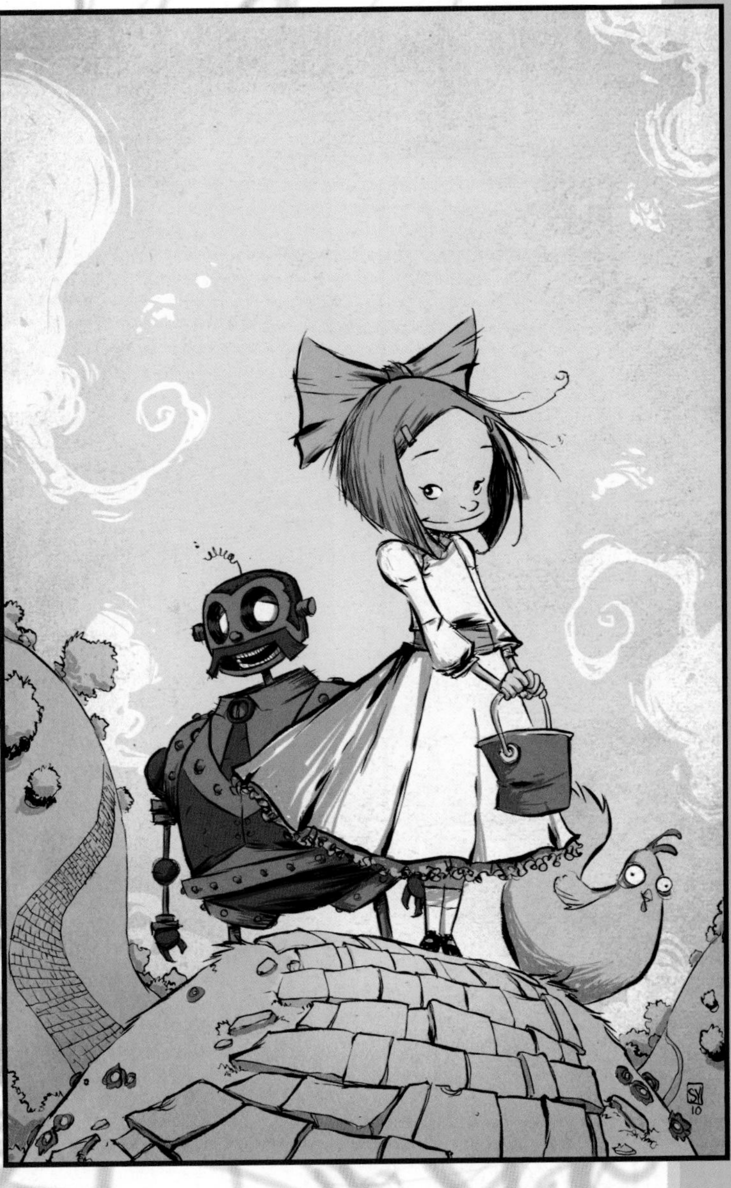

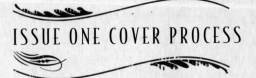

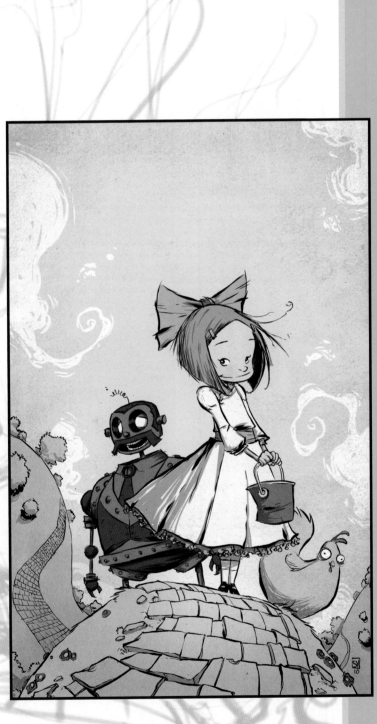

ISSUE TWO COVER PROCESS

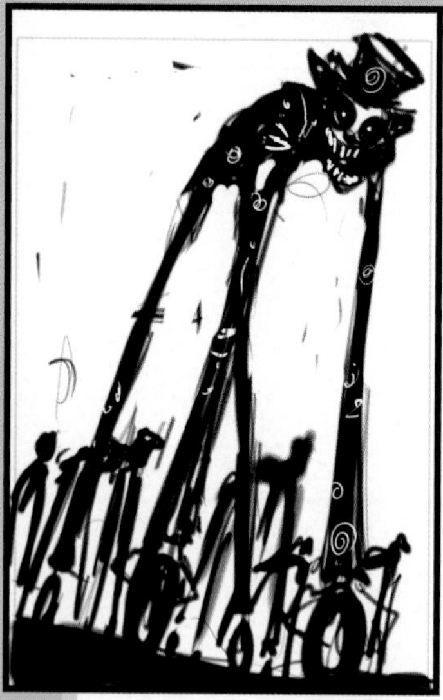

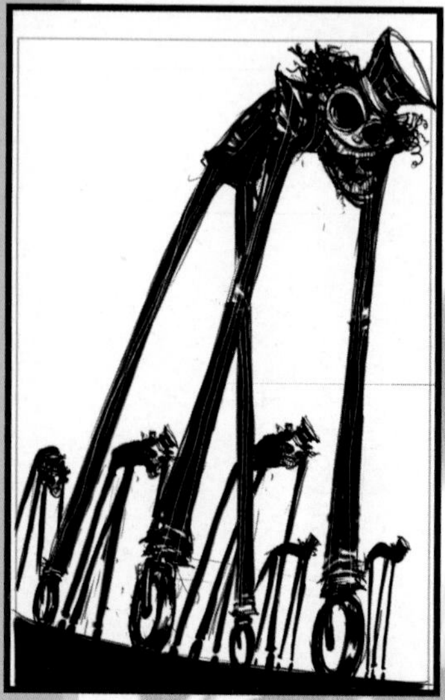

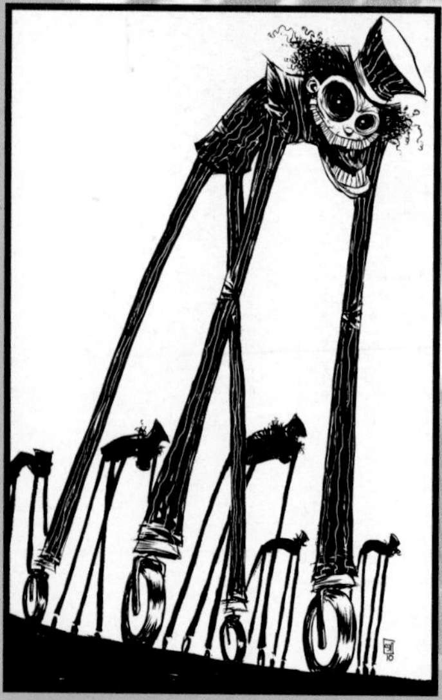

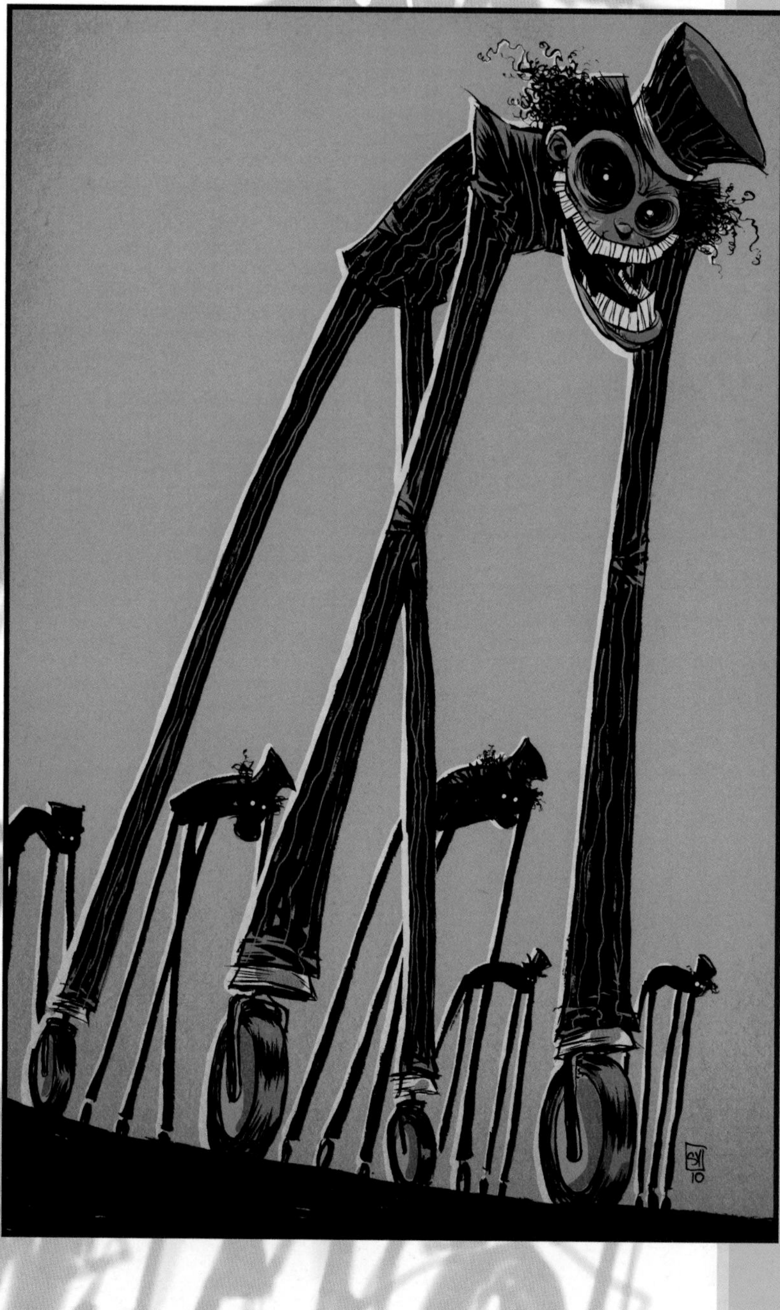

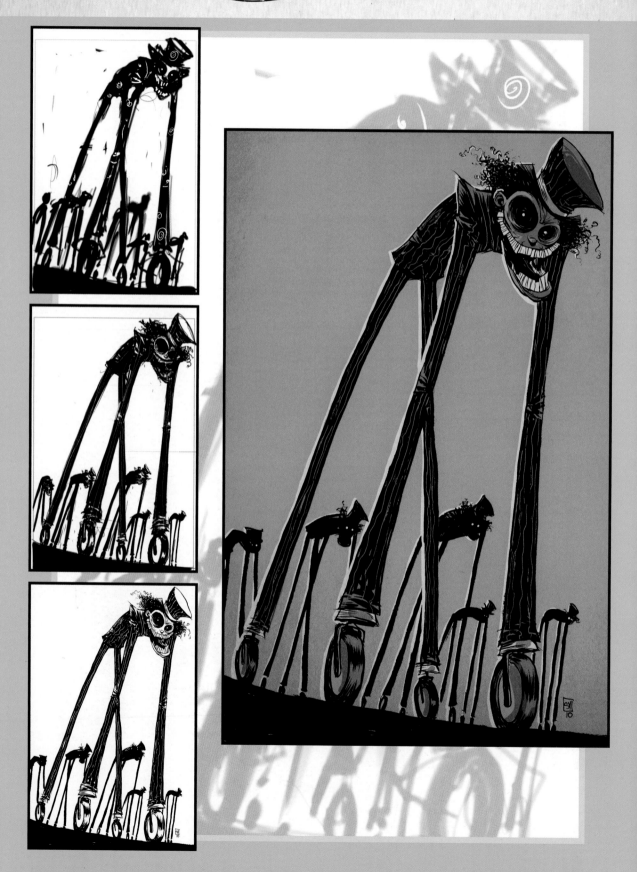

ISSUE ONE, PAGE 6 PROCESS

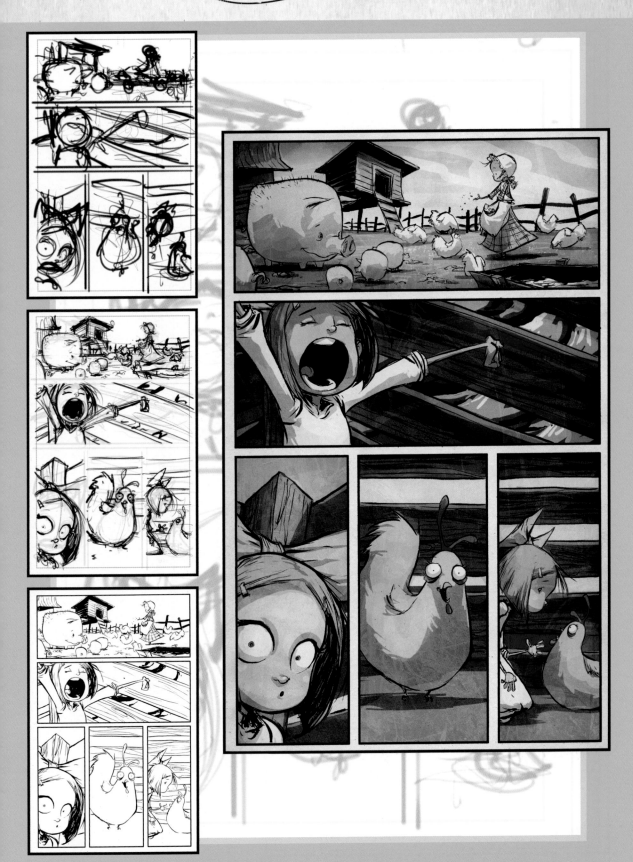

ISSUE THREE, PAGES 10-11 PROCESS

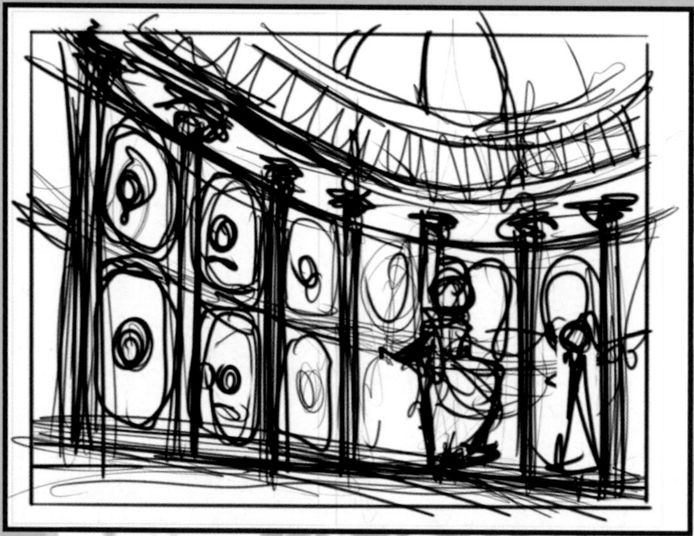

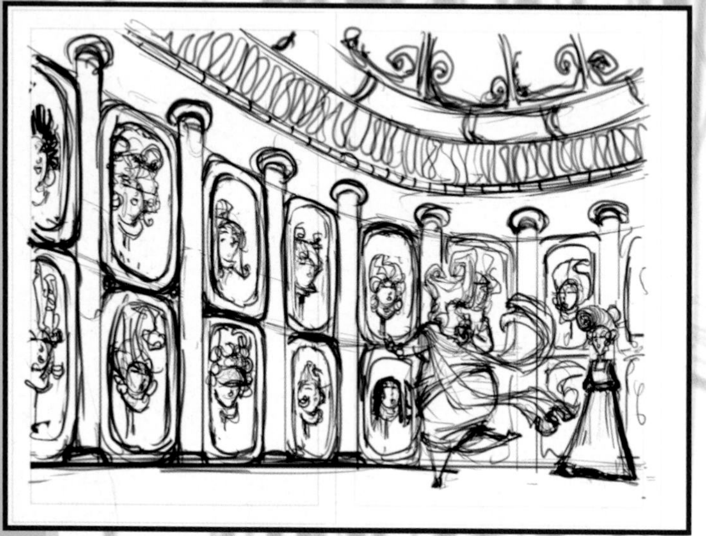

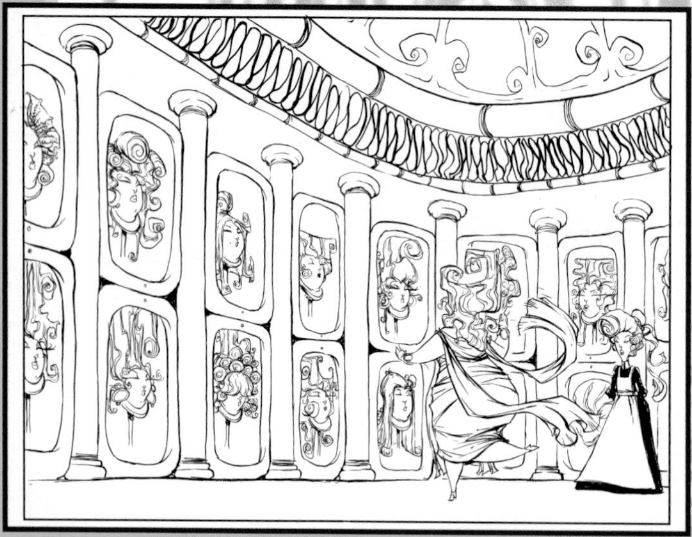

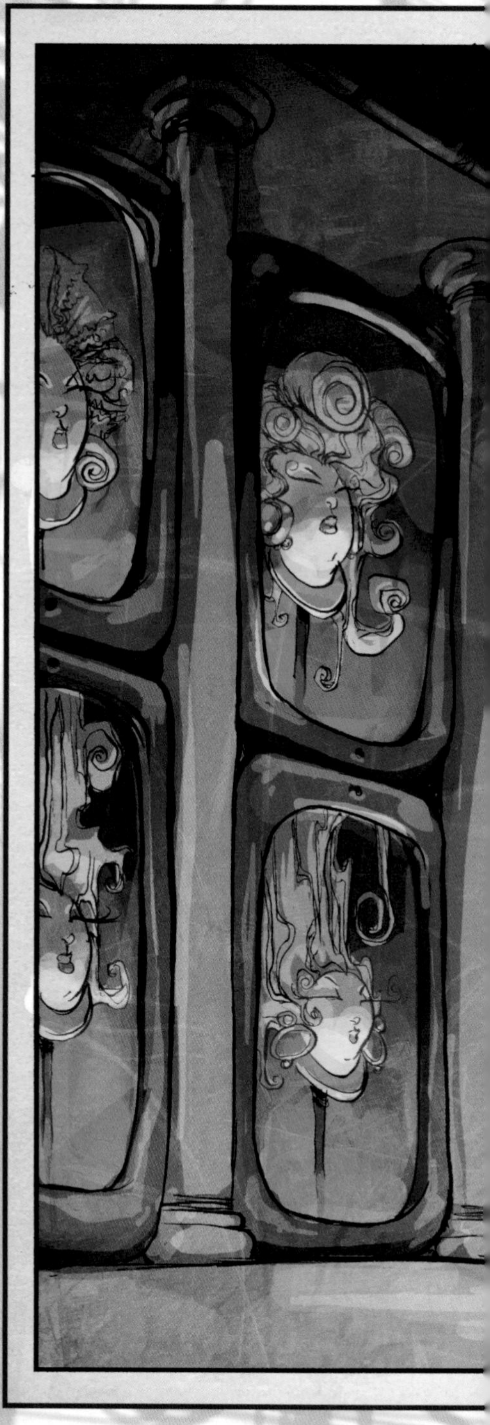

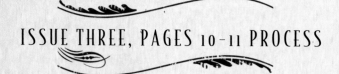

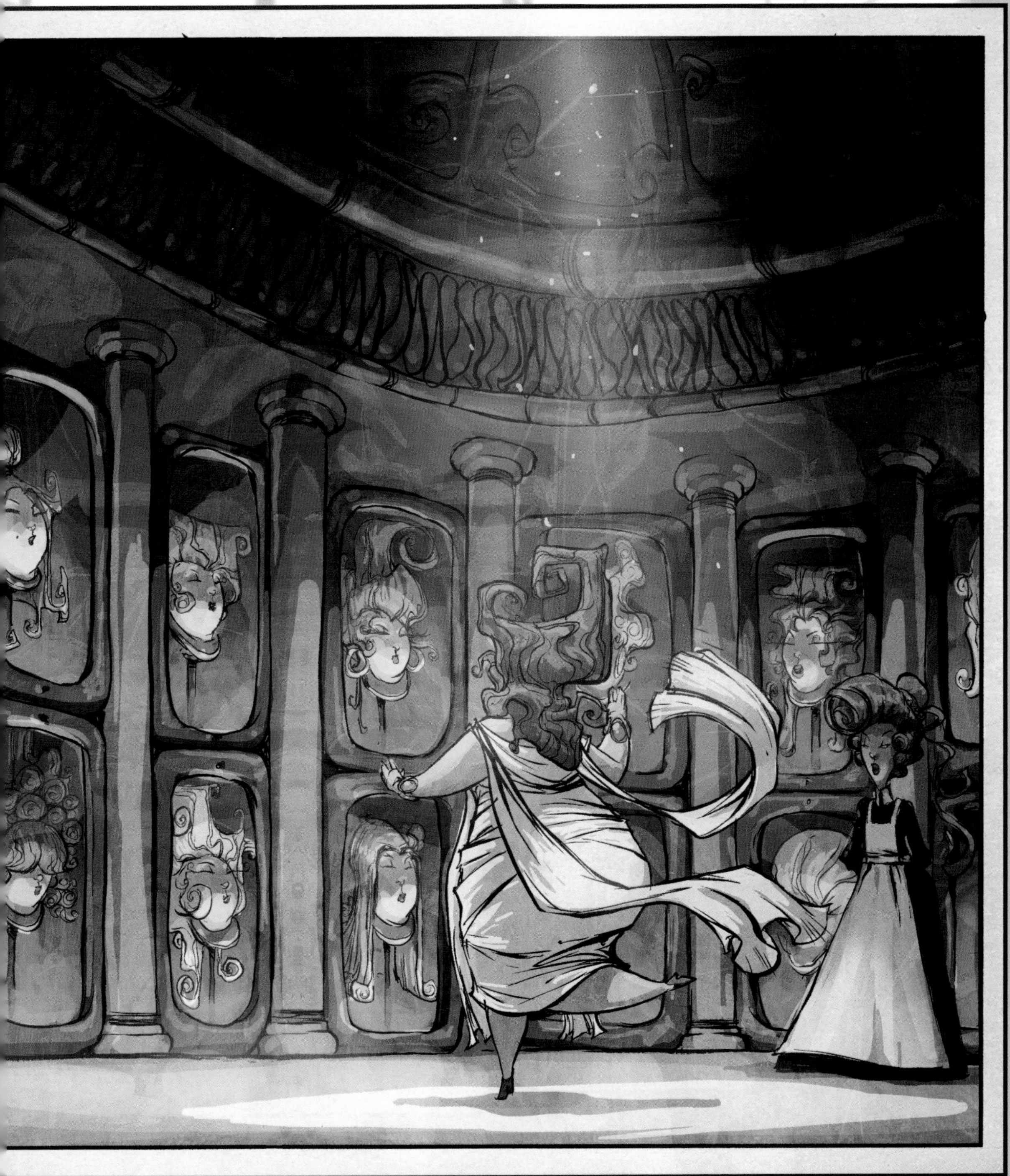

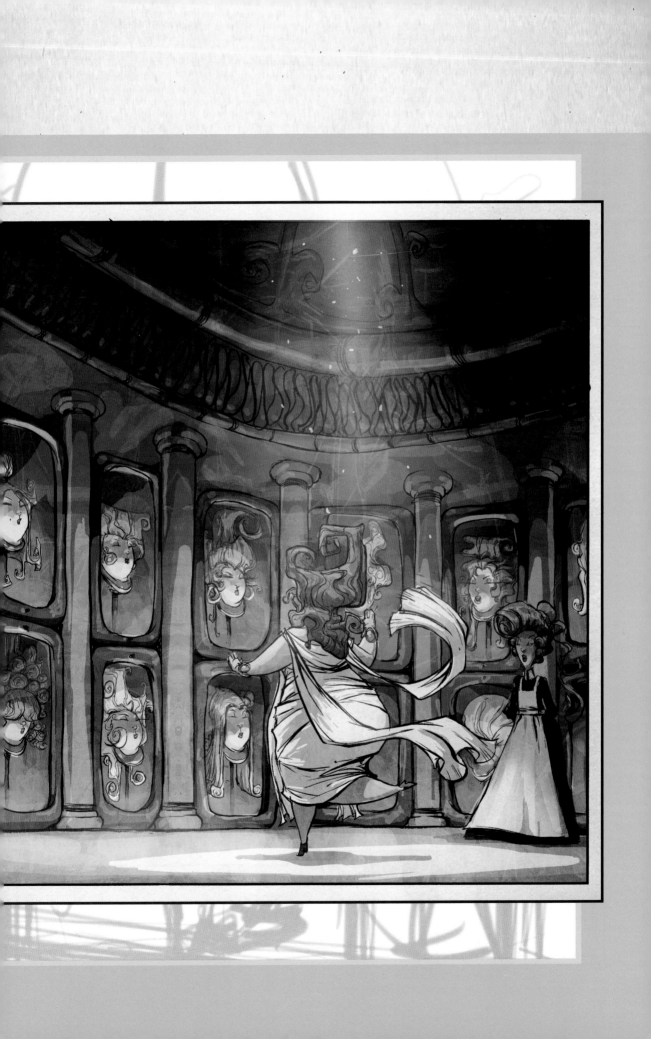

ISSUE SEVEN, PAGE 15 PROCESS

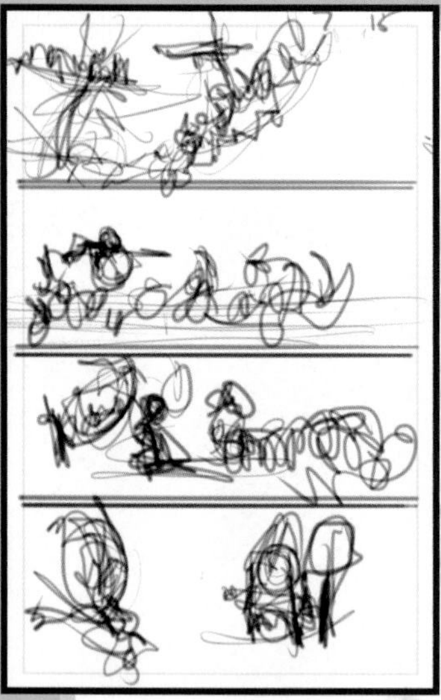

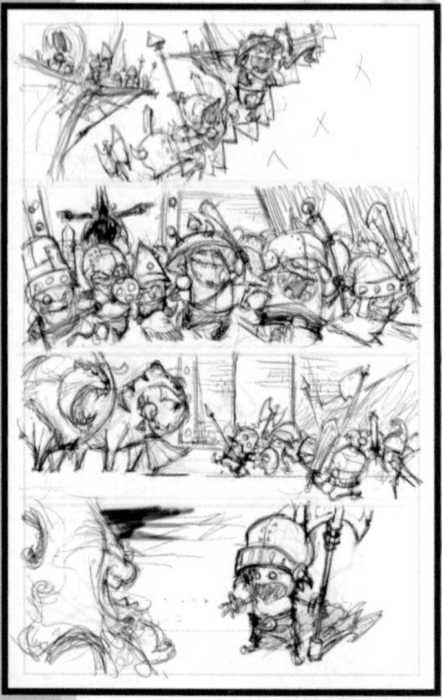

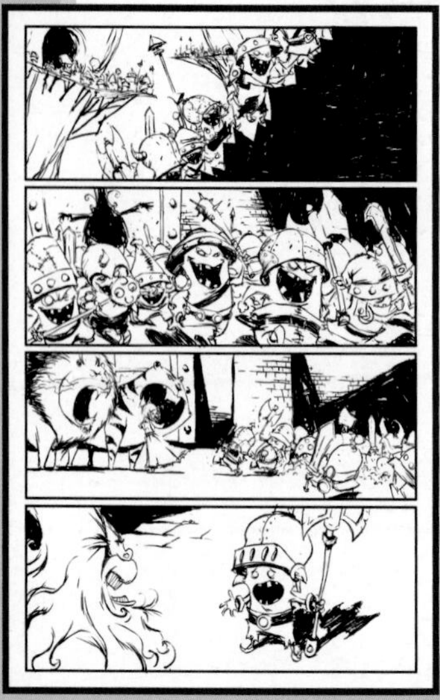

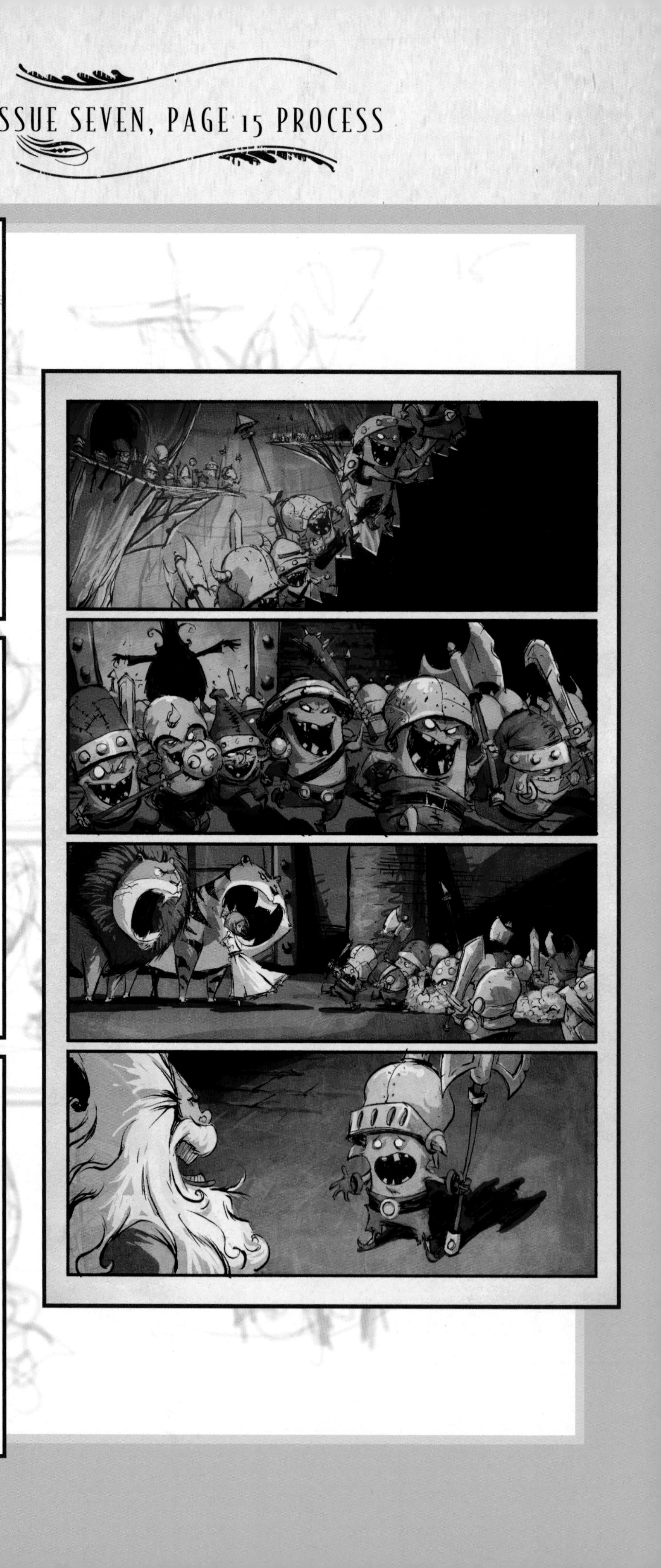